CiTY·SMaRT™

Anchorage

Second Edition

Donna Freedman

AVALON
TRAVEL

CiTY·SMaRT: Anchorage
2nd edition

Donna Freedman

Published by
Avalon Travel Publishing
1400 65th Street
Suite 250
Emeryville, CA 94608

Please send all comments,
corrections, additions,
amendments, and critiques to:

CiTY·SMaRT™
AVALON TRAVEL PUBLISHING
1400 65th Street, Suite 250
EMERYVILLE, CA 94608, USA
e-mail: atpfeedback@avalonpub.com
www.travelmatters.com

Printing History
Second edition—March 2000
5 4 3

ISBN 1-56261-511-4
ISSN 1096-0082

Editors: Sarah Baldwin, Peg Goldstein
Graphics Editor: Bunny Wong
Production: Marie J.T. Vigil
Design: Janine Lehmann
Cover Design: Suzanne Rush
Maps: Julie Felton
Typesetter: Marie J.T. Vigil
Front cover: © Mark Newman/Photo Network—Anchorage Performing Arts Center
Back cover: © Index Stock Imagery—Anchorage skyline

Distributed in the United States by Publishers Group West

Printed in the U.S. by RR Donnelley

CONTENTS

Restaurants, hotels, museums and other facilities marked by the
& symbol are wheelchair accessible.

See Anchorage the CiTY·SMaRT™ Way

The Guide for Anchorage Natives, New Residents, and Visitors

In *City•Smart Guidebook: Anchorage,* local author Donna Freedman tells it like it is. Residents will learn things they never knew about their city, new residents will get an insider's view of their new hometown, and visitors will be guided to the very best Anchorage has to offer— whether they're on a weekend getaway or staying a week or more.

Opinionated Recommendations Save You Time and Money

From shopping to nightlife to museums, the author is opinionated about what she likes and dislikes. You'll learn the great and the not-so-great things about Anchorage's sights, restaurants, and accommodations. So you can decide what's worth your time and what's not; which hotel is worth the splurge and which is the best choice for budget travelers.

Easy-to-Use Format Makes Planning Your Trip a Cinch

City•Smart Guidebook: Anchorage is user-friendly—you'll quickly find exactly what you're looking for. Chapters are organized by travelers' interests and needs, from Where to Stay and Where to Eat to Sights and Attractions, Kids' Stuff, Sports and Recreation, and even Day Trips from Anchorage.

Includes Maps and Quick Location-Finding Features

Every listing in this book is accompanied by a geographic zone designation (see the following pages for zone details) that helps you immediately find each location. Staying on Fourth Avenue and wondering about nearby sights and restaurants? Look for the Downtown label in the listings, and you'll know that that statue or café is not far away. Or maybe you're looking for the Alaska Zoo. Along with its address, you'll see a South Anchorage label, so you'll know just where to find it.

All That and Fun to Read, Too!

Every City•Smart chapter includes fun-to-read (and fun-to-use) tips to help you get more out of Anchorage, city trivia (did you know that the city's drinking water comes from a glacier?), and illuminating sidebars (for a Shopper's Glossary, see page 148). And well-known local residents provide their personal "Top Ten" lists, guiding readers to the city's best photo opportunities, best spots for kids, and more.

ANCHORAGE ZONES

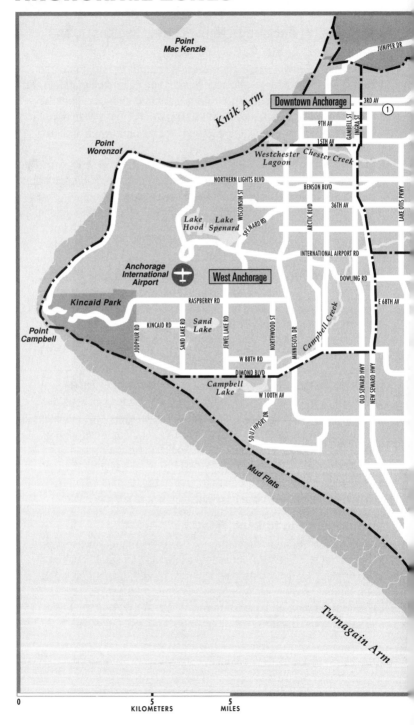

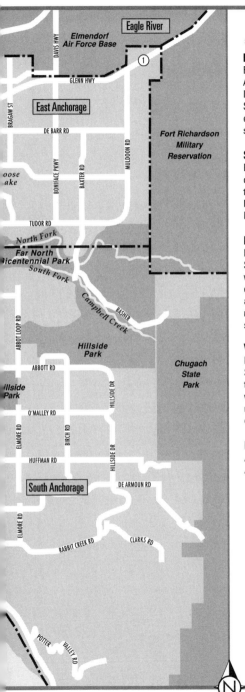

ANCHORAGE ZONES

DT—Downtown Anchorage
Bounded by the Port of Anchorage on the north, Cook Inlet on the west, Gambell Street/Seward Highway on the east, and 15th Avenue on the south

S—South Anchorage
Bounded by Dimond Boulevard on the north, Turnagain Arm on the west, the Chugach Mountains on the east, and Potter Marsh on the south

E—East Anchorage
Bounded by Gambell Street/Seward Highway on the west, Muldoon Road on the east, Elmendorf Air Force Base and Fort Richardson on the north, and Dowling Road on the south

W—West Anchorage
Bounded by Gambell Street/Seward Highway on the east, Cook Inlet on the west, 15th Avenue on the north, and Dimond Boulevard on the south

ER—Eagle River
Approximately 10 miles east of Anchorage

Alaska Division of Tourism

1

WELCOME TO ANCHORAGE

Many people choose to visit Anchorage because, as a local saying goes, "it's only half an hour away from Alaska." In some ways the city is like the rest of the United States: strip malls, traffic jams, fast-food restaurants, and cookie-cutter housing developments. Yet, while heading out for some Chicken McNuggets, you can admire the aurora borealis (or, on a really cold day, an Arctic mirage called Fata Morgana). City drinking water comes from a glacier. Local shops sell dogsleds, moose-nugget jewelry, and reindeer sausage. People fish for king salmon a stone's throw from downtown office buildings. One out of every 58 Alaskans is a pilot. The state has no official lottery, but you can wager $2 on when river ice will give way in Nenana.

Moose wander into yards and munch on ornamental plantings, and bears walk onto porches to eat from dog dishes. Lynx, wolves, Dall sheep, and coyotes also frolic within the city limits. You may glimpse whales as you drive along Seward Highway or from a kitchen window if you live near Turnagain Arm.

In February and March city workers actually *add* snow to downtown streets to facilitate sled-dog races, including the ceremonial start of the world-famous Iditarod. A citizens' race league stages regular races for mushers ages four and up; the sled-dog track is right across the street from a Quik Lube. At the winter carnival, called the Fur Rendezvous, locals play snowshoe softball and soar in the air during the blanket toss.

Residents ski and skijor, snowshoe and ice climb, trot up family-friendly Flattop, and make plans to tackle the formidable Denali. They hike and camp in the state park and national forest that are right in their backyards. They watch the boys of summer play on real grass in the semipro Alaska Baseball

A musk ox at the Musk Ox Farm

League, but they also cheer for athletes competing in the One-Arm Reach, Seal Hop, Stick Pull, and other games at the Native Youth Olympics.

Anchorage hosts take their houseguests to the Musk Ox Farm to see these improbable Stone Age beasts, and to the Reindeer Farm to pose for Christmas-card pictures with the friendly animals. They drive visitors to Portage Glacier for photo opportunities next to glowing blue-green icebergs and then stop at Crow Creek Mine on the way back to pan for gold.

No matter when you visit Anchorage, beauty, fun, and adventure await.

A Brief History of Anchorage

What is now Anchorage had long been used as a food resource by the Dena'ina Athabaskans, an Indian tribe, but there is no conclusive evidence that they actually lived here year-round. Visits were seasonal and involved dip-netting king, silver, and red salmon and hunting game animals. Historian Shem Pete notes that a Dena'ina word for the Anchorage area was *qatuk'e'usht*, which translates to "something drifts up to it." This name probably referred to the custom of traveling to the area via the incoming tide.

The first Euro-American contact in the region came in the mid-1700s, when Russian traders set up posts on the Kenai Peninsula, some 150 miles from Anchorage. The Russians did not have a good reputation among the local Native people, however. Oral accounts of murders and swindles have been handed down over the generations.

In 1778, Captain James Cook spent a week sailing up the River Turnagain, now Turnagain Arm. He met with groups of Natives along the way. Whom he met is the subject of some debate. Some historians believe he

ANCHORAGE TIME LINE

Russian traders establish posts in western and southcentral Alaska.	**1743**
Captain James Cook finds and names the river Turnagain (today's Turnagain Arm).	**1778**
Captain George Vancouver explores Southcentral Alaska.	**1794**
United States purchases Alaska from Russia.	**1867**
Congress extends the Homestead Act to Alaska.	**1898**
Alaska Central Railway construction begins in Seward.	**1902**
The first cabins show up on the flats of Ship Creek in what will become Anchorage.	**1910**
Alaska becomes a U.S. territory.	**1913**
Woodrow Wilson authorizes the Alaska Railroad Anchorage townsite auction.	**1915**
The first train runs between Anchorage and Seward.	**1918**
The city of Anchorage is incorporated.	**1920**
The first homestead is established in the wilds of South Anchorage; Peter "Russian Jack" Toloff sets up an East Anchorage homestead.	**1926**
Merrill Field airfield opens.	**1930**
First Fur Rendezvous winter carnival.	**1937**
Construction begins on Fort Richardson and Elmendorf Air Force Base.	**1940**
The first traffic lights are installed on Fourth Avenue.	**1949**
The highway between Anchorage and Seward is completed.	**1951**
Alaska becomes the 49th state.	**1959**
Good Friday Earthquake.	**1964**
A former Nike missile site becomes Kincaid Park.	**1968**
First modern Iditarod race.	**1973**
Construction of the Trans-Alaska Pipeline begins, triggering the free-spending oil boom.	**1974**
Oscar Anderson House, built in 1915, is restored and opened.	**1982**
Mount Redoubt erupts, coating the city in ash.	**1992**
Arctic Winter Games take place in the Eagle River/Chugiak area.	**1996**
Alaska Native Heritage Center opens.	**1998**

met Athabaskans; others say he met Chugach or Koniag Eskimos who happened to be traveling in the area.

After accounts of Cook's discoveries were published, a British company sent two ships to the area. The voyagers met with a group of Russians, men who had traveled up from the Aleutian Islands. Yet despite all this visiting, no permanent settlements were made in Anchorage until 1915, when the city became something of an overnight sensation. When President Woodrow Wilson ordered the creation of the Alaska Railroad, a tent city sprang up on the muddy banks of Ship Creek. About two thousand people materialized out of nowhere, all of them ready and willing to build America's only government railway.

Within a few months, town lots were being surveyed and auctioned. Mindful of the wide-open naughtiness of gold rush towns like Nome and Skagway, the fledgling town's fathers insisted that Anchorage lots could not be used "for the purpose of manufacturing, selling, or otherwise disposing of intoxicating liquors as a beverage, or for gambling, prostitution, or any unlawful purpose."

The federal government was a benevolent force in the new town, providing necessities such as city management, a hospital, schools, utilities, and even fire protection. Anchorage was incorporated in 1920, and for years the railroad remained the cornerstone of the local economy (even though the line wasn't finished until 1923 because of World War I–related delays).

Beginning in 1940, construction on Elmendorf Air Force Base and Fort Richardson—and the consequent arrival of both jobs and military personnel—had a major impact on Anchorage's economy. Fears of a Japanese invasion led to even more troops showing up after the start of World War II. When the Cold War began, Alaska's proximity to the Soviet

Wow, Look at the Colors

The aurora borealis, or northern lights, is produced when charged electrons and protons strike gas particles in the upper atmosphere of Earth. The aurora may appear in green, red, blue, or purple, and in patterns ranging from arcs of illumination to a shimmery curtain of light. Start checking the skies in late August. You may see the lights from your hotel window; if you do, consider hopping back in the car and driving up the Seward or Glenn Highways, or up Minnesota Drive, for a better view. If you don't see any northern lights while you're here, check department stores and souvenir shops for aurora videos.

Union necessitated a continued military presence.

Between 1940 and 1951, the population of Anchorage soared from 3,000 to 47,000. Oil had been discovered on nearby Kenai Peninsula, though the real oil finds had yet to be made. A quest for statehood began, and it was attained in 1959.

Alaska made headlines in the 1970s with the development of oilfields at Prudhoe Bay and the building of the Trans-Alaska Pipeline. Workers flowed north once again, in search of big-money jobs. Revenue began to flow, too, and Anchorage citizens used their share to build

Anchorage Museum of History and Art

Earthquake of 1964

parks and trails, a new library, a sports arena, and a performing arts center.

Things have changed since the early days. The population has grown, the housing stock has improved somewhat, and the feds have sold the railroad to the state. But Anchorage is still full of independent cusses who came north seeking a big grubstake, along with a fair number of folks dependent on government paychecks.

The People of Anchorage

Anchorage is a young city, with an average age of 32.1 years, compared to the national average of 36.2 years. With 258,782 people, the city contains 41.6 percent of Alaska's population.

Old-timers snort that the current generation has gone soft, and indeed Anchorage residents have become increasingly accustomed to creature comforts like espresso stands, health clubs, and cell phones. Yet the city still has a do-it-yourself mentality, that you wouldn't find in, say, New York City or San Diego. Spend any time here and you will almost certainly meet someone who is building a cabin in the woods. If your car goes off the road into the ditch, someone will stop and yank you out with a four-wheel-drive vehicle and a length of chain carried for just such an emergency. Should a coworker announce that he's quitting his job to train for the Iditarod or climb Mount McKinley, the reaction is likely to be, "Cool!"

People go cross-country skiing on their lunch breaks and winter camping over the weekend. They climb Flattop on the spur of the moment on a June evening—hey, the sun's still out, isn't it? And then there's the famous summer "suicide run": Right after work, people drive 150 miles to the Kenai Peninsula, fish most of the night, then drive back in time for work the next day. (That's where those espresso stands really come in handy.)

Incidentally, men outnumber women in Anchorage, where 51.5 percent of the population is male. That statistic has a lot to do with the city's two military bases, as well as industries (fishing, timber, oil) that tend to draw single males. Before women start rushing north, though, they should keep in mind a local adage about Alaska men: "The odds are good, but the goods are odd." A 1998 article in *Cosmopolitan* reiterated the usual stereotypes: Alaska men have a "mysterious quality," and they "seem to have secrets—hopefully not criminal ones—and have nonconformist lifestyles."

Note that this "nonconformist" credo might have as much to do with employment, social graces, or indoor plumbing as with personal philosophy. Certainly, some men do move to Alaska to become one with nature. They like the idea of hunting, fishing, ice- or mountain-climbing, snowboarding, and other manly pursuits. However, others reportedly come north because no one will look for them here.

Scratch an Alaska woman, especially an ex-wife, and you'll hear a different side to the "romance of the north" story. Jane Haigh, coauthor of *Catch and Release: An Insider's Guide to Alaska Men*, says that many men are looking for women who will both kill and cook game, stay home alone during the various fishing, hunting, and snowmachine seasons, and wash the men's clothes when they return. Another generalization, to be sure—but one that often fits.

For some women, especially outdoorsy types, a low-impact lifestyle sounds like a good deal. Those who think so should attend the Talkeetna Bachelors Auction, a fun and funky event held each December, then stick around until spring. After a couple of months, the romance of the north will

Anchorage Climate Chart

	Ave. High Temps (°F)	Ave. Low Temps (°F)
January	21.4	8.4
February	25.8	11.5
March	33.1	18.1
April	42.8	28.6
May	54.4	38.8
June	61.6	47.2
July	65.2	51.7
August	63.0	49.5
September	55.2	41.6
October	40.5	28.7
November	27.2	15.1
December	22.5	10.0

A floatplane lands on Lake Hood.

either wear thin or not. If Alaska, and Alaska men, are for you, that's great. You'll need that devotion to get you through mosquito season.

About 81 percent of the community is white. African Americans and Alaska Natives account for 6 percent each, and Asians and Pacific Islanders make up 5 percent of the population. Mexicans and other groups comprise another 2 percent.

Almost 19 percent of the state's Natives live in Anchorage. Some are born here, and some move here for employment or educational opportunities. Maintaining their Eskimo, Indian, and Aleut cultures in a large, impersonal city has been a continuing challenge. The new Alaska Native Heritage Center, a number of Native churches, music and dance groups, and even the Alaska Native Medical Center (long a place to meet friends in from the village) all provide a bridge from rural to urban ways. Native sports, arts and crafts, and storytelling are taught in local elementary and secondary schools. Many Native foods—moose, caribou, fish, waterfowl, berries, wild greens, even beluga whale (hunted in Cook Inlet)—are available within or just outside the city limits. Annual events like Spirit Days, the Native Youth Olympics, Quyana Alaska, the Alaska Federation of Natives convention, and the Fur Rendezvous help city Natives stay connected to traditions, and relatives and neighbors from outlying areas.

Anchorage Weather

Locals joke that Anchorage has only three seasons—last winter, this winter, and next winter. However, the climate here isn't so bad compared to winters in Alaska's interior, where you can sample temperatures of 60 or 70 below. Now *that's* cold.

When reading "official" weather reports, keep in mind that temperatures vary widely around town. In 1997 a particularly chilly spell prompted a resident to monitor temperatures in several different locations. He found a 30-degree variance: zero at the airport and 30 below zero in Far North Bicentennial Park.

Generally speaking, a typical winter day reaches into the teens during the day and drops into the low single digits or colder at night. At least once each winter, the temperature dips below zero and stays there for a week or more, night *and* day.

The local attitude toward the winter cold is, basically, "big deal." Expect it to be cold and then live with it. Go skiing. Insulate your plumbing. Take the dog for a walk. Plug in your car. Stand outside and watch the aurora borealis at midnight. Invest in a decent hat and warm gloves. And be thankful that you don't live in Fairbanks.

Snow is a collective plaything to those who ski, skijor, snowshoe, and mush dogs. The snow can begin as early as September, continuing off and on until April. An average year's snowfall is about 69 inches. (Keep in mind, though, that snowfall reports vary as much as official versus actual temperatures.) But kids rarely get a "snow day" from school since road crews are fairly diligent about plowing—or at least on main streets.

Winters are pretty dark. At its lowest peak, the winter solstice, Anchorage gets 5 hours and 28 minutes of daylight. Cloudy days can be depressing, especially if you suffer from seasonal affective disorder. Some folks buy special high-intensity lamps to stave off the doldrums.

But let the sun come out, even for a little while, and the snowdrifts magnify the sunshine a hundredfold. Hoarfrost glitters, turning the humblest chainlink fence into a latticework of sparkling lace. When the sun

Anchorage skyline

Anchorage CVB

sets, flinging pink-orange "alpen-glow" onto the Chugach Range, the view is postcard perfect—and you get it for free.

Spring, as most of the country knows it, doesn't really exist here. Instead, we have an unofficial season called "breakup," as in the breaking up of accumulated ice and snow. Temperatures soar into the high 30s and low 40s, causing folks to walk around wearing T-shirts, shorts, and big, goofy grins. The snow goes through a gradual freeze-thaw cycle: melt all day, harden off at night. Usually, it's all gone by the end of April. Trees leaf out sometime in May, and by Memorial Day weekend residents are planting flowers and vegetables.

May and June are considered by many to be the best months of the year because the daylight has increased tremendously and because July and August tend to be rainy. The high point is summer solstice, with about 19 hours and 21 minutes of daylight. For much of the summer, light remains in the sky long after sunset, fading so gradually that by the time it's technically "dark" the sun is just about to rise once more. You may be startled by the sight of kids playing outdoors after 11 p.m. You can't blame them, though—they're soaking up all the sun they miss in winter, when they get up in the dark, go to school in the dark, and come home in the dark.

Summertime brings private homes ablaze with flowers, as part of Anchorage's "City of Lights and Flowers" campaign. (The lights are tiny white lights strung around city and private landscapes to dispel winter gloom.) The program also encourages residents to plant flowers according to specific themes, such as "Blue and Gold" (the state flag colors) or "Gone Fishin'" (pinks, reds, and silvers—the colors of salmon). Municipal gardeners tend hundreds of thousands of blooms in public plots and in hanging baskets along downtown streets.

Summer temperatures range in the 50s and 60s. Any time the mercury edges toward 70, you'll hear residents complaining about the oppressive heat wave. That's because the sun is bright, intense, and well-nigh endless. Cloudy days, however, will make you glad you packed a sweater.

Fall comes early, with none of the Indian-summer reprieves of the Lower 48. Fields and roadsides blaze with the bittersweet beauty of fireweed. Local legend has it that when the bright fuchsia blooms reach the top of the wildflower stalk, summer has come to an end. By mid-August the trees are turning gold, and the vegetation begins to die back.

Soon after, "termination dust"—local parlance for early snow on the mountains—makes its appearance. Residents shouldn't be surprised (but always are) by how quickly summer ends. Yet the brevity of the season makes it that much more glorious.

TRIVIA

Anchorage is on the same latitude as Helsinki, Finland, and on the same longitude as Honolulu, Hawaii.

Dressing in Anchorage

The only real rule is to cover yourself; how you do it is up to you. The city's fashion statement might well be described as "Carhartt Casual"—comfort, protection, and practicality are the watchwords. While you'll see black tie and tails at the Anchorage Opera, you'll see jeans and sweaters, too. A few restaurants may require a jacket, but plenty of folks wear T-shirts out to dinner. Tourists traveling light can easily get by with a bare minimum of formal wear: a jacket for men and a simple dress or skirt for women. (A blazer over slacks works for both genders.)

It's more important to consider your everyday wear. Start from the ground up, by wearing shoes or boots that offer plenty of support, whether you plan to wear them on a hiking trail or a walking tour. Break them in before you travel; blisters can make a vacation miserable pretty quickly.

As for the rest of your wardrobe, take a hint from this local joke: "Don't like the weather? Stick around for a few minutes—it'll change." You may walk out of your hotel to a warm, sunny summer day, then walk back through a windy, 45-degree downpour. And a 10-below-zero winter day may be followed by a 30-degree, icicle-dripping bluster if a Chinook wind blows through town.

To deal with changeable weather, be ready to change with it. Dress in layers that you can put on or take off as needed. For spring and summer, bring a sweater or sweatshirt and a waterproof windbreaker with a hood. If you have room in your day pack or tote bag, a folding umbrella provides additional peace of mind. People who are from warm climates or who have poor circulation may want to bring light gloves.

Sportfishing in Alaska

Alaska Division of Tourism

Fall and winter, you'll want to have long underwear, gloves or mittens, a hat, and good boots. Whatever the season, good sunglasses are a must. So is sunscreen.

Most tourists find that fanny packs or lightweight backpacks are most convenient for storing wallets, tissues, and the like. A few hard candies make sense since low humidity can dry out your mouth. The dry air also affects skin, so don't forget the lip balm and a travel-sized bottle of lotion.

When to Visit

Most people come to Alaska between late May and early September—when the weather is best. If you're an average visitor, you will definitely want to come during high season. Consider visiting in early to mid-May, though, to save money on accommodations and certain attractions. Those with special interests—hunters, mountain climbers, winter-sports enthusiasts—come year-round, hang the weather. In fact, the weather may be the very reason someone comes up—activities such as extreme snowboarding and aurora borealis viewing are available only in the winter.

Anchorage has been increasingly successful in capturing a share of the convention/special event market—and not only in spring and summer. Two upcoming examples are the Special Olympics World Winter Games, scheduled for March 3–10, 2001, and Left Coast Crime, a national mystery conference, set for February 15–18, 2001.

Calendar of Events

JANUARY
Alaskan Sled Dog and Racing Association season opens, Tozier Track; Robert Burns Dinner, Anchorage Hilton

FEBRUARY
Fur Rendezvous Winter Carnival, various locations; Iditarod Days Festival, Wasilla

In-town Wildlife Sightings

Here's some of the wildlife you might glimpse within the Anchorage city limits: moose, lynx, bears (black and grizzly), coyotes, wolves, fox, hares, eagles, hawks, squirrels, marmots, voles, shrews, several varieties of owl, and numerous waterfowl.

Recommended Reading

- **55 Ways to the Wilderness in Southcentral Alaska** *by Helen Nienhueser, Nancy Simmerman, and John Wolfe (Mountaineers): For any kind of hiking or climbing, this book is a must-have.*
- **The Alaska Almanac: Facts About Alaska** *(Alaska Northwest Books): Need to know who won the Iditarod in 1974? Ever wonder what our official state fossil is? Confused between a mukluk and muktuk? This book can help. (Incidentally: Carl Huntington was the 1974 winner; the state fossil is the woolly mammoth; and the mukluk is a skin boot, whereas muktuk is the outer skin layers and attached blubber of a whale—an Eskimo delicacy.)*
- **Alaska Bizarre** *by Mr. Whitekeys (Alaska Northwest Books): Read this book for a twisted look at the Last Frontier by Anchorage's most successful humorist/nightclub operator/musician.*
- **Alaska's History: The People, Land and Events of the North Country** *by Harry Ritter (Alaska Northwest Books): This slender volume covers the state's history, with plenty of interesting facts and photos.*
- **Fashion Means Your Fur Hat Is Dead** *and* **How to Speak Alaskan** *by Mike Doogan (Epicenter Press): These humor books are by a columnist for the* Anchorage Daily News.
- **Iditarod Classics** *by Lew Freedman (Epicenter Press): This book describes the real-life adventures of the men and women who run the 1,049-mile sled-dog race from Anchorage to Nome.*
- **The Last New Land: Stories of Alaska, Past and Present***, edited by Wayne Mergler (Alaska Northwest Books): This is an anthology of fiction, nonfiction, and poetry about the Last Frontier.*
- **A Walk-About Guide to Alaska: A First-Person Hiking Guide. Volume One: Kenai Peninsula and Turnagain Arm** *by Shawn Lyons: A local hiker, climber, and newspaper columnist offers essays on some of his favorite treks.*

MARCH
Ceremonial Iditarod start, downtown; International Ice Carving Competition, Town Square Park; Extreme Skiing and Snowboard Trials, Alyeska Resort

APRIL
Spring Carnival, Alyeska Ski Resort; Great Alaska Sportsman Show, Sullivan Arena; Native Youth Olympics, University of Alaska–Anchorage (UAA); Jazz Week, UAA

MAY
Saturday Market opens, downtown; Loon Festival, various locations; Alaska Women's Gold Nugget Triathlon, Bartlett High School; Miner's Days, Talkeetna

JUNE
Anchorage Festival of Music, Alaska Center for the Performing Arts; Ship Creek King Salmon Derby, downtown; Juneteenth celebration, Park Strip; Three Barons Renaissance Fair, Hilltop Ski Area; Summer Solstice celebrations, various city locations; Mayor's Midnight Sun Marathon, Bartlett to West High Schools; Alaska Run for Women, Mulcahy Stadium

JULY
Freedom Days Festival, Mulcahy Stadium; Girdwood Forest Fair, Girdwood; Bear Paw Festival, Eagle River; Sadler's Midnite Sun Ultra Challenge, from Fairbanks to Anchorage; Moose Dropping Festival, Talkeetna; Wasilla Water Festival, Wasilla

AUGUST
Ship Creek Silver Salmon Derby; Military Open House/Air Show, Elmendorf Air Force Base; Alaska State Fair, Palmer

SEPTEMBER
Make It Alaskan Festival, Sullivan Arena

OCTOBER
Quyana Alaska Native music and dance performance, Egan Center

NOVEMBER
Great Alaska Shootout basketball tournament, Sullivan Arena; Anchorage Opera season opens, Alaska Center for the Performing Arts; Crafts Emporium, Egan Center; Tree-Lighting Ceremony, Town Square

DECEMBER
Swedish Christmas, Oscar Anderson House; Colony Christmas Celebration, Palmer; Enchanted World, Egan Center; Bachelor Auction and Wilderness Woman Competition, Talkeetna

Business and Economy

Two words describe Alaska's economy: boom and bust. Whether its fortunes turn on gold, timber, fish, or oil, this is a state that alternates prosperity with belt-tightening. The most recent example is the pipeline years. Employment soared beginning in the mid-1970s and then augered in, finally hitting bottom in 1988. The recession was long and painful; not until 1993 did employment rates reach pre-1985 levels.

Without a doubt, the most important force in the Alaskan economy is the oil and gas industry, which fills 85 percent of the state's coffers. Locally, however, the effect isn't as obvious: Petroleum-industry employment accounts for just 2 percent of Anchorage jobs. And the situation just keeps getting weirder in "petroleum land" due to mergers and the declining price of oil. The trend now is toward layoffs, not hiring.

The majority of local jobs are in the service (28.4 percent), trade (24.3 percent), and government (22.2 percent) sectors. Tourism becomes more important each year. Some locals are seasonal workers employed in commercial fishing, construction, and logging.

Incidentally, Alaska still has the country's highest median household income: $49,717, compared to the nationwide median of $38,233. However, Alaska's median dropped $2,069 in the last four years, whereas the nationwide median rose by $1,000.

A large number of Anchorage's residents are part of the workforce. In 1990, 78 percent of residents ages 16 and older were working, as opposed to 65 percent in the rest of the country. Also, 70 percent of adult women were working in 1990, compared to only 57 percent nationwide.

Can you still make big bucks in Alaska? Possibly, if you luck into a commercial fishing or oil industry job. But fishermen sometimes make little or no money at all, and they risk a high rate of injury and death. In addition, it may be difficult to get a big-money job unless you know a fishing boat captain. You're more likely to end up on the "slime line"—fish cutting and packing—making little more than minimum wage.

As for the oil industry—well, once upon a time you could earn $1,000 a week just for keeping a bus engine running all day. But the swell of pipeline-era jobs had subsided even before the oil consolidations of 1999. Any positions that do remain are highly sought after by a much larger labor pool than existed during the late 1970s. In other words, don't come to Alaska with hopes of making your fortune. It could happen, but you could also wind up living in your car.

TRIVIA

Three of Alaska's 39 mountain ranges are visible from Anchorage: the Chugach, Kenai, and Alaska ranges. Mount McKinley, the tallest mountain in North America (20,320 feet), is 130 miles north but can be seen from downtown on a clear day.

Nothernmost Alaska has the longest period of daylight in the United States—no sunset for 82 days. It also has the longest period of darkness—no sunrise for 67 days.

For those who decide to settle in or just visit Anchorage, here's what you can expect to pay for a variety of goods and services:

- movie admission: $4–$4.75 matinees, $6–$7.25 evenings
- daily newspaper: 50 cents ($1.50 Sunday)
- average dinner: $20
- hotel room: $95
- five-mile taxi ride: $10

Taxes

According to a 1994 survey, a typical family of four earning less than $50,000 paid under $1,700 in taxes—in contrast to the national average of more than $4,400. The higher the family income, the greater the disparity between Anchorage and the rest of the country. That's partly because Anchorage residents pay neither a city nor a state income tax; additionally, no sales tax is charged in the city.

Housing

Anchorage homes aren't cheap, for several reasons: Building materials must be shipped a great distance, labor costs are high, and land is expensive and often needs soil improvement before a foundation can be laid. The Anchorage Home Builders Association defines a "lower-priced" home as any newly built house priced at less than $175,000.

To find real neighborhoods, you have to look in the older parts of the city—"older," of course, being a relative term. Areas like South Addition, Turnagain, Airport Heights, and Nunaka Valley are more mature and better landscaped since people have been living there longer—but only since the early 1940s to mid-1950s, which isn't very long at all by some cities' standards.

That doesn't mean the houses in these older areas are necessarily gracious. Early Anchorage housing emphasized shelter, not design. It's been called "the architecture of expediency"—get it built before snow flies, with the materials that you have on hand. Some Anchorage natives remember living all winter in the basement of a split-level house, while Dad worked nights and weekends to finish the upstairs.

These days, more and more residents are remodeling these "old" houses to bring them in line with modern standards. (And boy, do they need it: When remodelers open up walls, they're finding wiring that would make a code-enforcement officer break out into a cold sweat, as well as old-time, improvised insulation like newspaper and horschair.) Areas like Hillside and Westchester Lagoon still have their share of subdivisions and older split levels, but many people are hiring architects to design their dream houses.

Contractors still do a fair amount of single-family home building on private lots. However, the bulk of construction in Anchorage is in subdivisions and multifamily housing units such as condos and duplexes, which give builders the most bang for the buck on those expensive plots of land.

Plenty of people live in mobile homes. All types are represented: ancient paneling-and-aluminum "wobbly boxes," former traveling trailers set on blocks, and brand-new "manufactured homes" that look like regular houses. As the city moves toward a service economy, mobile homes are often the only way that some families can afford to own housing. In addition to the usual banks and mortgage brokers, a state-owned lender called Alaska Housing Finance Corporation also helps residents buy homes.

Schools

The Anchorage School District encompasses about 48,000 students and 85 public schools. The district offers special and gifted education; foreign language immersion programs on the elementary level; open-optional, basic-skills, and Montessori schools; vocational training; and several high schools especially for at-risk students (apparently these schools work since the city has one of the lowest dropout rates in the country).

Several charter schools, operating independent of regular schools yet receiving public funding, opened in the late 1990s. A handful of private schools, most of them religious, also exist in the city.

High schools field teams in sports such as swimming, diving, cross-country skiing, and riflery, in addition to the usual basketball, football, and volleyball. Football season, by the way, begins in mid-August and runs to the middle of October. Teams fully expect to play in or on snow, and the boosters sell a lot of hot chocolate.

Anchorage Trolley

2

GETTING AROUND ANCHORAGE

It *is* possible to drive to Anchorage via the Alaska Highway, which links Alaska, Canada, and the contiguous United States (also known as the Lower 48). But it's a long, long drive: Anchorage is 2,463 road miles from Seattle and 3,608 road miles from Los Angeles.

Most people fly in or take a cruise ship. The Anchorage International Airport is a destination for Delta, Northwest and other carriers, including, naturally, Alaska Airlines. Several cruise lines dock in Anchorage. You can also take the state ferry system, known as the Alaska Marine Highway, as far as Haines and then drive to Anchorage, a two-day car trip.

One of the first things you'll notice is that Anchorage is a darned big place. The municipal boundaries stretch more than 50 miles, encompassing some 1,955 square miles—about as much as the state of Delaware. Of course, much of that land is unoccupied wilderness. But Alaskans like to bandy about large numbers.

With so much space, you may wonder why homes and businesses tend to be built so close together. The reason is that buildable land is at a premium since a lot of local land is boggy. Construction companies would rather deal with sites they don't first have to drain, and drain, and drain, and then fill, and fill, and fill.

City Layout

You'll find the lion's share of historic and cultural attractions in downtown Anchorage. Orienting yourself is pretty simple: east-west routes are

Flight Times to Anchorage from Some Major Cities

Chicago: 5 hours and 30 minutes

Detroit: 6 hours

London: 7 hours

Los Angeles: 5 hours

Minneapolis: 5 hours and 15 minutes

New York City: 8 hours

St. Louis: 6 hours and 30 minutes

Salt Lake City: 5 hours

San Francisco: 4 hours and 30 minutes

Seattle: 3 hours

Seoul: 8 hours and 30 minutes

Tokyo: 6 hours and 30 minutes

Zurich: 9 hours and 30 minutes

---

numbered avenues, and north-south routes are mostly lettered streets. Even the named north-south streets, located east of A Street, follow a predictable pattern: Barrow, Cordova, Denali, Eide, Fairbanks . . . well, you get the idea.

Fourth and Fifth Avenues are the main east-west streets in the downtown area. Sixth Avenue becomes the Glenn Highway just east of downtown. The Glenn takes you to the suburbs of Eagle River and Chugiak, and to Palmer, a town that hosted an agricultural experiment during the Depression. The road eventually intersects the Parks Highway, leading to Wasilla (Iditarod headquarters) and such tourist destinations as Denali National Park and Fairbanks.

Going north-south, the main drags are C Street, L Street (which later turns into Minnesota Drive), and Gambell Street (which quickly becomes the Seward Highway). However, when downtown, you're more likely to go south since north consists only of the Port of Anchorage and two military bases.

One thing you'll notice right away is that Anchorage has no freeways as the rest of the world understands them. To get almost anywhere in the city, those three major north-south streets (C, L, and Gambell) are your best starting points. Gambell, which becomes the Seward Highway, will take you to South Anchorage, Girdwood, Portage, and all the way to—

surprise!—Seward. The Seward Highway is also the first part of the route to the Kenai Peninsula and its world-class salmon fishing.

Public Transportation

Anchorage residents like to make fun of their public transit system, the People Mover (schedules and route information, 907/343-6543; TTY/TDD, 907/343-4775), which some have dubbed "the People Ager." The sarcasm has some degree of truth since you may wait 25 to 90 minutes between buses, depending on the route.

Still, for many residents, the People Mover is the only way to travel. Tourists who don't want to rent cars find it useful for visiting attractions both downtown and elsewhere. Note that all of the city's buses are ramp-equipped "kneeling" buses, which let people with mobility problems board and disembark more easily. In addition, all buses offer both verbal and text announcements that tell riders where they are along the route. And all Anchorage city buses have bike racks, so you can take the bus to a park or some other attraction and then ride your bike from there.

Mostly moving around downtown? Ride for free within the Downtown Anchorage Short Hop (DASH) zone. This area is bordered by Fifth Avenue, Eagle Street, Eighth Avenue, and K Street. Buses on Fifth and Sixth run about every 10 minutes on weekdays, less frequently on weekends. If you're not sure where the free ride area ends, ask a driver.

At one point, tourists were perplexed that you couldn't take a city bus to or from the international airport. Route 6 now offers several trips per day.

A regular bus ride costs one dollar for adults and 50 cents for youths ages 5 to 18; transfers are 10 cents. Day passes are $2.50 and are available at the People Mover Transit Center and the Bus Stop Shop, both located in the parking garage at Sixth Avenue and H Street, and at the Dimond Transit Center at the west end of the Dimond Center mall. Seniors and the disabled can ride for 25 cents with a transit photo ID card. The photo cards cost two dollars and can be purchased at the front counter of the Transit Center, at Sixth Avenue between and G and H Streets.

Be absolutely vigilant about getting to your pick-up stop a few minutes ahead of time—if your watch is slow and you miss the last bus, it

Alaska Railroad

Kenai Fjords Tours

Top Ten Place Names in Alaska
by Dana Stabenow

Anchorage resident Dana Stabenow is an Edgar-winning author (the Kate Shugak and Liam Campbell series, among other books) who sets all her mysteries in the Last Frontier. A lifelong Alaskan, her favorite place names aren't limited to Anchorage because the choices around the state are just too good.

1. **Turnagain Arm:** In yet another flop at finding the Northwest Passage, Captain Cook had to "turn again" here.

2. **Denali:** The tallest mountain in North America. Not McKinley, not Big Mac—Denali. De-NAH-lee. It's a Tanaina word for "home of the sun" or "the high one."

3. **Alyeska:** An Aleut word distinguishing the Aleutian Islands from the mainland, or "the great land." 'Nuff said.

4. **Picnic Harbor:** So named because during an October blow, the harbor is a picnic compared to beating through Chugach Passage.

5. **Farewell Burn:** Between Rainy Pass and Rohn on the Iditarod Trail, it is "farewell" to sanity as mushers suffering from dehydration and sleep deprivation begin hallucinating about white lights, crying friends, dead relatives, and Hawaiian beaches.

6. **Salmon:** There are two Salmon Bays, one Salmon Bay Lake, two Salmon Berry Lakes, thirteen Salmon Creeks, one Salmon Creek Divide, one Salmon Creek Reservoir, one Salmon Flats, one Salmon Fork, one Salmon Fork Black River, one Salmon Island, one Salmon Lagoon, four Salmon Lakes, one Salmon Mountain, one Salmon Pass, one Salmon Point, one Salmon Ridge, seven Salmon Rivers, one Salmon Run, one Salmon Slough, one Salmon Trout River, and two villages named Salmon. And these are only the places that use the English word.

7. **Egegik:** A village on Bristol Bay, the name is possibly derived from the Yupik word iguugek, meaning "his testicles." I don't know the story here, but there is bound to be one.

8. **Killisnoo:** A village south of Angoon. Corrupted from the Tlingit word kootsnahoo, meaning "bear's rectum." A close second for Number 8 was Anaktuvuk Pass, which means either "caribou shit" or "where the caribou shit."

9. **Taiga:** The name of my father's hunting and fishing lodge on the Kichatna River and the setting of the ninth Kate Shugak mystery. Taigataiga means "bear shit" in some obscure Athabascan dialect.

10. **Dana Peak** (north of Petersberg) and **Mount Dana** (northeast of Pavlof Bay): But of course.

could be an expensive cab ride back to your lodgings. A schedule of all People Mover routes costs one dollar and can be obtained at the People Mover Transit Center, Sixth Avenue between G and H Streets, and at many area stores. Or check the Web site, www.peoplemover.org.

Anchorage Share-A-Ride (907/562-7665) offers free matching service to people who want to car- or van-pool to work. Van-pool drivers ride free each month in exchange for driving and collecting fees from passengers; drivers receive limited use of the vehicle on weekends for personal transportation.

Anchorage Museum of History and Art

Historic public transport

Taxis

Cabs regularly cruise the downtown area and the airport, but if you're looking for a taxi anywhere else, you'll have to call. Expect to pay about $15 for a cab from the airport to downtown. The following companies serve the area:

- Alaska Cab Co., 907/563-5353
- Anchorage Checker Cab, 907/276-1234
- Anchorage Taxicab, 907/245-2222
- Yellow Cab, 907/272-2422

A company called Borealis Super Shuttle (907/276-3600) operates a trio of vans almost around the clock to transportation hubs such as the Anchorage International Airport and the Alaska Railroad Depot, as well as to hotels, tourist attractions, and private homes. The cost is about half that of a cab, but you must be willing to share a ride in these 11-passenger vans. When calling for a ride, allow at least one hour's advance notice.

Driving in and Around Anchorage

If you're part of a packaged tour group or if you're interested mostly in downtown attractions, you probably won't be renting a car. However, if you want to see anything of the area, get yourself a vehicle and a map, and possibly a St. Christopher's medal. While not exactly combative, Anchorage drivers do tend to have a touch of attitude about their roads.

You'll see a lot of four-by-four vehicles, both sport-utility and pickups, and drivers who think four-wheel drive means that God is their copilot. Yield to these guys, but even if they're flaming bozos. Discretion is not only the better part of valor, but it may also keep you alive longer.

You may also notice that many of the drivers look really young. They might be: you can get a learner's permit at age 14 and a driver's license at 16. Those striplings you see behind the wheel may actually be quite skillful and cautious. But, to be safe, assume that every teen-driver stereotype is true and give them plenty of room.

Because Anchorage has no freeways, traffic can be heavy during morning and evening commute times. The situation is nothing like the rush-hour jams in big cities, but you should still allow yourself a few extra minutes to get where you're going.

Winter Driving Tips

Don't like winter driving? Then stay away from Alaska October through April, when snow is plentiful. Road crews usually swing into action when the snow begins to fall, but Anchorage is a sprawling city, and the plows can't be everywhere at once. Allow plenty of time to get to your destination, and, for heaven's sake, slow down. If you drive a stick, try downshifting before braking to avoid a skid. Automatic transmission drivers should tap their brakes gingerly to avoid one of those heart-stopping death spirals.

A cleared road may not be completely clear: "Black ice" can make you slide instead of stop when you hit the brakes. Watch the cars in front of you to see if they're skidding or fishtailing when the brake lights go on. Leave plenty of space between your front fender and the rear of the car in front of you. Don't speed.

Before you leave the rental car place, make sure a jack and spare tire are in the back, and know how to use them. If it's winter, make sure there's a scraper to remove frost and snow from the windows; the kind with a brush on one end is your best bet. And if you're driving out of town, think about buying a snow shovel and a bag of sand, too. These could be cheap insurance in the long run.

The right outdoor gear is good insurance, too. Should the car break down, warm clothes are essential. Even if you have to walk less than a mile to a telephone, you could be in trouble if the temperature is much below zero. And on an out-of-town trek you are quite likely to be many miles from

T i P

Your rental-car agreement may warn that you will be charged extra if the vehicle comes back with blood stains from hunting trips. Ditto for fish scales.

the nearest phone or tow truck. (Here's where that copy of *The Milepost*—see page 25—comes in handy.)

Make sure you're equipped to walk for help. Wear decent boots and a warm hat and see that whoever stays behind with the car is also protected from the cold. It's smart to carry a sleeping bag in the trunk since the car will get very cold very fast. It's even smarter to carry one sleeping bag per person, along with a few basic survival items such as matches, candles, water, and snacks (nuts, M&Ms, dried fruit, crackers, or freeze-dried food).

Sound alarmist? It isn't. Suppose you run out of gas late at night on a lightly traveled road. Suppose you break down during a bad storm. Suppose there is a serious earthquake. Although a state trooper or some highway samaritan might happen along, you simply can't count on it. In 1996, three Alaskans—a husband and wife and their young grandson—froze to death after their car broke down. They walked for as long as they could, but temperatures between 50 and 60 below zero finally killed them—within one mile of a roadhouse.

Major Domestic Airlines

Alaska Airlines, 800/426-0333

America West, 800/235-9292

American Airlines, 800/433-7300

Continental Airlines, 800/523-3273

Delta Airlines, 800/221-1212

Northwest Airlines, 800/225-2525

Reno Air, 800/736-6247

Sun Country Airlines (summers only), 800/752-1218

TWA (summers only), 800/221-2000

United Airlines, 800/241-6522

Parking in Anchorage

Parking made for some interesting politics in the 1997 municipal election. Some residents saw the Anchorage Parking Authority as an overly vigilant corps of meter maids, an image that was exacerbated by a controversial photo-radar program. In the end, voters booted the Authority off the streets, decreeing that only city police officers could write parking tickets.

For a while, it was a real free-for-all downtown. Alaskans realized that the average cop usually has more pressing concerns than expired meters. So downtown workers and shoppers were allegedly parking for free for hours at a time, sometimes all day long.

Free rides die hard, but they are, in fact, dead: The Anchorage Police Department has two officers assigned downtown to enforce parking. So get over it and plug those meters—unless, of course, you luck out and find a freebie. The city has approximately 500 downtown spaces with two-hour free parking. Metered parking spots cost 50 cents per hour; some of those meters accept nickels and dimes, some take only quarters.

Parking is enforced from 9 a.m. to 6 p.m., Monday through Friday. Note that enforcement is per square block—you can't simply move your car ahead a few spaces or right around the corner after your time is up. If you do and a ticket-writing officer notices, you'll get a souvenir you hadn't planned on.

Don't want to bother moving your car every two hours? The city boasts 46 private lots and two parking garages. Or utilize the Anchorage Parking Authority's remaining purpose in life: the municipal parking system. The parking garage at Fifth Avenue and C Street (entrance off B Street) is open 9 a.m. to 9:30 p.m.; if you get back later than that, you can pay by envelope.

Anchorage International Airport

Anchorage International Airport/Chris Arend

If you're going out of town, invest in a copy of *The Milepost* (Vernon Publications). This essential book, available at retailers, souvenir shops, and even grocery stores, provides mile-by-mile logs of all northern roads, offering vital information on scenic turnoffs, tourist attractions, campgrounds, state and national parks, and safe traveling in the north country.

It's quite a deal, really: 50 cents per hour, up to five dollars per day. This garage is attached via skybridge to the Anchorage Fifth Avenue Mall (see Chapter 9, Shopping).

Note: You can get up to two hours of free parking at either municipal garage if you shop at Nordstrom, JC Penney, or any of the stores at Anchorage Fifth Avenue Mall. Just ask a salesclerk to validate your ticket. The garage at Sixth Avenue and H Street (entrance on H) is open 9 a.m. to 6 p.m., also with after-hours envelope payments. The cost at this garage is 75 cents per hour, up to $5 per day. The Ship Creek Center (formerly Post Office Mall) parking lot is on Third Avenue between C and E; meters there run up to 10 hours. And if you drove your RV to Alaska? Park it at the A-C Couplet Lot, on Third Avenue between A and C Streets. The cost is five dollars per day.

Biking in Anchorage

The Department of Parks and Recreation frowns on the term "bike trails," preferring the name "multiuse trails." Bicyclists do use the 175 miles of paved trails in Anchorage and Eagle River, but so do walkers, runners, skiers, skijorers, in-line skaters, and folks out exercising the family dog. Ring a bell to warn others of your approach and call out, "Passing on the left!" before you make your move. (Remember that some of your fellow trail users are wearing headphones, though, and proceed with caution.)

Some people, but only a relative few, use the trails for commuting by bike. It's easiest to do so, of course, when it hasn't snowed recently since snow-removal crews can't get to every trail immediately. Besides, newly snow-covered byways quickly fill with happy Nordic skiers. Cold temperatures are also an issue; folks who would gladly pedal to work in San Diego tend to balk at riding when it's 10 below zero.

Only a couple of city streets, none of them major thoroughfares, have bike lanes. More may be forthcoming. Because Alaskan drivers tend to be a bit attitudinal, those who do cycle to work on city streets may face close, calls from drivers who believe that bikes belong on the bike—uh, multiuse—trails.

Anchorage International Airport

The Anchorage International Airport (907/266-2525) is owned and operated by the State of Alaska. It pays for itself through rates and fees. The approximately 5,000-acre complex hosts domestic and international passenger flights, commuter service, and national and international cargo.

The airport averages about 160 domestic passenger flights each day, from major carrier to regional commuter flights. You can take a commercial or private plane from Anchorage to anywhere else in the state. Because Alaska simply doesn't have many roads and its sheer size makes driving impractical, air travel, whether by commercial jet or glacier-hopping small plane, is very popular. Some rural communities do not even have road connections but do have airports, or at least their own airstrips, so companies like Reeve Aleutian Airways, Frontier Flying Service, and ERA Aviation can bring people back and forth.

Year-round international passenger service is surprisingly brisk, given the size of the city. You can fly to countries such as Korea, Russia, Germany, Switzerland, and Japan. Tourists are intrigued by the possibility of flying to Russia, as well they might be. Aeroflot currently has a weekly trip to Magadan and two trips each week to Khabarovsk.

The airport is also seeing considerable growth in carriers such as Federal Express and United Parcel Service, and in cargo traffic to more than 30 European, Asian, and North American cities.

Lake Hood air harbor

Anchorage CVB

Train Travel

The Alaska Railroad is the last full-service railroad in North America, transporting both people and freight. The railroad runs daily in summer and on an abbreviated schedule during winter. The tracks span 525 miles, from Seward to Fairbanks. From Anchorage, you can take a train to those two cities, as well as to Whittier, Wasilla, Denali National Park, Talkeetna, or to any points in between; it's the last "flag-stop" railroad in America, allowing people literally to flag down the train and hop on board. (People who live in outlying areas appreciate the convenience, and tourists love watching Bush rats hop off, loaded down with groceries and gear bought "in town.") Each railroad coach has reclining seats and large windows, so you can watch for moose and other wildlife. All cars are wheelchair-accessible. The northbound train (Anchorage–Denali–Fairbanks) features a full-service dining car.

From mid-May through mid-September, the railroad offers four different southern train rides: Anchorage to Whittier, Portage to Whittier, Anchorage to Seward, and the "Seward Swing," a trip from Seward to Portage and back. All routes follow the shoreline of Turnagain Arm, a beautiful ride with rugged mountains, alpine glaciers, and the chance to see mountain goats, moose, bears, Dall sheep, eagles, and, if you're lucky, beluga whales and bore tides. From Whittier, the gateway to Prince William Sound, you can connect with half-day cruises or other outdoor activities (see Chapter 13, Day Trips).

The railroad also offers a number of combination tours, which combine a train ride with helicopter flightseeing, a riverboat ride, fly-in fishing, glacier cruises, rafting, a tour of Denali National Park, and even an "Arctic Circle Air Adventure." Reservations are recommended; call 800/544-0552 or, in Alaska, 907/265-2494. Or check out the Web site at www.akrr.com.

Regal Alaskan Hotel

3

WHERE TO STAY

No room at the inn? Unlikely, these days. Between 1997 and 1999, the number of hotel rooms in Anchorage increased by 25 percent.

Most of the city's hotels huddle in two places: downtown and near the airport.

You can find very basic accommodations and extremely luxurious suites in both locations. Bed-and-breakfast establishments pick up the slack in the rest of the city.

Some area hotels go so far as to have a concierge, but in others you'll be lucky to find a desk clerk. Remember that things are sometimes done a little differently in Anchorage. For instance, you probably won't have the current New York Times with your breakfast because the paper has to be flown in. And if you select a relatively inexpensive downtown hotel, you probably won't have a dozen clerks dancing in attendance.

So remember the stranded seal hunter's motto: Go with the floe. If you are civil to the often overworked desk clerks, you'll be able to get their advice about the city later on. Who better to ask than the people who live here?

Rates are indicated by the symbols listed below. A dramatic difference between summer and off-season rates is shown as a range. Rates do not include the 8 percent city bed tax. (Most bed-and-breakfasts are exempt from this tax.)

Price-rating symbols:

$	Under $65
$$	$66 to $90
$$$	$91 to $140
$$$$	$141 and up

DOWNTOWN

Hotels and Motels

ALASKAN SAMOVAR INN
720 Gambell St.
Anchorage
907/277-1511
$–$$

This place isn't as fancy as some other downtown hotels, and it's a bit of a walk from the major attractions—which is the main reason why it's cheaper than those heart-of-the-action places. The Samovar has free local calls, cable, and room service delivered from its restaurant. It's also six blocks away from a grocery store. ♿ (Downtown)

ANCHORAGE HILTON
500 W. Third Ave.
Anchorage
907/272-7411
$$$–$$$$

It's a Hilton, and it's right in the thick of the downtown scene, so naturally it's a bit pricey. But for those seeking a convenient location and the guaranteed service of a known hotel chain, it's a winner. Ask for a room with a view of Cook Inlet or the mountains. When Mount McKinley is "out," you can see it from the West or Anchorage towers. The hotel has a health club and three places to eat: the Berry Patch for casual dining, the Sports Edition bar for snacks and the big game, and the Top of the World for an elegant evening. ♿ (Downtown)

ANCHORAGE HOTEL
330 E St.
Anchorage
907/272-4553
$$–$$$$

Built in 1916, with an addition in 1936,

The Anchorage originally included a kennel for dog mushers. This heart-of-downtown hotel once housed painter Sydney Laurence (look for his works at the Anchorage Museum of History and Art). You'll find a minibar in each room, free local phone calls, a morning newspaper delivered daily, and complimentary continental breakfast. Luggage storage and freezer space are available. Rumrunners Lounge serves lunch and dinner. ♿ (Downtown)

ANCHORAGE MARRIOTT DOWNTOWN
820 W. Seventh Ave.
Anchorage
800/228-9290
$$–$$$$

Each of the nearly 400 rooms in this brand-new hotel feature individual climate control, coffeemakers, cable TV, and irons and boards. Guests have a choice of smoking or non-smoking rooms and the use of an indoor pool, a fitness center, and a business center. The concierge level offers breakfast in the morning and cocktails and hors d'oeuvres at night. A full-service restaurant, a lounge, and a variety of retail shops are on the premises. The hotel is close to the city's Park Strip (see Chapter 8, Parks and Gardens) and the Coastal Trail, a favorite walking/jogging/biking thoroughfare (see Chapter 10, Sports and Recreation). ♿ (Downtown)

BLACK ANGUS INN
1430 Gambell St.
Anchorage
907/272-7503 or 800/770-0707
$–$$

This recently remodeled hotel is a long way from downtown attractions, but it has its advantages. The

DOWNTOWN ANCHORAGE

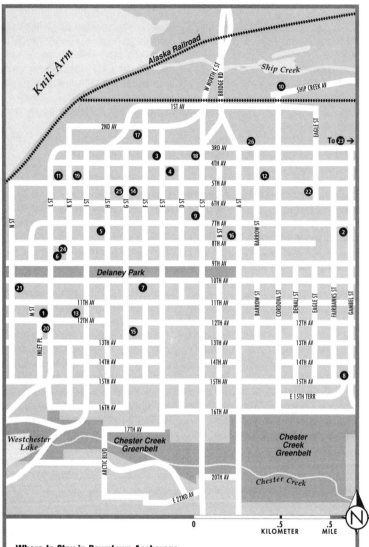

Where to Stay in Downtown Anchorage

1 12th & L Bed and
   Breakfast
2 Alaskan Samovar Inn
3 Anchorage Hilton
4 Anchorage Hotel
5 Anchorage International
   Hostel
6 Anchorage Marriott
   Downtown
7 Bed & Breakfast on the
   Park
8 Black Angus Inn
9 Clarion Suites

10 Comfort Inn Ship Creek
11 Copper Whale
12 Days Inn
13 Earth Bed & Breakfast
14 Econo Lodge
15 Gallery Bed & Breakfast
16 Hawthorn Suites
17 Historic Leopold David
   B&B Inn
18 Holiday Inn of Anchorage
19 Hotel Captain Cook
20 Inlet Tower Suites
21 Oscar Gill House

22 Sheraton Anchorage
23 Ship Creek Landing RV
   Park
24 Snowshoe Inn
25 Westmark Anchorage
   Hotel
26 Westmark Inn Third
   Avenue

rates are low, some rooms have kitchenettes, and a grocery store is two blocks away. The restaurant serves three meals daily and provides room service. The hotel offers free local calls and cable TV. Senior and military discounts are available, as are weekly rates in winter. Free shuttle to the airport and train station. ♿ (Downtown)

CLARION SUITES
325 W. Eighth Ave.
Anchorage
907/274-1000 or 888/389-6575
clarions@alaska.net
$$–$$$

These two-room suites offer microwaves, refrigerators, cable and Web TV (on two televisions), and telephones that provide personal voice mail, dataports, and speakerphones. Take advantage of the hotel's swimming pool and whirlpool, exercise room, and the "Choice Picks" food court, with nine restaurants that serve three "fast, fun, affordable" meals a day. The hotel is a block away from the Anchorage Museum of History and Art, and just a couple of blocks from downtown shops and restaurants. Free parking and free airport and railroad shuttle. ♿ (Downtown)

COMFORT INN SHIP CREEK
111 W. Ship Creek Ave.
Anchorage
907/277-6887 or 800/228-5150
$$–$$$

This new hotel is located a couple blocks from the Alaska Railroad Depot and even closer to Ship Creek, the city's premier urban salmon fishery (see Chapter 5, Sights and Attractions). From your window you can watch folks in hip waders grappling with 40-plus-pound king salmon. If you're tempted to join them, the hotel offers free fishing tackle. You can also rent a bike for a minimal fee and explore the downtown area, or stay indoors and exercise in the hotel pool. Dataports are available in many rooms, as are kitchenettes. The complimentary deluxe continental breakfast is served from 6 to 10 a.m. Free on-call shuttle service to airport and railroad depot. ♿ (Downtown)

DAYS INN
321 E. Fifth Ave.
Anchorage
907/276-7226 or 800/325-2525
$–$$$

Here you'll find basic, comfortable rooms in the center of downtown. For a fine view, ask for a room that opens onto Mount Susitna (also known as Sleeping Lady), Mount McKinley, or the Chugach Range. A dozen newly remodeled rooms even have air-conditioning. The Daybreak Café serves breakfast, lunch, and dinner. The hotel has a car rental place on the premises, making it easy to pick up and return your vehicle. Free shuttle service to and from the airport and railroad depot. ♿ (Downtown)

ECONO LODGE
642 E. Fifth Ave.
Anchorage
907/274-1515
$–$$

Though it has an edge-of-downtown location, hardy walkers will find the savings well worth the stroll. The hotel was recently renovated and offers free local calls and cable TV. "Senior rooms" feature digital alarm clocks with oversized numbers, telephones with extra-large keypads, and refrigerators and coffeepots. If you're in town for the fishing, the hotel will keep your catch in the freezer at no charge. Free 24-hour airport shuttle. & (Downtown)

HAWTHORN SUITES
110 W. Eighth Ave.
Anchorage
907/222-5005 or 888/469-6575
$$–$$$
These two-room suites have microwaves, refrigerators, minibars, cable and Web TV (on two screens), and telephones that provide fax, personal voice mail, dataports, and speakerphones (and if that's not enough, there's also a guest business center). Take advantage of the hotel's swimming pool, whirlpool, and exercise room, or head out the door and walk one block to the Coastal Trail (or rent a hotel bike). The hotel has a complimentary hot breakfast buffet as well as Benihana

restaurant. Free airport and railroad shuttle. & (Downtown)

HOLIDAY INN OF ANCHORAGE
239 W. Fourth Ave.
Anchorage
907/279-8671
$$–$$$$
Recently renovated, this conveniently located Holiday Inn provides such amenities as free cable, coffeemakers, irons and ironing boards, a health club and pool, and a coinop laundry. Its restaurant is open for breakfast, lunch, and dinner. Free airport transportation every hour. & (Downtown)

HOTEL CAPTAIN COOK
Fourth Ave. and K St.
Anchorage
907/276-6000 or 800/843-1950
$$$–$$$$
This stately hotel is close to all

downtown attractions and boasts wonderful views. Specify Tower 3 for the best city view or Tower 2 for the best glimpse of Cook Inlet. Guests have access to the excellent athletic club and can dine at three restaurants serving everything from light meals and pub-style food to gourmet cuisine. Hotel shops offer souvenirs, books, gifts, fine clothing, Native art, gourmet chocolates, jewelry, and cosmetics. Haircuts, shoeshines, therapeutic massage, travel reservations, tailoring, and valet parking are also available. ♿ (Downtown)

INLET TOWER SUITES
1200 L St.
Anchorage
907/276-0110
$$–$$$

This hotel is on the outskirts of downtown, within 10 to 12 blocks of most tourist attractions. Ask for a room facing the Inlet (west) or the Chugach Range (east). Every room has at least a queen-size bed (a king-size is just five dollars more) plus coffee fixings, a refrigerator, and a microwave; some also have whirlpool tubs. The hotel is near the Coastal Trail, and there's a small workout room with saunas on the premises. The restaurant serves lunch and dinner daily in summer, only dinner in winter; the lounge is open until 2 a.m. The Inlet Tower is also just a stone's throw away from New Sagaya City Market (see Chapter 9, Shopping), where you can buy international hot foods, fancy cheeses and deli items, freshly baked breads, and plenty of gourmet coffees. Other hotel amenities include an on-site laundry facility, free parking, and 24-hour airport shuttle service. ♿ (Downtown)

SHERATON ANCHORAGE
401 E. Sixth Ave.
Anchorage
907/276-8700
$$$–$$$$

Though slightly off the beaten track of downtown, the Sheraton is still an easy walk from local attractions (and closer to the Anchorage Museum of History and Art than most other downtown lodgings). Its photos and etched-marble murals and artifacts on each floor depict legends of Alaska Native groups. All rooms offer hairdryers, coffeemakers, and irons and ironing boards. Work off extra calories or travel kinks at the full-service health club. Enjoy fine dining at the Bistro 401, including a nightly seafood buffet in summer, or Asian food and drink at the Legends Lounge, whose menu includes sushi and saki. ♿ (Downtown)

WESTMARK ANCHORAGE HOTEL
720 W. Fifth Ave.
Anchorage
907/276-7676 or 800/544-0970
$$$–$$$$

All 200 guest rooms and suites have balconies that give you an above-it-all look at the city and its surroundings. Depending on which side of the hotel you're staying on, you'll view the city, mountains, or inlet. Some rooms have exercise equipment. On-site restaurants serve breakfast (Manor House Café) and lunch or dinner (Mesa Grill). The hotel is right downtown, just across the street from the Glacier Brew House brewpub. ♿ (Downtown)

WESTMARK INN THIRD AVENUE
115 E. Third Ave.
Anchorage
907/272-7561 or 800/544-0970
$$$–$$$$

B&B on the Park

Bed & Breakfast on the Park

Here's a funky bit of history: This building's grand opening took place on March 27, 1964—the day of the Good Friday Earthquake, the most devastating temblor on the North American continent. Obviously, the structure survived. The three-story hotel is open in summer only, and it's less expensive than some other downtown hotels. In part, that's because it's less elaborate: There are no coffeemakers, voice mail, computer hookups, or other frills, although you do get cable TV. The hotel's not right in the thick of things, but it's close to the train station and not a terribly long walk to most downtown attractions. And if you must have caffeine in the morning, go down to the lobby for a free cuppa joe. The hotel's lounge serves beer and wine, and its restaurant is open for breakfast and dinner. ⚹ (Downtown)

Bed-and-Breakfasts

12TH & L BED AND BREAKFAST
1134 L St.

Anchorage
907/276-1225
arcticimages@customcpu.com
$–$$$
A comfortable walk from downtown attractions, this inn has private baths, cable TV, a two-line telephone, and coded door locks for each room. Rooms sleep two to four people. Other amenities include luggage storage, laundry facilities, self-serve full breakfast all morning, and accessibility to the Coastal Trail, Park Strip, and municipal tennis courts. No smoking. (Downtown)

BED & BREAKFAST ON THE PARK
602 W. 10th Ave.
Anchorage
907/277-0878
$–$$
Located right on the Park Strip downtown recreational spot, this pleasant inn was once a log-cabin church. Each room has a phone and a private bath, and the common room has a refrigerator and microwave. Laundry facilities are available. (Downtown)

COPPER WHALE
440 L St.
Anchorage
907/258-7999
cwhalein@alaska.net
$–$$$
This B&B offers a prime location—most rooms have a view of Cook Inlet—and a pleasant, homey atmosphere. It has shared or private baths, with phones and voice-mail in every room (most phones are modem-compatible). The Coastal Trail is nearby, as is Surf City, an Internet café. ⚹ (Downtown)

EARTH BED & BREAKFAST
1001 W. 12th Ave.

Anchorage
907/279-9907
www.AlaskaOne.com/earthbb
earthtrs@alaska.net
$–$$$

Foreign visitors take note: The owner of this B&B speaks a half-dozen languages and is working on two more. Margriet van Laake is fluent in German, Dutch, French, Italian, Afrikaans, and Spanish and currently studies Russian and Japanese. Her B&B offers two rooms with private baths and two rooms with a shared bath. Guests have access to a sunny garden, bike paths, and lots of parking. The inn is within 10 blocks of most tourist attractions, so you may choose to forego a rental car. Van Laake's other business, Earth Tours, can help you reserve tours, vehicle rentals, lodges, cruises, outdoor adventures, and other activities in Anchorage and around the state. (Downtown)

GALLERY BED & BREAKFAST
1229 G St.
Anchorage
907/274-2567
lesevans@alaska.net
$–$$

This B&B has eight rooms, all with telephones and alarm clocks. Bathrooms are shared; laundry facilities are available. It's a seven-block walk downtown, but the price is right. A specialty grocery store with an extensive menu of cooked foods is nearby. Free luggage storage. ♿ (Downtown)

HISTORIC LEOPOLD DAVID B&B INN
605 W. Second Ave.
Anchorage
907/279-1917 or 888/279-1225

Welcome@AlaskaHoliday.com
$$–$$$$

This Victorian-style building was constructed in 1917 for the family of the first mayor of Anchorage. As a rooming house, its lower level was used by Alaska Railroad executives who came here to build the railway. Eight rooms and suites are available, all with private entries and varying views that include Cook Inlet, volcanoes, and downtown Anchorage. Depending on the accommodations you select, you will have one or more of the following options: coffeemaker, refrigerator, kitchen, library, phone with dataport, or fireplace. All rooms have cable TV and private baths. (Downtown)

OSCAR GILL HOUSE
1344 W. 10th Ave.
Anchorage
907/258-1717
TOGH@alaskabandb.com
$$–$$$

Oscar Gill was a pioneer who became, among other things, three-term mayor and speaker of the territorial house. His 1913 clapboard home was originally built in the town of Knik. Moved and renovated in cooperation with Anchorage Historic Properties, it's now a B&B located on Park Strip, within walking distance of all downtown attractions. It features luxuries such as bathrobes, down comforters, and Body Shop toiletries, plus such amenities as laundry facilities and the use of bicycles and skis for the nearby Coastal Trail. (Downtown)

SNOWSHOE INN
826 K St.
Anchorage
907/258-7669
$–$$$

TIP

Staying downtown? Take advantage of the People Mover's "Dash Zone"—free bus rides through the area bordered by Fifth Avenue, Eagle Street, Eighth Avenue, and K Street. Weekday buses on Fifth and Sixth run about every 10 minutes; weekend buses run less frequently.

This newly remodeled B&B is close to tourist attractions yet away from downtown noise and traffic. Enjoy a morning stroll on the Park Strip or a more ambitious walk on the nearby Coastal Trail. The inn offers gear and equipment storage, laundry facilities, and a shared or private bath. The rooms are basic and clean, and each has a small refrigerator, microwave, and TV/VCR combo. Two suites, with Jacuzzis, are available. Smoking is not permitted. (Downtown)

Hostels and Campgrounds

ANCHORAGE INTERNATIONAL HOSTEL
700 H St.
Anchorage
907/276-3635
$
Many travelers have fond memories of hostel stays, whether at home or abroad. The advantage, of course, is meeting people from all over the world who are interested in seeing Alaska, too. The disadvantage is living dorm-style and sharing a bathroom, but for these prices, who can complain? You're also asked to do a housekeeping chore in the morning. The hostel is located downtown within easy access of tourist attractions, the People Mover Transit Center, the Coastal Trail, and the Alaska Railroad Depot. Luggage storage space is available. &. (Downtown)

SHIP CREEK LANDING RV PARK
150 N. Ingra St.
Anchorage
907/277-0877
$
One hundred and fifty full hookups and tent spaces are available here, as are bathrooms, showers, and laundry facilities. You can walk to downtown attractions, and the park has easy access to Ship Creek fishing. (Downtown)

SOUTH ANCHORAGE

Bed-and-Breakfasts

15 CHANDELIERS
14020 Sabine St.
907/345-3032
chndlr15@alaska.net
www.alaska.net/~chndlr15
$$–$$$
Those crystal chandeliers hang from 10-foot ceilings in this manor-style house. Each room has a theme—Victoria, King George, Scottish Royals, Queen Mary Doll—and they all have queen-size beds, phones, TVs, and private baths. The B&B is located close to the Alaska Zoo and the Potter Marsh Bird Sanctuary. German is spoken here. Send correspondence to P.O. Box 110528, Anchorage 99511. (South Anchorage)

AURORA WINDS B&B
7501 Upper O'Malley

Anchorage
907/346-2533
awbnb@alaska.net
www.aurorawinds.com
$–$$$

This tastefully decorated B&B was drastically enlarged in 1999. It offers an indoor swimming pool, an exercise room, a sauna, a pool table, a home theater with surround sound, and an outdoor hot tub, plus a meeting room and banquet facility. Its suites are large, each with a private bath, sitting area, TV, optional VCR, and phone; one suite also has a kitchenette. The two-acre lot is beautifully landscaped with wildflower, formal, and water gardens. It's located close to ski and golf areas and to the Alaska Zoo. Smoking is permitted in designated areas. (South Anchorage)

GOURMET FLEURS
10000 Hillside Dr.
Anchorage
907/346-1758
jstranik@alaska.net
www.alaska.net/~jstranik
$$$$

A private suite in this beautiful home, set on a two-acre lot, offers panoramic views of the city and mountains. The suite sleeps up to six people in the bedroom and sitting room and has a full kitchen; it has a private deck next to a fragrant herb garden. The house also has a pool table, an exercise room, beautiful gardens, and true gourmet cooking (a former caterer runs the place). Since there's only one B&B suite, visitors are treated as exclusive guests. (South Anchorage)

IVY INN
13570 Westwind Dr.
Anchorage

907/345-4024
www.alaska.net/~ivyinn/
$$

The private-entry rooms, accommodating up to six people, have complete kitchens with well-stocked refrigerators so that you can fix breakfast at your own pace. The inn provides storage for outdoor gear and a barbecue grill for anglers who wish to cook their catches. Located close to Chugach State Park, the inn offers quick access to tennis, skiing, horseback riding, shopping, and bird-watching at Potter Marsh. (South Anchorage)

LITTLE RABBIT CREEK
5420 Rabbit Creek Rd.
Anchorage
907/345-8183
$$–$$$

In this beautiful hillside setting, paths from the garden lead down to a cedar swing and guest deck by a creek. Rooms are decorated with antiques and Alaskan art, and each has a private entry, phone, and cable TV. The common area is

Oscar Gill House, p. 35

Oscar Gill House

GREATER ANCHORAGE

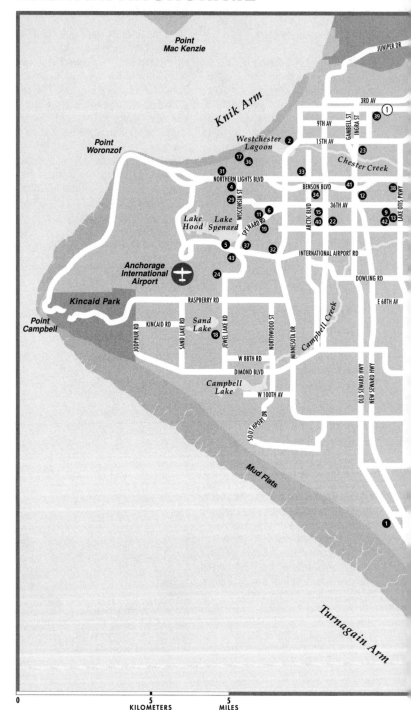

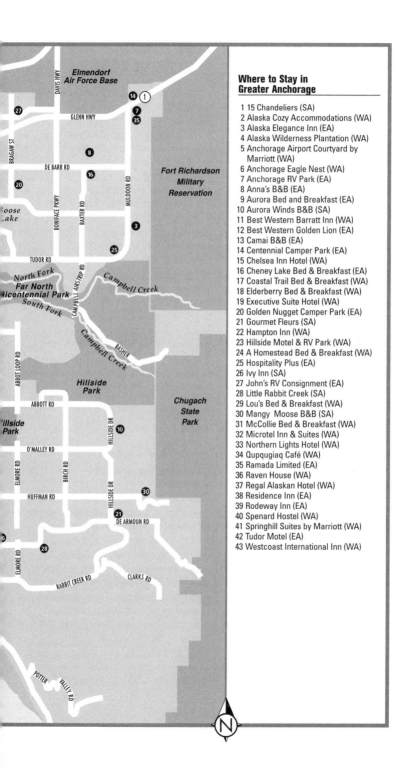

Where to Stay in Greater Anchorage

1 15 Chandeliers (SA)
2 Alaska Cozy Accommodations (WA)
3 Alaska Elegance Inn (EA)
4 Alaska Wilderness Plantation (WA)
5 Anchorage Airport Courtyard by Marriott (WA)
6 Anchorage Eagle Nest (WA)
7 Anchorage RV Park (EA)
8 Anna's B&B (EA)
9 Aurora Bed and Breakfast (EA)
10 Aurora Winds B&B (SA)
11 Best Western Barratt Inn (WA)
12 Best Western Golden Lion (EA)
13 Camai B&B (EA)
14 Centennial Camper Park (EA)
15 Chelsea Inn Hotel (WA)
16 Cheney Lake Bed & Breakfast (EA)
17 Coastal Trail Bed & Breakfast (WA)
18 Elderberry Bed & Breakfast (WA)
19 Executive Suite Hotel (WA)
20 Golden Nugget Camper Park (EA)
21 Gourmet Fleurs (SA)
22 Hampton Inn (WA)
23 Hillside Motel & RV Park (WA)
24 A Homestead Bed & Breakfast (WA)
25 Hospitality Plus (EA)
26 Ivy Inn (SA)
27 John's RV Consignment (EA)
28 Little Rabbit Creek (WA)
29 Lou's Bed & Breakfast (WA)
30 Mangy Moose B&B (SA)
31 McCollie Bed & Breakfast (WA)
32 Microtel Inn & Suites (WA)
33 Northern Lights Hotel (WA)
34 Qupqugiaq Café (WA)
35 Ramada Limited (EA)
36 Raven House (WA)
37 Regal Alaskan Hotel (WA)
38 Residence Inn (EA)
39 Rodeway Inn (EA)
40 Spenard Hostel (WA)
41 Springhill Suites by Marriott (WA)
42 Tudor Motel (EA)
43 Westcoast International Inn (WA)

stocked with gourmet hot drinks and juices, and guests have access to a mini-kitchen. (South Anchorage)

MANGY MOOSE B&B
5560 E. 112th Ave.
Anchorage
907/346-8052
mmoose@arctic.net
www.bnbweb.com/
mangymoose.html
$$–$$$
This nonsmoking B&B, on a wooded lot on a sparsely populated street, features specialized decor: The Denali Room is decorated with Alaskan art, the Bush Pilot Room has aviation decor, and the Gone Fishin' Room has fish netting and a piscine theme. All rooms have private baths. Other features include a guest deck, private entrances, and proximity to the Alaska Zoo. (South Anchorage)

EAST ANCHORAGE

Hotels and Motels

BEST WESTERN GOLDEN LION HOTEL
1000 E. 36th Ave.
Anchorage
907/561-1522
$$–$$$
Located close to the University of Alaska–Anchorage and Alaska Pacific University, the Golden Lion has large rooms with coffeemakers, cable TV, and free local calls. The hotel's Garden Café serves breakfast, lunch, and dinner, and live bands play in the lounge on weekends. Free parking. ᕃ (East Anchorage)

RAMADA LIMITED
207 Muldoon Rd.
Anchorage
907/929-7000 or 800/2-RAMADA
$–$$$$
On the outskirts of Anchorage, this hotel is about 11 miles from the airport, adjacent to military bases and just a stone's throw from the Glenn Highway, which takes you to the Mat-Su Valley, Denali National Park, and Fairbanks. The hotel has a full-service restaurant on the premises and is located near a string of fast-food restaurants and two major supermarkets. Rooms at the Ramada Limited have cable TV, coffeemakers, and voice mail. Business rooms have all those amenities plus two-line business phones with dataports, hairdryers, and irons and ironing boards. Suites have queen-size beds and sleeper sofas, refrigerators, microwaves, coffeemakers, irons, hairdryers, and Jacuzzis. The hotel offer a complimentary hot breakfast buffet and free parking. Freezer space is available. ᕃ (East Anchorage)

RESIDENCE INN
1025 E. 35th Ave.
Anchorage
907/563-9844 or 800/331-3131
www.residenceinn.com
$$$–$$$$
This hotel, which opened in 1999, provides room to stretch out, whether you're traveling with family or on an extended business trip. Studio, one-bedroom, and two-bedroom suites are available. All have separate sleeping and living areas (the two-bedroom suites have two bathrooms), generous work space with dataports and Internet access, full kitchens, coffeemakers, cable TV, irons and boards, a complimentary grocery-shopping service, guest laundry, and a free daily newspaper.

Regal Alaskan Hotel, p. 47

The hotel also has a pool, spa, and an exercise room. It offers a continental breakfast buffet daily and, on Monday through Thursday evenings, a complimentary dinner hour, with informal meals. A number of restaurants are nearby, with offerings ranging from Mexican to Japanese to steakhouse fare. The hotel shuttle will take you to the airport or any other destination within five miles. &. (East Anchorage)

RODEWAY INN
1104 E. Fifth Ave.
Anchorage
907/274-1655
$–$$

You'll find basic rooms in this recently renovated hotel, located a brisk walk from downtown attractions and close to the best fried-chicken restaurant in town, the Lucky Wishbone (see Chapter 4, Where to Eat). Each room has a refrigerator, and freezer space is provided for fish you catch. Free local calls and cable, plus free shuttle to the airport or train depot. (East Anchorage)

TUDOR MOTEL
4423 Lake Otis Pkwy.
Anchorage
907/561-2234
$–$$

Each room at this motel has a kitchenette and free cable and local calls. Located at a very busy intersection, it's close to several fast-food restaurants and the University of Alaska–Anchorage. Weekly rates are available. &. (East Anchorage)

Bed-and-Breakfasts

ALASKA ELEGANCE INN
8501 Brookridge Dr.
Anchorage
907/338-0453
$–$$

Enjoy a great view from this B&B in the foothills of the Chugach Mountains, next to a greenbelt. Each of the inn's large rooms has a phone and a TV/VCR (video library

Earthquake!

On March 27, 1964, the earth moved big-time in Anchorage. That was the day of the Good Friday Earthquake, which even today gets uppercase pronunciation. The temblor, the strongest ever felt in North America, measured 9.2 on the Richter scale. How strong was that, exactly? Think of the bomb that leveled Hiroshima and multiply that energy times 10 million.

The earthquake had a surprisingly low death toll—115 people in all, including those killed in outlying areas by the resulting tsunamis. Many downtown buildings were damaged or destroyed, however. Citywide, property damage was estimated at $205 million.

Alaska is the most seismic of the 50 states. The Alaska Earthquake Information Center in Fairbanks records about 120 temblors every week. Since most of them are of low magnitude or located far from towns or cities, they go unnoticed by the general population.

Still, if you feel an earthquake, even a small one, it'll certainly get your attention. If you're indoors, stay put unless you're clearly in danger. Get under a heavy table or desk; a doorway will do only if it doesn't appear to be buckling and has no swinging door to knock you down or crunch your fingers.

Outside? Get away from trees, phone and power lines, fuel tanks, potential avalanche areas, and buildings—especially brick and glass ones. Down by the waterside? Head for high ground immediately. Driving? Get as far off the road as you can, and stick with your car unless you're in obvious peril.

If you'd like to know more about earthquakes, visit the University of Alaska-Fairbanks Web site at www.giseis.alaska.edu/Seis/.

available), and guests have the choice of a private or shared bath. You'll enjoy homemade breakfasts, and the owners can accommodate special diets. Some German is spoken. Smoking is not permitted indoors. Open summers only. (East Anchorage)

ANNA'S B&B
830 Jay Circle
Anchorage

907/338-5331
annas@alaska.net
www.alaska.net/~annas
$$

Guests sigh over waffles made with real Alaskan sourdough—so good that the hostess offers souvenir sourdough starter. Rooms have refrigerators, phones, and TVs; two of them also have microwaves. German is spoken. (East Anchorage)

AURORA BED AND BREAKFAST
1916 E. 37th Ave.
Anchorage
907/562-2411
aurorabnb@customcpu.com
www.customcpu.com/
commercial/aurora
$–$$

"A new home with an old country feeling" is the way that the hosts describe this B&B. They built the house themselves, incorporating into their design two fully disabled-accessible rooms and bathrooms. All rooms have private baths, queen-size beds, and radiant floor heating. Aurora is located in a quiet neighborhood, close to the University of Alaska–Anchorage and Providence Medical Center and just a few minutes from downtown; it also has easy access to public transit. ♿ (East Anchorage)

CAMAI B&B
3838 Westminster
Anchorage
907/333-2219 or 800/659-8763
camai@alaska.net
www.camaibnb.com
$$–$$$

This beautifully landscaped B&B was selected for the 1998 Anchorage Garden Tour. Camai's two suites each have a private entry, sitting room with daybed, bathroom, phone

(can be hooked up to modem), TV, radio, and mini-fridge. The wheelchair-accessible suite has a kitchenette with a refrigerator, microwave, and cook-top range. This B&B is close to a neighborhood park with a playground, trails on the Alaska Pacific University campus, and a greenbelt frequented by moose. ♿ (East Anchorage)

CHENEY LAKE BED & BREAKFAST
6333 Colgate Dr.
Anchorage
907/337-4391 or 888/337-4391
cheneybb@alaska.net
www.alaska.net/~cheneybb
$$

Surrounded by a lake, mountains, and a quiet neighborhood, this inn offers king-size beds, private baths, phones, TVs, and VCRs (an extensive video library is available). Juices, teas, and other beverages are free. The Alaska Botanical Garden (see Chapter 8, Parks and Gardens) is nearby. No smoking. (East Anchorage)

HOSPITALITY PLUS
7722 Anne Circle
Anchorage
907/333-8504
jbudai@alaska.net
www.alaska.net/~jbudai/
$–$$

Your hosts at this B&B are long-time Alaskans and willing storytellers. Hospitality Plus offers three rooms with either a shared or a private bath. The master suite, a double-size room, has a phone, TV, and refrigerator. The wooded backyard is popular with moose, and skiing/bike trails are closeby. Amenities include luggage storage, freezer space, big family-style breakfasts, and a gift shop with items made by family

Have trouble sleeping in a light room? The sun sets late here in the summer, and light lingers in the sky for hours afterward. Consider bringing a sleep mask, or a roll of aluminum foil and some tape to "darken" your room windows each evening.

members. Hungarian is spoken. No smoking, no alcohol. (East Anchorage)

Campgrounds

ANCHORAGE RV PARK
7300 Oilwell Rd.
Anchorage
907/338-7275
$
The 195-site park has full hookups, a dump station, showers, restrooms, a laundry facility, and a cable TV hookup. Some grocery and RV supplies are available. (East Anchorage)

CENTENNIAL CAMPER PARK
8300 Glenn Hwy.
Anchorage
907/333-9711
$
The city runs this campsite, which allows tent camping only. Water and dump stations are available. Seven-day limit. (East Anchorage)

GOLDEN NUGGET CAMPER PARK
4100 DeBarr Rd.
Anchorage
907/333-2012
$
Choose from full hookups or electricity only. Dry campsites are available too. The park has showers and a Laundromat. (East Anchorage)

JOHN'S RV CONSIGNMENT
3453 Mountain View Dr.
Anchorage
907/277-4332
$
A short drive from downtown, this park has full hookups, showers, a Laundromat, phone jacks, and a dump station. (East Anchorage)

WEST ANCHORAGE

Hotels and Motels

ANCHORAGE AIRPORT COURTYARD BY MARRIOTT
4901 Spenard Rd.
Anchorage
907/245-0322 or 800/321-2211
$$$–$$$$
Just one-and-a-half miles from the airport, this beautiful hotel is brand-new. Each room has a queen- or king-size bed, large work desk, coffeemaker, clock-radio, and hairdryer; king suites have refrigerators and microwaves. A full-service restaurant and a fitness center with a heated indoor pool are also on-site. Other amenities include same-day valet service, guest laundry facilities, and a complimentary airport shuttle. ⅍ (West Anchorage)

ANCHORAGE EAGLE NEST
4110 Spenard Rd.

Anchorage
907/243-3433
$–$$

This recently renovated hotel in the Spenard district is close to both a family-style restaurant and the notorious Fly By Night Club (see Chapter 12, Nightlife). Studio rooms are available. The hotel offers free coffee and doughnuts in the morning, plus a courtesy shuttle to the airport and train station. & (West Anchorage)

BEST WESTERN BARRATT INN
4616 Spenard Rd.
Anchorage
907/243-3131 or 800/221-7550
$$–$$$

Enjoy free cable, a fitness center, luggage storage, and freezer space for fish at this Best Western. The inn is close to Lake Hood, the world's busiest floatplane base—great for photo opportunities or flightseeing. In summer, the hotel's on-site coordinator will book tours and charters both locally and statewide. The Susitna Restaurant and Lounge serves breakfast, lunch, and dinner. Free shuttle to the airport. & (West Anchorage)

CHELSEA INN HOTEL
3636 Spenard Rd.
Anchorage
907/276-5002
$–$$

This former church is something of an oddity: a hotel in which some of the rooms share baths. If price means more to you than convenient tooth-brushing, this is the place. However, some rooms with private baths are available. Amenities include cable TV, local calls, freezer space, and morning coffee and fruit. Coin-op laundry facilities are available, and a number of fast-food

restaurants are closeby. Free 24-hour shuttle service to the airport and train station. (West Anchorage)

EXECUTIVE SUITE HOTEL
4360 Spenard Rd.
Anchorage
907/243-6366 or 800/770-6366
$$–$$$$

Almost all the rooms at this hotel are suites (the rest are studios), about half have kitchens, and all have coffeemakers, cable TV, VCRs, and free local calls. The hotel is located near Lake Hood, a pleasant place to stroll and watch floatplanes take off and land. Although it has no restaurant, you can walk to nearby Gwennie's Old Alaska Restaurant and charge meals to your room. Courtesy shuttle to the airport and downtown. & (West Anchorage)

HAMPTON INN
4301 Credit Union Dr.
Anchorage
907/550-7000 or 800/HAMPTON
$$$$

Located three miles from the airport

Alaska Wilderness Plantation, p. 48

One of the B&B units at A Homestead Bed & Breakfast, p. 50

and three miles from downtown, this hotel is within walking distance of several restaurants. Each room has cable TV, iron and board, hairdryer, microwave, refrigerator, and coffeemaker. Rooms also have three phones each, including a two-line speakerphone with a dataport. Downstairs, a business center offers faxing, copying, and Internet access. Other amenities include a coin-op laundry, freezer storage, swimming pool, Jacuzzi, and exercise room. A complimentary continental breakfast is served from 6 to 10 a.m. daily, and a shuttle offers free rides to the airport and downtown. ♿ (West Anchorage)

HILLSIDE MOTEL & RV PARK
2150 Gambell St.
Anchorage
907/258-6006
info@hillside-alaska.com
www.hillside-alaska.com
$–$$
The park offers an odd combination—hotel rooms and campers—but the price is right. So is the location: It's right off the Chester

Creek bike trail, and you can walk to a movie theater, shopping center, and grocery store. All rooms have microwaves, coffeemakers, and refrigerators; several have kitchenettes. Free local calls and cable TV. ♿ (West Anchorage)

MICROTEL INN & SUITES
5205 Northwood Dr.
Anchorage
907/245-5002
$$–$$$
If you'd like to see Mount McKinley (aka Denali), ask for a north-facing room. All guest rooms have extra-long beds, phones with modem jacks, work space, window-seat sitting areas, and cable TV. Depending on the kind of room you select, you can also get such amenities as a refrigerator, microwave, coffeemaker, kitchen, or whirlpool. Five wheelchair-accessible "junior suites" have lower countertops, wide doorways, and bathrooms with assists. The hotel also offers guests a business meeting room, laundry facilities, passes to a nearby recreation center with gym and weight room,

continental breakfast, and an airport shuttle. ♿ (West Anchorage)

NORTHERN LIGHTS HOTEL
598 W. Northern Lights Blvd.
Anchorage
907/561-5200
$$–$$$

This hotel isn't close to downtown attractions, but it offers free parking and car rental on the premises. It's standard hotel decor, but how many places can claim a world-record moose mount standing in their lobbies? Amenities include free local calls, satellite TV, freezer space, and luggage storage; each room has a coffeemaker and minifridge. Cusack's Brewpub, a microbrewery and restaurant, serves appetizers, full meals, and a variety of brews. ♿ (West Anchorage)

QUPQUGIAQ CAFÉ
640 W. 36th Ave.
Anchorage
907/562-5681
qupq@alaska.net
www.alaska.net/~qupq
$

Pronounce it "koop-koo-gee-ak" and look for it eight minutes away from the international airport. The Qupqugiaq is a most unusual lodging house, with the privacy of a hotel and the community of a hostel. Its common reading area encourages lodgers to get to know one another, and full kitchen privileges help stretch vacation dollars. (A large supermarket, Asian grocery, and European-style bakery are within walking distance.) Rooms are very inexpensive but still offer free local calls and satellite TV. The city's main library is a block away; also within walking distance are several fast-food restaurants and a movie theater. The Qupqugiaq is located upstairs from a pleasant restaurant/coffeehouse that sponsors lectures and community meetings and hosts live music (tending toward folk and acoustic) on Friday and Saturday. This is a no-smoking, no-alcohol establishment. (West Anchorage)

REGAL ALASKAN HOTEL
4800 Spenard Rd.
Anchorage
907/243-2300 or 800/544-0553
$$$$

Located on Lake Spenard just one mile from the airport, the Regal is a beautiful hotel with an excellent restaurant (the Flying Machine) and a friendly, cozy bar (the Fancy Moose; see Chapter 12, Nightlife). The lobby is full of taxidermy specimens that will have you whipping out your camera even before you check in ("Honey, take my picture in front of the polar bear!"). Its rock fireplace and cozy chairs make it a very agreeable place, indeed. Go up to the third floor to enjoy stunning wildlife pictures by local photographer John Pezzenti. Rooms have refrigerators, coffeemakers, cable TV, hairdryers, and 24-hour room service; the hotel also has a health club with sauna, whirlpool, and steambath. In summer you'll enjoy relaxing on the deck outside the Fancy Moose and watching floatplanes take off and land. If you're visiting in March, you'll meet some pretty interesting people—the Regal serves as Anchorage headquarters for the Iditarod Trail Sled Dog Race. The hotel staff will help you arrange flightseeing or sport-fishing expeditions and will freeze your catch until your departure. Free shuttle to the airport and downtown. ♿ (West Anchorage)

SPRINGHILL SUITES BY MARRIOTT
3401 A St.
Anchorage
907/562-3247 or 800/287-9400
$$–$$$$

All rooms at this hotel have separate areas for sleeping, eating, and working; choose from one king or two double beds plus pull-out sofa bed. Each suite has a work desk, dataport, free local calls and voice mail, cable TV, iron and board, hair dryer, and coffeemaker. Guest services include fax and copying, same-day dry cleaning, laundry, and continental breakfast. The hotel is close to several restaurants and to a 16-screen movie theater. Non-smoking rooms are available. Free airport shuttle. ♿ (West Anchorage)

WESTCOAST INTERNATIONAL INN
3333 W. International Airport Rd.
Anchorage
907/243-2233
$$$–$$$$

Very close to the airport and rental car agencies, the newly remodeled inn sports a nice view of Lake Hood. All rooms have free cable TV, irons and boards, hairdryers, and coffeemakers. Other amenities include a 24-hour exercise room, Nintendo rentals, dataports for computers, and freezer space for fish. Piper's Restaurant serves breakfast, lunch, and dinner, with room service available during restaurant hours. Complimentary airport shuttle. ♿ (West Anchorage)

Bed-and-Breakfasts

ALASKA COZY ACCOMMODATIONS
1029 W. 16th Ave.
Anchorage
907/272-7723 or 800/272-7733
ccs@alaska.net
www.alaskacozy.com
$$

Located in the Westchester Lagoon area just south of downtown Anchorage, this home is convenient to the Coastal Trail and serves a full breakfast each morning. All three rooms have down comforters and pillows, bathrobes, fresh flowers, phones, cable TV, and VCR and use of the video library. Two of the rooms share a bath, but each has a vanity sink. No smoking. (West Anchorage)

ALASKA WILDERNESS PLANTATION
2910 W. 31st Ave.
Anchorage
907/243-3519 or 800/478-9657
plantatn@alaska.net
$$–$$$$

Also known as "the Spenard White House," this enormous B&B has more than 10,000 square feet of living space and more than three acres of wooded grounds. All rooms have private baths, and the suite has whirlpool tub, fireplace, king-size bed, and breakfast table and chairs. An indoor swimming pool, sauna and whirlpool, and numerous taxidermy specimens are also on the premises. Other amenities include an expanded continental breakfast, coin-op laundry services, freezer space, and storage for gear and luggage. Five minutes from the airport. (West Anchorage)

COASTAL TRAIL BED & BREAKFAST
3100 Iliamna Dr.
Anchorage
907/243-5809

Elderhostel Alaska

Elderhostel's mission is to enable older people to travel and enjoy new and exciting experiences. Elderhostel Alaska sponsors adventures in several areas around the state; in Anchorage they're headquartered at Alaska Pacific University.

Past Elderhostel programs have included "The 200-Year Legacy of the Russian Orthodox Church in Alaska," "The Geology of Southcentral Alaska," "The Untold Story of the Aleut People During World War II," "Alaska's Russian Connection," "Glaciers, Volcanoes and Gold: How They Change Our Lives," "Alaska Natives: Their History and Culture," and "Alaska Native Art: A Close-Up Look." Participants go everywhere from the Anchorage Museum of History and Art to a local glacier and Denali National Park. Many programs are held in conjunction with other cities in Alaska.

Accommodations and meals in the university dorms and cafeteria are included in the program cost. Costs ranges from about $1,200 to $4,000, depending on the adventure. Participants must be at least 55 years old; younger spouses are welcome. For more information, write to Elderhostel, Alaska Pacific University, 4101 University Dr., Anchorage, AK 99508, or call 907/564-8203.

info@coastaltrail.com
www.coastaltrail.com
$$

Coastal Trail is less than three miles from both the airport and downtown, on a quiet side street off a main road. Its Garden Room has a queen-size bed, private bath, and private entry, and it overlooks an English cottage-style garden that won an award in the "City of Flowers" contest. The Backpacker Suite is a living area plus bedroom that sleeps four (one queen bed, two twins); it has a private bath and a TV/VCR. In-

cidentally, all beds are featherbeds (but they can be switched if need be). Full breakfasts are served using the owners' best dishes and silver. An outdoor hot tub is available. The B&B is in the Turnagain section, one of the city's older and more family-oriented neighborhoods, and is close to its namesake. It's also fairly close to a major supermarket and fast-food restaurants. Smoking is not permitted. (West Anchorage)

ELDERBERRY BED & BREAKFAST
8340 Elderberry Rd.

Anchorage
907/243-6968
elderberrybb@compuserve.com
www.alaskan.com/elderberrybb
$–$$

Located near the airport, a grocery store, and fast-food restaurants, this B&B has rooms with Victorian, wildflower, and nautical themes. Each room has a private bath, phone, and TV/VCR. Breakfasts feature hot homemade bread and homemade strawberry jam. If you catch a fish, they'll freeze it for you. No smoking. (West Anchorage)

A HOMESTEAD
BED & BREAKFAST
6141 Jewel Lake Rd.
Anchorage
907/258-1717
homestead@alaskabandb.com
$–$$$

Stay in a real log cabin or in the "country suite" that sleeps up to four people. Both have private entrances and baths, TVs, and refrigerators. A stocked lake sits just across the street, and the Homestead is close to Kincaid Park's cross-country skiing and hiking trails. (West Anchorage)

LOU'S BED & BREAKFAST
3246 Wiley Post Loop
Anchorage
907/243-5197
cacytwo@alaska.net
$–$$

The host at this bed-and-breakfast is a certified city guide who is extremely knowledgeable about Alaska and can provide travel brochures to local and regional attractions. She has a library of books about the state that guests are encouraged to use. Each room has a private bath; there's a TV in the common area as well as gardens for guests' enjoyment. The B&B also offers laundry facilities and use of a computer. On a restricted diet? Ask for sugar-free jams at breakfast. Smoking is not allowed. (West Anchorage)

McCOLLIE BED & BREAKFAST
3010 McCollie Ave.
Anchorage
907/258-1717
$–$$

This cozy home in a quiet neighborhood features views of Cook Inlet, Sleeping Lady, and, on clear days, Mount McKinley. The guest room has antique furniture, a private bath, and a beautiful flower garden right outside its window. Across the street is the Coastal Trail, which is great for biking, skating, and walking in summer and cross-country skiing in winter. The hosts offer free transportation to a nearby fitness center. Smoking is not allowed at the B&B. (West Anchorage)

RAVEN HOUSE
3315 Iliamna Ave.
Anchorage
907/258-1717
$$–$$$

Looking for a special experience? Ask for the suite, which features a queen-size bed, a sitting room with leather furniture and an entertainment center, a private luxury bath with a two-person whirlpool, and views of a beautifully landscaped yard, a lovely stand of birch, and Cook Inlet. Special packages available for honeymoons (or second honeymoons) and anniversaries. The other two rooms at Raven House have queen beds and shared baths. (West Anchorage)

Hostels and Campgrounds

SPENARD HOSTEL
2845 W. 42nd Pl.
Anchorage
907/248-5036
$

This converted fourplex features dorm-style accommodations and common bathrooms. Kitchen and laundry facilities are available, and some food (salads, fruit, doughnuts) is included in the rate. You are requested to do 10 minutes of light housekeeping chores as part of your stay. Reservations are recommended in summer. Weekly and monthly rates are available in winter. The hostel is close to a bus line. (West Anchorage)

HILLSIDE MOTEL & RV PARK
2150 Gambell St.
Anchorage
907/258-6006
$

Located next to Chester Creek bike trail and within walking distance of a movie theater, shopping center, and grocery store, the 67-site park provides full and partial hookups, showers, a laundry facility, and propane refills. (West Anchorage)

EAGLE RIVER

Hotels and Motels

EAGLE RIVER MOTEL
11111 Old Eagle River Rd.
Eagle River
907/694-5000
$–$$

Accommodations are basic in this family-run hotel located close to restaurants and banks. If you like to stretch out, ask for a room with a queen-size bed. Free local calls and cable TV. Kitchenettes and freezer space available. (Eagle River)

Bed-and-Breakfasts

ALASKA ARCTIC B&B
17501 Toakoana Way
Eagle River
907/696-4027
$–$$

You'll find basic rooms, all with shared baths but private entrances, in this clean, quiet B&B located in the Eagle River Valley, close to the Eagle River Nature Center and just a 15-minute ride from Anchorage. Each room has a TV, VCR, and phone. No smoking. (Eagle River)

ALASKA CHALET B&B
11031 Gulkana Circle
Eagle River
907/694-1528
akchalet@alaska.net
www.alaska.net/~akchalet
$$

This B&B offers an 800-square-foot suite including a bedroom, sitting room, private bath with whirlpool tub, and eat-in kitchen. The room sleeps up to four people and has a TV, VCR, and phone. Laundry facilities are available. German is spoken here. (Eagle River)

BIRCH TRAILS ADVENTURES B&B
22719 Robinson Rd.
Chugiak
907/688-5713
thamill@micronet.net
$$

This inn offers private entrances, kitchenettes, and private living areas, as well as phones, TV/VCRs, an exercise room, a shared bath, and plenty of Alaska books and videos. It is close to Mirror Lake and

EAGLE RIVER

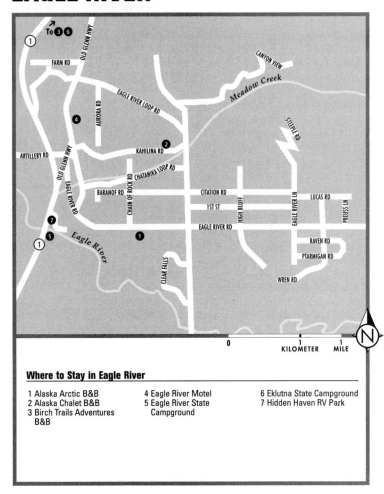

Where to Stay in Eagle River

1 Alaska Arctic B&B
2 Alaska Chalet B&B
3 Birch Trails Adventures
  B&B

4 Eagle River Motel
5 Eagle River State
  Campground

6 Eklutna State Campground
7 Hidden Haven RV Park

hiking trails, and it also offers optional dogsled adventures. Smoking outdoors only. (Eagle River)

Campgrounds

EAGLE RIVER STATE CAMPGROUND
Mile 10 Glenn Hwy.

Eagle River
907/694-1074
$
Located on the banks of the Eagle River, this 50-site campground has drinking water, flush toilets, and an emergency phone. Near the Eagle River Nature Center, it also offers opportunities for river rafting, taking

photographs, backpacking, wildlife-viewing, biking, hunting, and berry-picking. Four-day camping limit. (Eagle River)

EKLUTNA STATE CAMPGROUND
Mile 26 Glenn Hwy.
Eklutna
907/688-0908
$
About 10 miles off the highway, on the shores of Eklutna Lake in Chugach State Park, this campground features great hiking and boating. Drinking water, pit toilets, and a 15-day camping limit. (Eagle River)

HIDDEN HAVEN RV PARK
10011 Aleden Lane
Eagle River
907/694-7275
$
Located right next to a greenbelt and the Eagle River, the park has full hookups. (Eagle River)

Marx Brothers Cafe

4

WHERE TO EAT

Although Anchorage is an isolated city, creative chefs do work here, leading to some pretty exciting food styles along with the usual American menus. That doesn't mean you'll have to struggle to decide among numerous trendy restaurants. Trends take a while to reach the Last Frontier, so don't be surprised if food styles that recently died out in the Lower 48 are still going strong in Anchorage. Not surprisingly, Anchorage offers some great seafood. If halibut and salmon seem to appear on every menu you see, just remember that they're simply too good for cooks to pass up.

This chapter begins with a list of restaurants organized by cuisine type. Each restaurant name is followed by a zone abbreviation and a page number where the complete listing can be found. Dining spots are then listed alphabetically within zones, with descriptions of menus and atmosphere.

Dollar-sign symbols indicate the cost of one meal (appetizer, entrée, and dessert). Unless otherwise noted, all restaurants accept credit cards.

Price-rating symbols:
$	Under $12
$$	$13 to $22
$$$	$23 and up

American/Contemporary

Chris' Mixed Grill (SA), p. 65
Eric's (SA), p. 68
Europa Bakery (WA), p. 75
F Street Station (DT), p. 59
Gallery Café (DT), p. 59
Harley's Old Thyme Restaurant (WA), p. 75
Humpy's Great Alaska Ale House (DT), p. 60
Kodiak Kafe (DT), p. 60
Momma O's (WA), p. 77
Sacks Café (DT), p. 62
Snow City Cafe (DT), p. 63
Southside Bistro (SA), p. 69

Breakfast

Alaska Bagel Restaurant (WA), p. 73
Alaska Breakfast Club (EA), p. 70
Bagel Factory (WA), p. 74
Hogg Bros. (WA), p. 76
Jackie's Place (WA), p. 76
Judy's Cafe (SA), p. 68
Snow City Cafe (DT), p. 63

Brewpubs

Brewmaster's Room (WA) p. 75
Cusack's Brewpub (WA), p. 75
Glacier Brew House (DT), p. 60
North Slope Restaurant (ER), p. 85
Regal Eagle Brewpub (ER), p. 85
Snow Goose Restaurant and Brewery (DT), p. 64

Delis/Sandwiches

Arctic Roadrunner (SA, WA), p. 73
Atlasta Deli (WA), p. 74
Downtown Deli (DT), p. 59
Dianne's (DT), p. 58
Europa Bakery (WA), p. 75
L'Aroma (WA, DT), p. 76
Qupqugiaq Café (WA), p. 80
Sweet Basil Cafe (DT), p. 64

Diner-style

Double D's (SA), p. 68
Jackie's Place (WA), p. 76
Judy's Cafe (SA), p. 68

Lucky Wishbone (EA), p. 71
Peggy's (EA), p. 71
Phyllis's Café & Salmon Bake (DT), p. 62

Ethnic

Arigato (WA), p. 74
Campobello (WA), p. 74
Catfish Haven (EA), p. 71
Don Jose's (EA), p. 71
Garcia's Cantina & Cafe (ER), p. 83
Greek Corner (WA), p. 75
Hacienda (EA), p. 71
La Mex (SA, DT, WA), p. 68
Mexico in Alaska (SA), p. 69
The Noodle House (WA), p. 78
Olga Russian & European Delicatessen (WA), p. 78
Pho MaiLee (WA), p. 80
Pizza Olympia (WA), p. 80
Roscoe's Skyline Restaurant (WA), p. 81
Saigon (EA), p. 72
Siam Cuisine (SA), p. 69
Siam Spicy (EA), p. 72
Taco del Mar (WA), p. 83
Taco King (WA), p. 83
Tempura Kitchen (WA), p. 83
Twin Dragon Mongolian Bar-B-Que (DT), p. 65

Fine Dining

Corsair (DT), p. 56
Crow's Nest (DT), p. 56
Marx Bros. (DT), p. 61
Turnagain House (SA), p. 78

Quick Eats

Moose's Tooth Pub & Pizzeria (WA), p. 78
Red Robin Burger & Spirits Emporium (EA, SA, WA), p. 72
Souper Bowl (DT), p. 64
Uncle Joe's Pizzeria (ER), p. 85
Wings 'n' Things (DT), p. 65

Seafood

Garmel's Seafood Gallery (ER), p. 84
Momma O's (WA), p. 77
Phyllis's Café & Salmon Bake
(DT), p. 62
Simon & Seafort's (DT), p. 62

Steaks

Club Paris (DT), p. 56
Lone Star Steakhouse (WA), p. 77
Outback Steakhouse (WA), p. 79
Pepper Mill (WA), p. 80
Stuart Anderson's Cattle Company
(WA), p. 82

Vegetarian

Downtown Deli (DT), p. 59
L'Aroma (WA, DT), p. 76
Middle Way Café & Coffee House
(WA), p. 77
Organic Oasis (WA), p. 78
Snow City Cafe (DT), p. 63
Sweet Basil (DT), p. 64

DOWNTOWN

CLUB PARIS
417 W. Fifth Ave.
Anchorage
907/277-6332
$$$
At first glance, this storefront restaurant doesn't seem to be anything special. The windows are dark glass, and if you peek in the door you'll see a bar and a dimly lit eatery with fewer than 20 small tables. However, you may also notice that it's crammed with happy diners—locals who know that this is one of the best places in town to get a steak. Do consider getting the blue-cheese stuffing, which is out of this world. And while you're at it, you might as well order the creamy cheese sauce on your baked potato, too. Though the steaks are

exceptional, do not expect a fine-dining ambiance—waiters drop a basket of cellophane-wrapped crackers on your table when they take your order, and cigarette smoke really can't be avoided in such a small place. But Club Paris has an agreeably dark, funky, old-Alaska atmosphere. You'd probably hear some pretty amazing stories if you spent any time at the bar—and some might even be true. Lunch Mon–Sat, dinner daily. (Downtown)

CORSAIR
944 W. Fifth Ave.
Anchorage
907/278-4502
$$$
Come here for fine European dining, and to heck with your diet. Chef Hans Kruger just loves to feed people rich sauces, oysters topped with pâté, rack of lamb, châteaubriand, and other culinary indulgences. Try the Oysters Christian appetizer: oysters lightly sautéed in lemon butter with fresh dill. Another signature dish is the venison in blueberry sauce. Most courses are "done" tableside, from marvelously constructed salads to incendiary after-dinner drinks like the Café Diablo (coffee, liqueurs, and skewers of marinated orange, lemon, and lime peels). The waiters wear tuxedos, and the clientele takes its time. There's a full bar, including an extensive wine list. Reservations recommended. Dinner only Mon–Sat. (Downtown)

CROW'S NEST
Top of the Hotel Captain Cook
939 W. Fifth Ave.
Anchorage
907/276-6000
$$$

DOWNTOWN ANCHORAGE

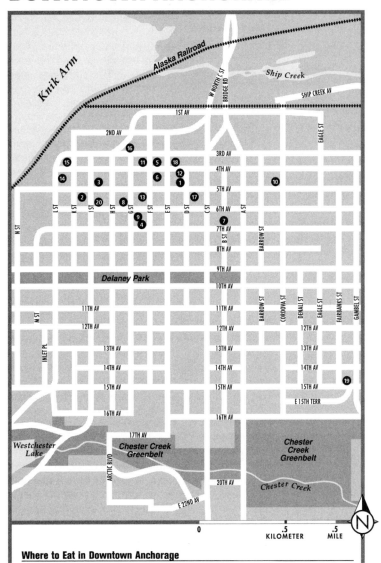

Where to Eat in Downtown Anchorage

1 Club Paris
2 Corsair
3 Crow's Nest
4 Dianne's
5 Downtown Deli
6 F Street Station
7 Gallery Café
8 Glacier Brew House
9 Humpy's Great Alaska Ale House
10 Kodiak Kafe
11 Marx Bros.
12 Phyllis's Café & Salmon Bake
13 Sack's Café
14 Simon & Seafort's Saloon & Grill
15 Snow City Cafe
16 Snow Goose Restaurant & Brewery
17 Souper Bowl
18 Sweet Basil Cafe
19 Twin Dragon Mongolian Bar-B-Que
20 Wings 'N' Things

Hotel Captain Cook

The Crow's Nest at the Captain Cook, p. 56

All tables have views—of the city, the Inlet, or the Chugach Range. Ask for a table with a potential Mount McKinley view—if you're lucky, the mountain will be out and fabulous enough almost to distract you from your food. But it would take one heck of a view to keep your eyes away from a plate of Alaska Dungeness crab marinated in horseradish and served with vine-ripened tomato gazpacho, avocado, and basil oil, or a salad of arugula, baby spinach, duck prosciutto, spiced pecans, Stilton cheese, and 18-year old balsamic vinegar. Save room for the oven-roasted Copper River salmon, served with horseradish-infused potato puree and sautéed tat soy with plum-tomato vinaigrette. For a truly unique taste, try the pepper-crusted Nunivak Island venison, along with Yukon Gold potato puree, braised Swiss chard, and ragout of wild mushrooms, accented with a lowbush-cranberry

reduction sauce. Or try the steamed Alaska king crab legs, along with a potato puree and a ragout of spring vegetables topped with citrus butter. It's difficult to ignore a dessert list that features goodies like Berry Financier (a French cake served with a warm berry compote and house-made buttermilk ice cream) or the Crow's Nest banana split (a Florentine tux filled with homemade banana ice cream, bourbon butterscotch sauce, bittersweet chocolate, fresh bananas, pistachios, fresh berries, and spun sugar). All desserts are made from scratch on the premises. The weekly brunch features the usual omelets, pastries, and Belgian waffles but adds some nifty touches like salmon Benedict, reindeer sausage, sushi, salmon gravlax, and fresh oysters, crab legs, and shrimp. Full bar, including a list of 1,175 wines. Reservations recommended. Dinner only Mon–Sat, brunch Sun. &. (Downtown)

DIANNE'S
Bank of America Building
550 W. Seventh Ave.
Anchorage
907/279-7243
$
Dianne's serves marvelously fresh and inventive soups, salads, pastas, sandwiches, and (especially) desserts. The round sandwich breads are baked fresh daily. It's tough to list house specialties because the menu is so changeable; every day brings tasty new options. These days, how often can you drop in at a casual dining place and find a slab of spice cake waiting just for you? And be sure to take one of those cartwheel-sized cookies back to your hotel

room for a late-night snack. Breakfast, lunch (to 4 p.m.) Mon–Fri. (Downtown)

DOWNTOWN DELI
525 W. Fourth Ave.
Anchorage
907/276-7116
$

Blintzes! Matzo-ball soup! Bagels and lox! And reindeer stew, and sourdough pancakes, and fresh Alaska salmon. Yes, tried-and-true deli specials like Reuben sandwiches and chopped liver bump up against those regional delicacies. The Downtown Deli also makes concessions to modern eating habits, such as blueberry oat-bran muffins, black-bean chili ("guaranteed insulation against the Alaska chill"), a quiche of the day, and espresso. The deli offers two specifically vegetarian sandwiches: The Veggie Works has layers of artichokes marinated in garlic vinaigrette, avocado, cucumbers, green peppers, lettuce, and a creamy herb-spinach spread; and the Garden Sandwich has avocado, lettuce, tomato, alfalfa sprouts, and cheddar cheese. The nice salad lineup includes Chinese chicken, shrimp with tortellini, and grilled chicken breast with fresh spinach and fruit; the most popular one, however, is the Calico Salad—a bed of shredded lettuce topped with sliced turkey, avocado, tomato, blue cheese, chopped bacon, egg, and cucumber in sour cream. Desserts are homemade and comforting, including deep-dish green-apple cobbler, fudge pie, carrot cake, and Tony's chocolate chip cookie. (The "Tony," by the way, refers to owner Tony Knowles, who was mayor of Anchorage and is now the governor of the state.) Beer and wine available. Breakfast, lunch, dinner daily. ✦ (Downtown)

F STREET STATION
325 F St.
Anchorage
907/272-5196
$

It looks like a bar, but it's got a nifty kitchen, too. The food reviewer for the *Anchorage Daily News* rated F Street's cheeseburgers and hand-cut fries the best in the city—ditto the eggs Benedict. Take a chance on the daily special—it's almost certain to be good. Full bar service. Lunch, dinner daily (open until 1 a.m.). ✦ (Downtown)

GALLERY CAFÉ
Anchorage Museum of History and Art
121 W. Seventh Ave.
Anchorage
907/343-6190
$$

This is not your usual museum canteen. The chef prepares European-style cuisine with a Pacific Rim influence, including such dishes as pan-seared halibut cheeks with a fireweed honey beurre blanc drizzled with sweet chili sauce and sweet soy. Tired museum patrons perk right up when they sample the "lacquered salmon"—fresh fish marinated in sweet soy and rice wine, seared and topped with soy-ginger beurre blanc, and served with jasmine rice and stir-fried vegetables. Locals often come to the café on their lunch breaks because of dishes like the house-smoked trout served over fresh spinach, thinly sliced red onions, and cucumbers with a blood-orange vinaigrette, or the seared sesame-crusted scallops

on a bed of vegetable-mint cous-
cous. If you're a sandwich fan, how
about a mesquite chicken club or
a roasted-vegetable sandwich on
focaccia with sun-dried-tomato
spread? Desserts vary, but two local
favorites are sourdough bread pudding with Tahitian-vanilla caramel
sauce and Key-lime pie made with a
macadamia–graham-cracker crust.
Fresh muffins and croissants are
available for breakfast or a midmorn-
ing coffee break. Open during museum hours, serving breakfast and
lunch. & (Downtown)

GLACIER BREW HOUSE
737 W. Fifth Ave.
Anchorage
907/274-2739
$–$$
This brewery and restaurant is located an easy walk from downtown
hotels. It focuses on wood-grilled
seafood, rotisserie-grilled meats,
and wood-fired pizzas. These aren't
just sauce-and-mozzarella pies, either. Try the spinach-artichoke
pizza, on a medium-thin crust made
with amber ale, topped with feta
cheese, roasted garlic, Kalamata
olives, sun-dried tomatoes, fresh
oregano, and herbed olive oil. Or
savor a pizza made with a roasted
garlic cream sauce, wild-mushroom ragout, oven-roasted porta-
bellas, and a blend of five cheeses,
served with arugula in sherry vinaigrette. The cioppino is made with
Alaska king crab legs in a spicy
tomato-saffron broth with fennel
and grilled lemons. The clams are
oven-roasted with shallot butter
and roasted tomatoes. The prime
rib is cured with a dry rub of three
kinds of peppercorns, thyme, brown
sugar, and kosher salt, then spit-
roasted and served with oven-

roasted vegetables and mashed
potatoes. The pork-loin chops are a
local favorite, made with a hearty
wild-mushroom sauce and served
with garlic mashed potatoes. Beer
and wine only. Lunch Mon–Sat,
dinner daily. & (Downtown)

HUMPY'S GREAT ALASKA
ALE HOUSE
610 W. Sixth Ave.
Anchorage
907/276-2337
$–$$
This casual local bar has interesting
light dining, including half a dozen
dinner specials nightly. One of the
most popular appetizers is the
smoked-salmon spread, made with
white and cayenne peppers and
Worcestershire sauce, and served
with fresh French bread. Halibut
tacos are made with fish marinated
in amber ale then sautéed with
black-bean salsa and served in a
flour tortilla with shredded cabbage,
guacamole, sour cream, and salsa.
Halibut also shows up as a burger.
King crab legs are available nightly.
For dessert, try homemade apple or
peach cobbler, or carrot cake.
Humpy's has more than 40 microbrews on draft, including cask-con-
ditioned ales. The full-service bar
also has the second-largest selection of single-malt scotches in town.
Lunch, dinner daily. & (Downtown)

KODIAK KAFE
225 E. Fifth Ave.
Anchorage
907/258-5233
$–$$
The Western/Alaskan decor may
give pause, but the food is definitely
serious. The sandwiches, salads,
and homemade soups are great for
lunch; the Reuben and the crab club

Brewpubs Move North

Food trends tend to move north pretty slowly, but when they hit, they're hot. A bunch of brewpubs have sprung up locally in the last few years, both downtown and in areas nearby. Since Anchorage residents have traditionally favored proletarian-style beers, some folks predicted that these new places wouldn't all survive. But so far, so good—not a single brewpub entrepreneur has ended up sadder Budweiser.

That's probably because these places have interesting foods and playful atmospheres as well as microbrews. Downtown, there's the Snow Goose Restaurant and Brewery, Third Ave. and E St., 907/277-7727. A few blocks away is the Glacier Brew House, 737 W. Fifth Ave., 907/274-2739. In West Anchorage, try Cusack's Brewpub, Northern Lights Hotel, 598 W. Northern Lights Blvd., 907/278-2739. Look for full descriptions in this chapter.

are particularly wonderful. Evenings, the place turns into a for-real dining spot, with light dining or a full-dinner menu. Fresh Alaska halibut and salmon are done differently each day. The filet mignon is grilled with a roasted-onion demiglace. Chicken Tartuffo is cooked with mushrooms, sun-dried tomatoes, cream, and white wine, finished with truffle oil, and served over fresh fettucine. Shrimp are grilled and presented on a bed of tomato-garlic chutney, with almond-raisin basmati rice on the side. All desserts are homemade. There's a good selection of beers and an extensive wine list. Breakfast, lunch Mon–Sat; dinner Tue–Sat. & (Downtown)

MARX BROS.
627 W. Third Ave.
Anchorage

907/278-2133
$$$
Some of the most innovative food in Alaska has come from this small historic (1916) house in the past dozen years. Greens, herbs, and edible flowers grown right outside pep up summer dishes, and Alaska products are emphasized year-round. The wine cellar is 10,000 bottles strong, the waiters are friendly, and the owner does much of the cooking (including a signature Caesar salad made tableside). Try the halibut in a macadamia nut crust with coconut curry and mango chutney or the pepper-crusted roasted king salmon served with crab-infused mashed potatoes and shellfish broth. Or how about some tea-smoked duck or deviled crab cakes? The restaurant offers many homemade ice creams and sorbets; for the best of both

worlds, check out the warm berry crisp with birch syrup–butter pecan ice cream. This is a very small place, so be sure to call ahead for a reservation. Ask for a view table and you'll be rewarded with a look at Cook Inlet. Dinner daily; closed Sun Oct–May. (Downtown)

PHYLLIS'S CAFÉ & SALMON BAKE
436 D St.
Anchorage
907/274-6576
$

Phyllis's serves good food, both for casual bites and full dinners. Try the Alaskan breakfast, which includes reindeer sausage, so you can tell your friends that you had Rudolph for breakfast. Scones are freshly baked and very tasty, particularly when smeared with raspberry jam. Tourists love the outdoor (also served indoors) salmon bake, whose best advertisement is the succulent aroma that drifts over the area. It's not just salmon out there, though— other seafood, steak, burgers, and even prime rib are grilled to order. You can also enjoy king or snow crab, shrimp, or chowder served in a sourdough bread bowl. For a lighter meal, try the salmon salad or choose from the sandwich/ burger side of the menu. Beer and wine available. Breakfast, lunch, dinner daily; closed Oct–Apr. &
(Downtown)

SACKS CAFÉ
625 W. Fifth Ave.
Anchorage
907/276-3546
$$

Intriguing and adventurous food rules here. For lunch, how about some creamy tomato soup with Gor-

gonzola cheese, or a homemade vegetarian chili topped with avocado, sour cream, scallions, and cheese? Consider the Caesar salad made with smoked halibut or the spinach salad with warm chèvre and a lemon or balsamic vinaigrette. For dinner, start with an appetizer of baked polenta gratin made with Gorgonzola and mascarpone and served with greens, sun-dried tomatoes, and roasted tomato vinaigrette. For your entrée, consider thinly sliced lamb loin braised in red-curry sauce, served with saffron rice and apple-mango compote. Or splurge on a buttery-soft filet of venison, peppered, oven-roasted, topped with Brie and deep-fried leeks, and served with a sauce of currants and a pork-and-veal-stock reduction. Sacks always has at least one vegetarian entrée, such as the penne pasta baked with fresh and sun-dried tomatoes, spinach, fontina, Parmesan, and Gorgonzola, and topped with roasted peppers and fresh herbs (if that sounds good to you meat-eaters, ask the chef to add chicken). For dessert, the chocolate gâteau is dense and moist, and you'll long remember the crème brûlées: ginger, or chocolate topped with blackberries. Wine and beer available. Dinner reservations recommended. Lunch, dinner daily; brunch Sun. & (Downtown)

SIMON & SEAFORT'S SALOON & GRILL
420 L St.
Anchorage
907/274-3502
$$$

This is one of the busiest places in town for seafood, and not just because it's a quick and pleasant walk from the major downtown hotels.

The food is uniformly good, sometimes terrific, and the views of Cook Inlet and Sleeping Lady are out of this world. Ask for a table near the window—but be prepared to wait a bit because everyone else wants one, too. The full bar includes the city's largest selection of single-malt scotches. A variety of wood-smoked beef and seafood selections are available, along with pasta dishes, salads, and prime rib roasted in rock salt. The from-scratch Key-lime pie is one of the most popular desserts, along with the chocolate indulgence cake, the fresh-berry coeur de crème, and the brandy ice, a "sipping dessert" made with brandy, dark crème de cacao, Kahlua, and ice cream. Reservations strongly recommended for dinner. Lunch Mon–Sat, dinner daily. ♿ (Downtown)

SNOW CITY CAFE
1034 W. Fourth Ave.
Anchorage
907/272-2489

$
This friendly, laid-back place features breakfast all day (a boon to groggy travelers), gourmet soups, salads, sandwiches, Alaska seafood, and chicken and pasta dishes. A number of vegetarian and heart-healthy selections are always available. For breakfast, you can choose from among dishes such as omelets, huevos rancheros, tofu scramble, the regional taste of salmon cakes and eggs, or the comfort-zone goodness of a bowl of oatmeal. Lunch sandwiches include meatloaf, smoked salmon, Italian classic, veggie loaf, garden, and turkey; salads include spicy noodle, tabouli, and hummus; and daily specials include Thai-chicken wrap, stuffed French toast, Mexican casserole, and vegan black-bean chili.

Start your dinner with a roasted-veggie platter, grilled Alaska salmon cakes served with black-bean-and-corn relish, or roasted garlic with Brie. Entrées are light but satisfying, with selections such as

Club Paris, p. 56

Club Paris

TIP Traveling with your canine? Check out the Doggie Diner, 3940 Spenard Rd., 907/248-9663, an establishment that not only permits but encourages dogs on the premises. It's a full-service dog-treat bakery, and it offers fancy coffees, teas, and light refreshments for human companions, too.

pan-seared halibut or salmon with wild-rice pilaf; pasta pomodoro; tofu stir-fry on brown rice; pasta with smoked Alaska halibut, sun-dried tomatoes, green onion, garlic, olive oil, and Parmesan cheese; and meatloaf (or veggie loaf) served with garlic mashed potatoes and steamed veggies.

Ice cream is "imported" from Hot Licks, a Fairbanks ice-cream parlor, and added to desserts such as the apple or mixed-berry crisp, the brownie sundae, and the Barq's root-beer float. Try an espresso or other specialty coffee drink, or a fruit smoothie, if you're in need of a pick-me-up. Beer and wine also available. Breakfast, lunch, dinner daily. ও (Downtown)

SNOW GOOSE RESTAURANT AND BREWERY
Third Ave. and G St.
Anchorage
907/277-7727
$–$$
Good beer and a new menu that features seafood, free-range chicken, and Alaskan beef have made this downtown brewpub quite popular. Half a dozen fresh brews are available, as is homemade root beer. The Snow Goose also offers unusual beers from Belgium. The filets and New Yorks, from a farm in Delta Junction, are tender and well-marbled. The Thai oysters (fresh shellfish served with basil, fish

sauce, and vinegar) are among the most popular appetizers. Try the pepper steak, made with a sauce of cream and brewery ale. Upstairs, you can smoke a cigar while taking in views of Mount McKinley—when it's out—and Sleeping Lady from the deck. No smoking downstairs. Lunch, dinner daily; closed Sun during winter. ও (Downtown)

SOUPER BOWL
Fifth Avenue Mall
Anchorage
907/278-7687
$
Don't be put off by its mall location—this place has some terrific surprises. Consider the Alaska steamer clams with rice-stick noodles, the homemade won-ton soup scented with ginger and bursting with veggies and tender pork and shrimp dumplings, or the chicken soup with either egg or rice-stick noodles. The little containers of hot chili paste add an edge. Loose-leaf teas are a specialty. Open during mall hours, lunch and dinner. ও (Downtown)

SWEET BASIL CAFE
335 E St.
Anchorage
907/274-0070
$
This nouvelle-cuisine café emphasizes fresh ingredients, especially Alaskan ones. Lunches are light fare

such as salads, a "hummus of the day," wraps, and sandwiches on homemade breads, including the sweet-basil variety that gives the café its name. Dinners are heartier, with fresh seafood, veal and pork chops, lamb, beef, and pasta dishes. The café always offers at least one vegetarian and/or vegan offering; in addition, the pastas are egg-free and the breads are made without dairy products. Sweet Basil has a full juice bar, as well as beer and wine. Lunch, dinner daily. ⅆ (Downtown)

TWIN DRAGON MONGOLIAN BAR-B-QUE
612 E. 15th Ave.
Anchorage
907/276-7535
$

This place has a Chinese buffet that is tasty and satisfying. But it's just so much more fun to enjoy the Mongolian Bar-B-Que (that's the way it's spelled on the sign). You fill up a bowl with whatever veggies you like (peppers, carrots, cabbage, sprouts, celery, onions, broccoli, etc.), then add slivers of chicken, beef, or pork, and let the counter person add whatever sauce (teriyaki, mild, or spicy) you like. Then watch the cook, armed only with a pair of long thin sticks, throw your meal onto a large round cooktop. He's serious and absorbed and vastly entertaining as he somehow gets everyone's meal perfectly stir-fried. Watch him at the end, as he lines up one dinner after another and then flings it off the stove and into a clean bowl. You'll want to applaud. The Mongolian barbecue also includes a pot of tea, soup, rice, and some spring rolls. Lunch, dinner daily. ⅆ (Downtown)

WINGS 'N' THINGS
529 I St.
Anchorage
907/277-9464
$

The spicy wings here range from pleasingly mild to punishingly nuclear. Listen to staffers when they explain the hotness quotient or your mouth may be startled by the result (a pullet surprise, so to speak). This tiny, casual eatery also does a very decent rendition of a Philly cheesesteak. The grilled Italian link sausage with provolone is another good bet. Dine in or, in fine weather, out on the deck. Beer and wine available. No credit cards accepted. Lunch Mon–Sat, dinner Thu–Sat. ⅆ (Downtown)

SOUTH ANCHORAGE

CHRIS' MIXED GRILL
6728 Lake Otis Pkwy.
Anchorage
907/344-3949
$–$$

This casual neighborhood dining room offers mixed-grill specials like the Roma (ribeye steak, scampi, and herbed chicken) or the Far Eastern (beef and chicken teriyaki and shrimp tempura). Fajitas, baby-back ribs, and pork chops are also available. A house specialty is Halibut Stroganoff, made with a low-fat yogurt-based sauce, white wine, and mushrooms. At lunchtime, popovers are popular, whether they're stuffed with vegetarian sauté, chicken à la king, or seafood gumbo. An even more popular lunch is the Philly Dip: sautéed marinated flank steak served on homemade bread with the jus on the side. For dessert, try the Bumbleberry Pie, a mix of apples,

GREATER ANCHORAGE

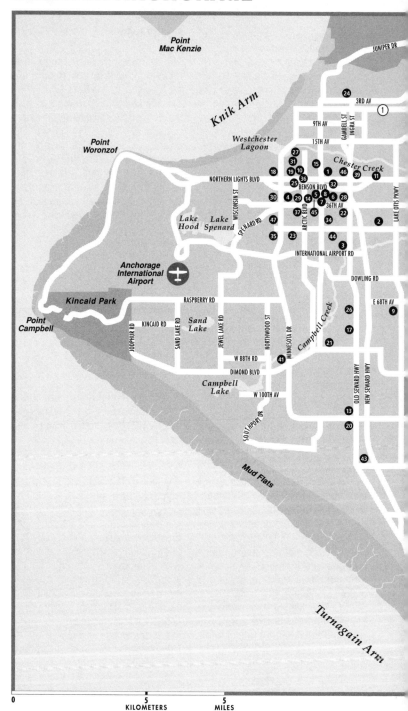

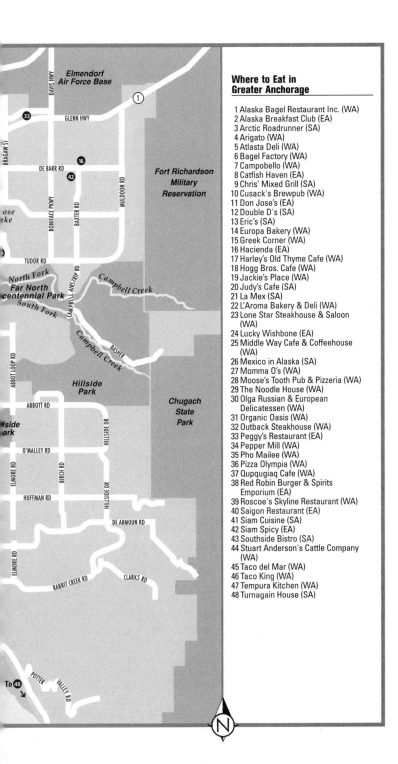

Where to Eat in Greater Anchorage

1 Alaska Bagel Restaurant Inc. (WA)
2 Alaska Breakfast Club (EA)
3 Arctic Roadrunner (SA)
4 Arigato (WA)
5 Atlasta Deli (WA)
6 Bagel Factory (WA)
7 Campobello (WA)
8 Catfish Haven (EA)
9 Chris' Mixed Grill (SA)
10 Cusack's Brewpub (WA)
11 Don Jose's (EA)
12 Double D's (SA)
13 Eric's (SA)
14 Europa Bakery (WA)
15 Greek Corner (WA)
16 Hacienda (EA)
17 Harley's Old Thyme Cafe (WA)
18 Hogg Bros. Cafe (WA)
19 Jackie's Place (WA)
20 Judy's Cafe (SA)
21 La Mex (SA)
22 L'Aroma Bakery & Deli (WA)
23 Lone Star Steakhouse & Saloon (WA)
24 Lucky Wishbone (EA)
25 Middle Way Cafe & Coffeehouse (WA)
26 Mexico in Alaska (SA)
27 Momma O's (WA)
28 Moose's Tooth Pub & Pizzeria (WA)
29 The Noodle House (WA)
30 Olga Russian & European Delicatessen (WA)
31 Organic Oasis (WA)
32 Outback Steakhouse (WA)
33 Peggy's Restaurant (EA)
34 Pepper Mill (WA)
35 Pho Mailee (WA)
36 Pizza Olympia (WA)
37 Qupqugiaq Cafe (WA)
38 Red Robin Burger & Spirits Emporium (EA)
39 Roscoe's Skyline Restaurant (WA)
40 Saigon Restaurant (EA)
41 Siam Cuisine (SA)
42 Siam Spicy (EA)
43 Southside Bistro (SA)
44 Stuart Anderson's Cattle Company (WA)
45 Taco del Mar (WA)
46 Taco King (WA)
47 Tempura Kitchen (WA)
48 Turnagain House (SA)

raspberries, blackberries, and rhubarb. You can also start the day here, with such classic breakfast fare as omelets, pancakes, biscuits and gravy, and eggs Benedict. Or try the breakfast specials, such as the Zucchini Mix (sautéed zucchini and onions with scrambled eggs), Breakfast Club (a fried-egg sandwich with ham and bacon served triple-decker club style), or Buffalo Muffin (an English muffin with a ground buffalo patty, scrambled eggs, and cheddar cheese). Beer and wine available. Breakfast, lunch, dinner daily; brunch Sun. ♿ (South Anchorage)

DOUBLE D'S
2101 Abbott Rd.
Anchorage
907/349-5134
$$

This small eatery specializes in from-scratch cooking. Fortify yourself for a day's touring with an omelet, breakfast steak, or plate of biscuits and gravy. Lunch sandwiches include the cheesesteak (made with top sirloin), the Paris Sandwich (eight ounces of ground sirloin, with cheddar cheese served like a French dip), or the Henpecker (broiled chicken breast with jack cheese and Dijon). A couple of variations on the Philly cheesesteak are the Chicken Philly (diced chicken sautéed with mushrooms and Dijon, served on a French roll with melted jack cheese) and the Vegetarian Philly (sautéed peppers, mushrooms, and onions, served on a French roll with melted cheddar and jack cheeses). Daily specials, all rib-stickers, include chicken and dumplings and pot roast with real mashed potatoes. Cheesecake, pies, and cakes are also homemade. Beer and wine available. Breakfast,

lunch, dinner daily (limited dinner hours). ♿ (South Anchorage)

ERIC'S
11541 Old Seward Hwy.
Anchorage
907/344-7512
$$

Eric's offers casual dining in a family-friendly environment (they have an inexpensive kids' menu, for starters). Try the baby back ribs, which are so meltingly tender they slide off the bone without protest. The fajitas—beef or chicken—are extremely popular, too. The fettucine, cooked to order for each diner, is made with real cream and comes with vegetables, chicken, or shrimp. Most desserts are made on the premises, including mud pie, crème brûlée, and profiteroles. Beer and wine available. Lunch, dinner daily; breakfast buffet Sun. ♿ (South Anchorage)

JUDY'S CAFE
11620 Old Seward Hwy.
Anchorage
907/349-5500
$

Large portions, low prices, friendly service, and no pretenses make this eatery the kind of place where people will wait in line for a seat (always a good sign). Judy's serves tasty, hearty, diner-style food, and you can get breakfast any time the place is open—particularly helpful when you're suffering from jet lag. Try the biscuits and gravy, but a word of advice: Unless you're really, really, really hungry, get the half-order. No credit cards. Breakfast, lunch daily. (South Anchorage)

LA MEX
8330 King St.

Phyllis's Café & Salmon Bake, p. 62

Anchorage
907/344-6399
$$

The newest location in a chain of three family-owned eateries, La Mex makes its own tortillas, corn chips, and salsa daily. Try the tostaditos: corn chips covered with beans, cheddar cheese, lettuce, house dressing, more cheese, and jalapeños, plus beef or chicken if you're really hungry. Fajita-dillas are grilled flour tortillas filled with cheddar and Monterey Jack cheeses, zucchini, broccoli, mushrooms, onions, tomatoes, and marinated chicken breast, all brushed with Parmesan garlic butter and served with your choice of sour cream or jalapeño cream cheese. The restaurant offers many other typical Tex-Mex treats, plus a number of American-style appetizers and entrées, including prime rib, fresh Alaska seafood, burgers, and baby-back ribs. Full bar service. Lunch, dinner daily. Other locations are downtown, 900 W. Sixth Ave.,

907/274-7678, and in West Anchorage, 2550 Spenard Rd., 907/274-7511. &. (South Anchorage)

MEXICO IN ALASKA
7305 Old Seward Hwy.
Anchorage
907/349-1528
$$

This is traditional, home-cooked Mexican food, not the Tex-Mex stuff of national chains. The chicken in mole sauce, carnitas, and chile rellenos are truly special. For a change of pace, try the nopales con huevos or the tacos al pastores, made with lamb, pork, beef, chicken, or beef tongue. There's also an all-you-can-eat lunch buffet weekdays and an all-you-can-eat dinner buffet Sunday. Beer and wine available. Lunch, dinner daily. &. (South Anchorage)

SIAM CUISINE
1911 W. Dimond Blvd.
Anchorage
907/344-3663
$$

Siam serves rewarding Thai food along with a few Vietnamese and Laotian dinners. Don't let the restaurant's inelegant outside appearance throw you: This is the genuine article, with some of the best spring rolls in town and a marvelous do-it-yourself dish called nam nuong—chicken meatballs, cold vermicelli, and fruits and vegetables you encase in rice-flour wrappers. Wine and beer available. Lunch Mon–Sat, dinner daily. &. (South Anchorage)

SOUTHSIDE BISTRO
1320 Huffman Park Dr.
Anchorage
907/348-0088
$$$

Tucked into an industrial park, the

Bistro offers intriguing ingredients and creative presentation, whether you're seeking a snack or a full meal. For appetizers, you can choose from among items such as Brie flatbread served with apple spears and watercress salad; prosciutto pizzetta topped with mushrooms, garlic, and fontina cheese; charbroiled eggplant with sun-dried tomatoes, roasted red-pepper relish, and goat cheese; and polenta fritters with grilled Kodiak scallops, oven-roasted red-pepper sauce, and ocean salad. Salads are far from iceberg-ian—you'll see field greens, heart of romaine, watercress, and fresh herbs. Entrées based on free-range chicken breast, venison loin, rack of lamb, Asian-style roast duck, or fresh Alaska seafood are prepared with savory touches like shallot–red-wine butter, black-currant demi-glace, rosemary-corn relish, apple–sundried-apricot compote, braised sweet red cabbage, and wild lingonberries. Desserts are punishingly rich, including the banana-caramel Napoleon, the chocolate-chip bread pudding, and the flourless triple-chocolate cake. For lunch, a lighter menu focuses on dishes such as burgers, wood-fired nachos, Caesar salad, angel-hair pasta, oysters or clams, and create-your-own pizzas with add-ons like artichoke hearts, sun-dried tomatoes, grilled chicken, Kalamata olives, Bay shrimp, prosciutto, wild mushrooms, and roasted garlic. Full bar service. Lunch, dinner Tue–Sat. & (South Anchorage)

TURNAGAIN HOUSE
Mile 103 Seward Hwy.
Indian
907/653-7500

$$$
Turnagain House is about 18 miles south of Anchorage, but the drive, along Turnagain Arm, is flat gorgeous. And the restaurant—a linen-tablecloth kind of place with a varied menu of beef, poultry, fish, and pork—is worth the drive. Try one of their tasty appetizers, such as the crab cakes in a tequila-lime sauce that's heartened by a roasted–red-pepper puree. If you want a nice spin on that old Alaska favorite, fresh seafood, consider the salmon or halibut done piccata-style or cooked with teriyaki ginger or cilantro salsa. Or spring for the roast duckling with cherry–port-wine sauce sparked with whole cherries. A local favorite is roasted pork loin topped with mushrooms in a Madeira sauce. The view while you eat is spectacular. Note: If smoke bothers you, ask for a table away from the bar since smoking is permitted there. Dinner daily. & (South Anchorage)

EAST ANCHORAGE

ALASKA BREAKFAST CLUB
1440 E. Tudor Rd.
Anchorage
907/561-3805
$–$$
As the name implies, this place does breakfast in a big way, literally: As a local restaurant reviewer noted, you could eat half of one of their omelets and save the rest for lunch. You can even buy the Farm—an omelet that includes mushrooms, bell peppers, onions, tomatoes, bacon, sausage, ham, and cheddar. Pancakes, waffles, eggs, and various breakfast meats

are also available, either singly or in combos. Lunches and dinners tend toward sandwiches, burgers, halibut, steaks, and the like. Breakfast, lunch, dinner daily. ⅃ (East Anchorage)

CATFISH HAVEN
360 Boniface Pkwy.
Anchorage
907/337-2868
$

Come here for down-home Southern cooking, and hang the calories! This family-style restaurant offers the titular catfish, plus smothered pork chops; ribs; barbecued beef, chicken, and shredded pork; and shrimp baskets. Side dishes are a real Sunday-dinner array: collard greens, candied yams, cabbage, corn bread, fried okra, macaroni and cheese, potato salad, black-eyed peas, baked beans, and red beans and rice. And what would a southern-style meal be without desserts like lemon pound cake, sweet-potato pie, and peach cobbler? Lunch, dinner Mon–Sat. ⅃ (East Anchorage)

DON JOSE'S
2052 E. Northern Lights Blvd.
Anchorage
907/279-5111
$$

Family-style dining thrives at this Mexican restaurant that offers such non–Tex-Mex specialties as fajitas, shrimp or crab enchiladas, carnitas, and carne asada. All the food is homemade, from the refried beans to the salsas and the chile rellenos. Kids who don't want "hot" food can be easily pacified with pizza or hamburgers from the children's menu. Full bar. Lunch, dinner daily. (East Anchorage)

HACIENDA
6307 DeBarr Rd.
Anchorage
907/338-6109
$$

This family-owned restaurant specializes in homemade chile verde, salsa, refried beans, tamales, chile rellenos, and fajitas. The margaritas aren't to be sneezed at, either. A relaxed atmosphere and friendly staff make this a good place to bring children. Full bar. Lunch, dinner daily. ⅃ (East Anchorage)

LUCKY WISHBONE
1033 E. Fifth Ave.
Anchorage
907/272-3454
$

This enduring restaurant is "family-owned and operated, and family-oriented." Its claim to fame is the best fried chicken in town, bar none: Made only from fresh chicken—never frozen—it's juicy, crispy, and just greasy enough to reassure you that it was fried, not baked. And if you have a hankering for fried gizzards or livers, you can get them here. The supporting cast is the usual batch of quick eats—sandwiches and burgers. The milkshakes are nice and thick, and the strawberry shortcake, pies, and sundaes provide satisfying ends to a great chicken dinner. Note that the Wishbone fills up quickly at lunchtime, but don't let that deter you; service is reliably swift and efficient, and lunchtime patrons are considerate of others waiting for a seat. Lunch, dinner Mon–Sat. ⅃ (East Anchorage)

PEGGY'S RESTAURANT
1675 E. Fifth Ave.
Anchorage
907/258-7599

$

At this unpretentious little place located near Merrill Field, the city's small-plane airport, the eats might be best described as "American coffee shop." You can get breakfast all day and salads, sandwiches, and soups at lunch and dinnertime. Salmon and halibut are also offered when they're in season. But all that food is just a prelude to the real reason everyone goes to Peggy's. The restaurant is "famous for pies," with as many as 18 varieties available at any given time. If you're looking for a cup of coffee during your visit, by all means have it here—along with a hunk of pie. Beer and wine also available. Breakfast, lunch, dinner daily. & (East Anchorage)

RED ROBIN BURGER & SPIRITS EMPORIUM
3401 Penland Pkwy.
Anchorage
907/276-7788
$$

This casual chain specializes in burgers, and it makes one for every taste: beef, chicken, fish, and even veggie. But it also offers sandwiches, soups, and light entrées— pretty much something for everyone. The burgers and appetizers are a bit pricey, but they come with free refills on the steak fries and soft drinks. Busy tourists will appreciate the turbo-powered service: You can be seated, eat, and get out within 30 minutes. However, lingerers won't be rushed; the friendly waitstaff will simply keep refilling your soda glasses. Red Robin's inexpensive kiddie menu and free crayons and balloons make it a popular family destination. And softball teams tend to gather here for post-game nibbles on late summer evenings. Full bar.

Lunch, dinner daily; food service to midnight. Also at 4140 B St., 907/563-1515, and 401 E. Dimond Blvd., 907/552-4321. & (East Anchorage)

SAIGON RESTAURANT
3561 E. Tudor Rd.
Anchorage
907/563-2515
$

Here you can enjoy a wide range of tasty Vietnamese food, some of which costs as little as a buck (a healthful bowl of anise-flavored clear broth with a few slices of white onion and jalapeño). Try the beef noodle soup, the spicy shrimp with lemongrass and red chili, or the fried chicken breasts, which come with steamed rice and sautéed vegetables. The menu also features barbecued pork chops, ribs, or chicken, again with veggies and rice. Fans of Vietnamese spices will enjoy the hot chicken, beef, and pork noodle dishes. Saigon also features plenty of vegetarian dishes. Lunch, dinner Mon–Sat. & (East Anchorage)

SIAM SPICY
6311 DeBarr Rd.
Anchorage
907/338-0757
$

At this small, family-run restaurant you're served a cup of soup as soon as you're seated, and waitstaff pay careful attention to your needs. The spring rolls are crisp but not oily and served with a cool, tasty dipping sauce of pickled garlic, pepper, and pineapple. Cook your own beef satay on a small grill at your table, or let the restaurant do the cooking with dishes like yum neau (onions, cucumbers, tomatoes, celery, lettuce, and hot peppers in a lime-juice dressing tossed with thinly sliced

Anchorage Area Cybercafés

- **Café Fonte**, *224 W. 34th Ave., Anchorage, 907/563-1700. Sip your brew and enjoy free Internet access.*
- **Sleepy Dog Coffee Co.**, *11525 Old Glenn Hwy., Eagle River, 907/694-6463. Cruise the Internet for free at this suburban coffeehouse.*
- **Surf City**, *415 L St., Anchorage, 907/279-7877. An Internet café with comfy furniture, coffee, juices, and snacks. There's a charge for computer use, but you can send or check e-mail and create your own home page at the multimedia station.*

barbecued beef) or gang panang (chicken, pork, or beef cooked with hot curry, Kaffir lime leaves, bell peppers, coconut milk, and a surprising touch of sweet basil, served with rice). Liquor license pending. No smoking. Lunch Tue–Fri, dinner Tue–Sat. & (East Anchorage)

WEST ANCHORAGE

ALASKA BAGEL RESTAURANT INC.
113 W. Northern Lights Blvd.
Anchorage
907/276-3900
$

A sometimes bewildering array of flavors—do you suppose God really meant for bagels to be available in chocolate-chip or pesto?—and a tasty selection of toppings make this restaurant a fine choice for breakfast or lunch. The sandwiches are good, and the eggs, potatoes, and bagel breakfast is the perfect fuel for a long morning of sightseeing.

Stop in on weekends, when bialys and cheese boards are available. Breakfast, lunch daily. & (West Anchorage)

ARCTIC ROADRUNNER
5300 Old Seward Hwy.
Anchorage
907/561-1245
$

The onion rings are good, but be sure to try the absolutely wonderful "onion pieces"—slivers and slabs of sweet onions so soft and oily that most of the breading has given up the ghost. Just don't tell your personal trainer. This local institution has fine, beefy burgers with Alaskan names, from the intimidating Lord Baranof (mozzarella, salami, ham, onion rings, and a special relish sauce atop two quarter-pound patties) to the kid-friendly Attu (a three-ounce patty with catsup, mustard, and onions). Salmon and halibut burgers are served in summer when the fish are running. And speaking of fish: If weather permits, eat outdoors alongside Campbell Creek and watch for salmon swimming upstream. No credit cards. Lunch, dinner Mon–Sat. Also in West Anchorage, 2477 Arctic Blvd., 907/279-7311. & (South Anchorage)

ARIGATO
3315 Spenard Rd.
Anchorage
907/561-4510
$$

This Japanese restaurant offers diners the familiar along with the exotic. The nervous among you can fall back on standbys like chicken teriyaki or vegetable tempura. But those with a sense of adventure might want to try sashimi, sea urchin, or hijiki (marinated tuna cooked in a nest of seaweed). The portions are large and the atmosphere comfortable and quiet. Wine and beer available. Lunch, dinner daily. & (West Anchorage)

ATLASTA DELI
701 W. 36th Ave.
Anchorage
907/563-3354
$

This deli has more than a hundred meats and cheeses, most of them imported, as well as salads and desserts made on the premises. Try the McKinley sandwich, with capocollo (a spicy ham), mortadella, Sicilian and Genovese salamis, and provolone; or the spicy Mount Redoubt (named after a volcano that blew its top a few years back), with dry coppa (pork sausage), soppressata (a wine-and-garlic-cured ham), Sicilian salami, and provolone. The smoked-salmon salad is very popular, as are the seafood and chicken-salad sandwiches. Desserts include the nut-brown chocolate Kodiak

cheesecake, Key-lime cheesecake, and various fruit pies. Beer and wine available. Continental breakfast, lunch Mon–Sat. & (West Anchorage)

BAGEL FACTORY
100 W. 34th Ave.
Anchorage
907/561-8871
$

As with the Alaska Bagel Restaurant (see previous page), some of the flavors available here may make bagel purists turn pale. If you're a traditionalist, stick with the tried-and-true favorites. Or go ahead and take a chance on a blueberry bagel, lightly toasted with a little butter—the color may be offputting, but the flavor is terrific. The restaurant has good soups and chili as well as tasty bagel sandwiches. Breakfast, lunch daily. & (West Anchorage)

CAMPOBELLO
601 W. 36th Ave.
Anchorage
907/563-2040
$–$$

With white tablecloths and plenty of Alaskan art on the walls, this bistro serves good, uncomplicated, mostly Northern Italian food. A typical evening menu might feature dishes such as penne with fresh Roma marinara, veal saltimbocca, halibut Rossini, and crispy salmon over fresh spinach with a garlic and Roma beurre blanc. Campobello has beer and an extensive wine list, with 30 wines available by the glass. Reservations suggested, particularly for midday. Lunch Mon–Fri, dinner Tue–Sat. & (West Anchorage)

CUSACK'S BREWPUB
THE BREWMASTER'S ROOM
Northern Lights Hotel
598 W. Northern Lights Blvd.
Anchorage
907/278-2739
$$

Both restaurants feature 9 to 12 house brews, microbrews from Alaska and the Lower 48 on tap, and an unusual root beer made with, among other things, Alaskan birch syrup, for a richer taste. The brewpub's appetizer bar features savory items like "Rasta wings," made with Jamaican seasonings; grinders; buffalo burgers; and a Reuben on dark rye with meats and cheeses sliced in-house. Lunch Mon–Sat, dinner daily; food service to midnight.

The Brewmaster's Room serves classic breakfast dishes, including omelets and eggs Benedict. Lunches consist of gourmet sandwiches similar to those served at the brewpub; wraps such as bacon, turkey, lettuce, tomato, and avocado; homemade soups; and mixedgreens salads. For dinner, sample steaks, prime rib, fresh seafood, and pastas. The desserts, including cheesecake, carrot cake, and fruit pies, are made in-house. Be prepared to defend turf—the cute little individual pies tend to induce others to ask for a bite. Full bar service. Breakfast, lunch, dinner daily. ⅝ (West Anchorage)

EUROPA BAKERY
601 W. 36th Ave.
Anchorage
907/563-5704
$

The specialty sandwiches here come on fresh baked breads: rustic sourdough, dark peasant, spentgrain made with barley from a local brewpub, and simple baguettes. One of the bakery's most popular sandwiches is the Meat Grinder: salami, prosciutto, ham, red onions, red peppers, provolone, and rémoulade. All sandwiches come with a side salad and a cookie. You can also choose from three daily homemade soups (the tomato-basil with feta cheese is superb) and two hot specials such as casseroles, vegetarian lasagna, steamed vegetables over rice, and stuffed peppers. Their Omelets of the World include the Hungarian (paprika, kielbasa, red peppers, and Jarlsberg), the Homer (halibut sautéed in butter and wine, with snow peas, celery root, and sour cream), and the French (mushrooms, fresh basil, fresh sage, and Gruyère). The bakery produces fabulous desserts, including chocolateraspberry truffle cake, muffins, scones, cream-cheese crowns, raspberry-nut squares, and French pastries. Lunch daily, breakfast Sat and Sun. ⅝ (West Anchorage)

GREEK CORNER
302 W. Fireweed Ln.
Anchorage
907/276-2820
$$

This tiny, cozy restaurant dishes up hearty and tasty fare, mostly rich Greek foods such as souvlaki, pastitsio, and gyro platters, as well as the seemingly inevitable Italian items like spaghetti and pizza. The Greek salad is absolutely massive—unless you're really hungry or making it your entire meal, plan to split it with a loved one. Beer and wine available. Lunch Mon–Sat, dinner daily. (West Anchorage)

HARLEY'S OLD THYME CAFE
7550 Old Seward Hwy.

Anchorage
907/349-8878
$
This family-style restaurant serves down-home cooking at low prices. Try the brisket, a house specialty that's cooked for 12 hours and then thinly sliced and served with a dipping sauce. And have fun choosing from the 20 side dishes. Beer and wine available. Lunch, dinner daily; breakfast Sat, brunch Sun. & (West Anchorage)

HOGG BROS. CAFE
1049 W. Northern Lights Blvd.
Anchorage
907/276-9649
$
A lovable local institution, this café serves enormous omelets and other wonderful breakfast treats, including a thick delicious French toast and biscuits with sausage gravy (the biggest, whitest plate of comfort food imaginable—just the thing for stressed travelers). In fact, the breakfasts are so pleasing that it

can be hard to remember the lunch side of the menu, which features some of the most satisfying burgers around. And while you're waiting for your meal to arrive, do wander around the restaurant to enjoy the pig-themed decor. Breakfast, lunch, dinner daily. & (West Anchorage)

JACKIE'S PLACE
2636 Spenard Rd.
Anchorage
907/274-3211
$
Anchorage doesn't have any real diners, but Jackie's is darned close. This no-nonsense eatery in the Spenard section of town has reasonably priced soups, sandwiches, and breakfasts. The waitresses are friendly and the iced tea is real. Breakfast, lunch (to 3:45 p.m.) daily. & (West Anchorage)

L'AROMA BAKERY & DELI
3700 Old Seward Hwy.
Anchorage
907/562-9797

Glacier Brew House, p. 60

Glacier Brew House

$

L'Aroma serves fabulous sandwiches on fresh-baked rustic breads and gourmet pizzas baked in an applewood-fired oven; try the four-cheese (fragrant and memorable) and the barbecued-chicken varieties. Lunch, dinner daily. The same pizzas and sandwiches, plus international hot foods, can be found downtown at New Sagaya City Market, 900 W. 13th Ave., 907/274-6173. ♿ (West Anchorage)

LONE STAR STEAKHOUSE & SALOON
4810 C St.
Anchorage
907/562-7827
$$

This eatery is part of a national chain that not only permits but encourages its waiters to break into spontaneous country-western dancing. Don't let it frighten you. Enjoy the Texas-themed decor while you peruse the large menu. The steaks and chicken are tasty, and by all means substitute a sweet potato for the ordinary baked potato—these "sweets" are baked until they're cloud-soft, then drenched in melted butter and cinnamon sugar; it's like being allowed to have a big slice of sweet-potato pie as a side dish. Another indulgence is the appetizer made up of a bale of fresh-cut French fries covered with melted cheese and bacon, served with a spicy ranch dressing—a heart attack on a platter, to be sure, but it's just too darned good to pass up. Full bar service. Lunch, dinner daily. ♿ (West Anchorage)

MIDDLE WAY CAFE & COFFEE HOUSE
Northern Lights Center

1200 W. Northern Lights Blvd.
Anchorage
907/272-6433
$

This small, laid-back restaurant specializes in healthy fare that tastes great, with an emphasis on vegan and vegetarian foods. Try the "Pestorica" wrap, with brown rice, pesto, sun-dried tomatoes, and scallions on mixed greens. Other popular wraps are the falafel, with tomatoes, cucumbers, red peppers, sprouts, parsley, Kalamata olives, and lemon-tahini sauce, all wrapped up in a whole-wheat chapati; and the "Quantum"—organic pinto beans, brown rice, red cabbage, carrots, avocado, scallions, and cheddar cheese served in a whole-wheat chapati with homemade salsa. The Spicy Veggie sandwich is made with leaf lettuce, tomatoes, cucumbers, red onion, avocado, pumpkin seeds, and cream cheese blended with sun-dried tomatoes, green onions, and jalapeños. A few non-vegetarian sandwiches are also available, such as turkey, chicken, or tuna. All the burgers are meatless, and one of the two daily soups is always vegetarian. The Middle Way's "micro-bakery" churns out lovely baked goods, such as carrot cake, banana bread, cardamom-cinnamon coffee cake, lemon bread, and scones. Vegan baked goods are available on Sunday, although the kitchen is closed that day. Fancy coffees and teas are served, and you can substitute soy- or rice milk in your drinks if you so desire. No credit cards. Lunch, dinner Mon–Sat. ♿ (West Anchorage)

MOMMA O'S
2636 Spenard Rd.
Anchorage

907/278-2216
$

The sign reads, "Where Batter-Dipped Halibut Is King." So why are all those bodybuilders going inside? Because you can also get that flavorful fish grilled or steamed, with a side of plain rice, that's why. If you're not watching your figure, do try the batter-dipped variety, as a sandwich or an entrée. Or check out the clam strips, oysters, calamari, or shrimp. For a lighter meal, you can have udon noodles, chicken teriyaki, or grilled chicken breast (again, as a sandwich or an entrée). Lunch, dinner Mon–Sat (limited Sat dinner hours). & (West Anchorage)

MOOSE'S TOOTH PUB & PIZZERIA
3300 Old Seward Hwy.
Anchorage
907/258-2537
$

This restaurant's location requires a tricky right turn off the New Seward Highway; if you miss it, creep up to 36th Avenue and turn right, then turn right again on Old Seward. You definitely don't want to miss the hand-tossed crusts and fabulous pizza combos—including a dozen vegetarian numbers—that set this pizzeria/brewpub apart. Try the Popeye, made with spinach, red and green peppers, mushrooms, two cheeses, and the chef's "Denali" sauce. Those on dairy-free diets might select the cheeseless Very Veggie or Purple Haze pizzas. Or you can make up your own creation. Try the soups and salads, too. Wine and brewpub beers available. Lunch, dinner daily. & (West Anchorage)

THE NOODLE HOUSE
3301 Spenard Rd.
Anchorage

907/563-9880
$–$$

This unassuming restaurant serves the best steamed dumplings in town. The homemade noodles are tops, too. If you're a fan of really spicy food, you may have to say so, emphatically and more than once; otherwise, waiters who think they're acting in your best interests will automatically bring you the toned-down versions. Lunch, dinner daily. (West Anchorage)

OLGA RUSSIAN & EUROPEAN DELICATESSEN
3020 Minnesota Dr.
Anchorage
907/279-1133
$$

Come here to sample the agreeable dishes of a different culture, such as pirozhki (bread-like dumplings stuffed with meat, cabbage, or flavored scrambled eggs), winter salad (meat, potatoes, eggs, peas, pickles, onion, and mayonnaise), okroshka (a cold soup made with kvass, cucumbers, green onions, potatoes, eggs, meat, sausage, and sour cream), solianka (cabbage, carrots, beets, and pickles fried with sausage), and galuptzi (beef, pork, and rice wrapped in cabbage leaves, then baked and served over shredded carrots). Or you can eschew restaurant dining and take home some deli food to make your own dinner: bologna, cheeses, dried whole fish, sardines, hams, sausages, filleted fish, kasha, or pickled tomatoes. Lunch, dinner Mon–Sat. & (West Anchorage)

ORGANIC OASIS
2610 Spenard Rd.
Anchorage
907/277-7882

Marx Brothers Cafe, p. 61

$–$$

Soft New-Age music plays and water trickles slowly into a small pond at this clean, mellow, healthy restaurant. Although the bulk of the menu is vegetarian or vegan, a consistent best-seller is the organic turkey sandwich—lean and delicious. The soups, salads, and sandwiches are 100-percent organic, and you can choose from a selection of smoothies and freshly made juices. Thanks to the miracle of shade-grown coffee and organic milk, you can even have an organic latte. If you're looking for meal-in-your-room supplies, the restaurant's "micro-bakery" produces vegan whole-wheat bread and cookies, and be sure to check out the coolers and shelves of good-for-you goodies such as chapati, pumpkin seeds, dried fruits, soy milk, non-dairy burritos, bottled juices, and even organic cola! Organic beer and wine available. Lunch, dinner daily. ♿ (West Anchorage)

OUTBACK STEAKHOUSE
101 W. 34th Ave.
Anchorage
907/562-8787
$$

A pleasant and very popular chain restaurant with an Australian theme, the Outback is always crowded; if need be, you'll be given a beeper to take with you to the bar, so you'll know when your table is ready. The tender steaks are coated with a peppery rub (if you like your steak unadorned, be sure to tell the server when you place your order). The chicken and the pork chops are good eating, too. "Jacket potatoes" are baked on a bed of rock salt, and the salads are large, crisp, and colorful. Note: All of the meals have coy little Aussie names, so if you are offended by cute, this might not be the place for you. Try to look past the adorableness, though, and you'll get a reliably tasty meal. Dinner nightly, lunch Sun only. ♿ (West Anchorage)

PEPPER MILL
4101 Credit Union Dr.
Anchorage
907/561-0800
$$$

This place specializes in pepper steak, but not just with your garden-variety pepper. Try French pepper, garlic pepper, jalapeño pepper, whiskey pepper, or blackened pepper, among others. Or go for the tournedos served with artichoke hearts, stuffed mushrooms, and béarnaise sauce. The Kodiak is another favorite: a center-cut filet served with Alaska crabmeat, asparagus, and béarnaise sauce. Ribeye, New York, Porterhouse, and teriyaki steaks are available, too, as are pastas, seafood, pork chops, prime rib, and chicken. Full bar. Dinner daily. ⅙ (West Anchorage)

PHO MAILEE
3020 Minnesota Dr.
Anchorage
907/258-4746
$$

Noodles are the staff of life at Pho MaiLee, a Vietnamese restaurant tucked anonymously into a strip mall off busy Minnesota Drive. You can get noodle soup with a variety of meats, including brisket, chicken, meatballs, tripe, or "soft tendon." Sautéed noodles and pad Thai dishes come with chicken, pork, beef, or seafood and mixed vegetables. Cold noodles (made with delicate rice vermicelli) with salad come in combinations such as grilled pork, lettuce, cucumber, and sprouts; and marinated prawns, grilled pork, and lettuce. Other dishes include pork chops marinated in lemongrass and served over steamed rice with savory sauce, curry chicken with carrots

and bamboo, spicy squid with onions and celery, and a Vietnamese sandwich of barbecued pork, pork meatloaf, and vegetables. Cool your inflamed palate with iced French coffee (served with or without condensed milk), Thai iced coffee or tea, soybean milk, or coconut juice. You could also select an ordinary soft drink—but how dull! Lunch, dinner daily. ⅙ (West Anchorage)

PIZZA OLYMPIA
2809 Spenard Rd.
Anchorage
907/561-5264
$$

This family-run restaurant has excellent homemade Greek food and some of the best pizza in town. Try the gyros, either as a lunchtime sandwich or a dinnertime platter. The moussaka is excellent, as is the leg of lamb served with oreganato potatoes and a side of marinara spaghetti. For appetizers, plenty of people opt for an order of tzatziki (yogurt, cucumbers, olive oil, and fresh seasonings), scooped up on fresh bread, or the saganaki, a baked dish of sheep's-milk cheese and egg that's flamed with brandy. Lunch Mon–Sat, dinner daily. ⅙ (West Anchorage)

QUPQUGIAQ CAFE
640 W. 36th Ave.
Anchorage
907/563-5634
$

Food is only part of this coffee-house-school-inn-restaurant (it's pronounced "koop-koo-gee-ak"). But the food they do sell is well worth a munch. Try sandwiches grilled on thick slices of rustic bread, in combos like ham and provolone with sprouts and sun-dried tomatoes; or roasted red peppers, summer squash, Gorgonzola, and mushrooms. Soups are intriguing and homemade; salads go far beyond the usual iceberg lettuce. If you're in for breakfast, you can get bagels and eggs—and coffee, of course. Breakfast, lunch, dinner daily. ⚬ (West Anchorage)

ROSCOE'S SKYLINE RESTAURANT
The Mall at Sears

Northern Lights Blvd.
and Seward Hwy.
Anchorage
907/276-5879
$
This renowned Government Hill soul-food restaurant, destroyed by arson in 1997, reopened in 1998 in a different location but with the same mission: to provide real homestyle cooking. This family-run eatery features food dear to the hearts of Southerners and to those who are

---

City Market

This "foods of the world" market, located at 13th Avenue and I Street, sells meats, cheeses, produce, seafood, breads, condiments, pastas, sauces, and other carefully chosen foodstuffs.

Owners Paul and Kathleen Reid don't call it a gourmet store. It's closer to the sorts of shops that used to be more common— small neighborhood groceries that sold homemade sausage or fresh cheese and olives from the old country.

Travelers looking for that morning wake-up call can buy fancy coffee and freshly baked breads, bagels, and sweets. While you're there, grab some items for a great picnic—bread, imported cheese, smoked duck, fresh cookies, and maybe some of those blood oranges or air-fresh peaches.

You can also eat at the market, in a sunny yellow dining area or at an outdoor table. Since the market is a de facto neighborhood center, you may have to wait for a seat outside—Alaskans tend to linger whenever sun is available.

If you're too tired to sit up politely in a restaurant, stop in for some takeout with a distinctly international flair: vindaloo chicken, tamales, beef ragout, and the like, along with comfort foods like meatloaf, baked Alaskan halibut, and garlic mashed potatoes. Gourmet pizzas from the wood-fired oven are a treat, too.

Top Ten Places to Cool Your Cerebellum

(in no particular order) by Mark Dudick, editor of "8,"
the *Anchorage Daily News*'s entertainment magazine

1. **Mead's Coffeehouse**, 405 E. Herring Ave., Wasilla,
   907/357-5633

2. **Bernie's Bungalow**, 626 D St., 907/276-8808

3. **Snow City Cafe**, 1034 W. Fourth Ave., 907/272-2489

4. **Tudor Road Bingo Center**, 3411 E. Tudor Rd.,
   907/561-4711

5. **Border's Books and Music**, 1100 E. Dimond Blvd.,
   907/344-4099

6. **A-K Korral Saloon**, 2421 E. Tudor Rd., 907/562-6552

7. **Blues Central**, The Chef's Inn, 825 W. Northern Lights Blvd.,
   907/272-1341

8. **Humpy's Great Alaska Alehouse**, 610 W. Sixth Ave.,
   907/276-2337

9. **Vagabond Blues Coffeehouse**, 642 S. Alaska St., Palmer,
   907/745-2233

10. **The Wave**, 3103 Spenard Rd., 907/561-9283

smart enough to try the food that Southerners eat—catfish, greens, North Carolina barbecue sandwiches, mesquite-smoked ribs, red beans and rice, and gumbo. Save room for made-on-the-premises desserts, including pound cake, peach cobbler, sweet-potato pie, and bread pudding. And do bring the kids: The children's menu includes smaller portions of the grownup foods, plus peanut-butter-and-jelly sandwiches for non-adventurous young palates (although don't be surprised if your formerly picky kids start snitching bits of food off your plate). Beer and wine available. No smoking. Lunch, dinner daily. &
(West Anchorage)

STUART ANDERSON'S CATTLE COMPANY
300 W. Tudor Rd.
Anchorage
907/562-2844
$$
This chain restaurant has a way with steaks, chicken, prime rib, and seafood. Go for the baked-potato soup every time: It's thick and rich and sprinkled with sour cream, bacon, cheddar, and chives. And don't let it stop you from having a potato dish with your dinner, particularly the garlic mashed potatoes. The Caesar salad is massive and tangy, and desserts are enormous—you may need a spotter to help you finish the Mile-High Mud Pie. The at-

mosphere is family-friendly, and if your kids get a little cranky when they're hungry, don't worry—the high-backed booths provide their own soundproofing until your meal arrives. Full bar service. Lunch Mon–Fri and Sun, dinner daily. ♿ (West Anchorage)

TACO DEL MAR
343 W. Benson Blvd.
Anchorage
907/563-9097
$

"Burritos so big you don't need a fork—you need a forklift" is the motto of this small, friendly restaurant. These Mission-style (steamed) burritos are available in beef, chicken, pork, fish, and other varieties. And yes, they really are huge, so consider sharing one with a friend. About those title tacos—the "del Mar" part refers to the kind made with Alaskan cod, shredded cabbage, a spicy white sauce, cheese, and homemade salsa. The restaurant also serves hard and soft tacos made of beef, braised chicken, or roasted pork in mole. Lunch, dinner daily. ♿ (West Anchorage)

TACO KING
Northern Lights Blvd. and A St.
Anchorage
907/276-7387
$

The food here is more Mexican than Tex-Mex. The carne asada tacos are lightly toasted corn tortillas piled with seasoned grilled beef, hot sauce, cilantro, and onions. Be brave and try the grilled-tongue tacos. And be sure to dunk some homemade corn chips in any of the five freshly made salsas. Lunch, dinner daily. (West Anchorage)

TEMPURA KITCHEN
3826 Spenard Rd.
Anchorage
907/277-2741
$$

This gracious and pleasant restaurant has sushi chefs who can turn simple ingredients into beautifully arranged works of art. Anywhere from 25 to 30 kinds of sushi are available at any given time. If you're lucky enough to be in town when the Alaska side-striped shrimp are running—well, then you are indeed lucky, whether you choose them fried whole or as part of a sushi order. Don't worry if you've never eaten Japanese food before—the wait staff will help you select the right kind. Beer (including Japanese beer) and wine available. Reservations suggested for Fri and Sat nights, and for parties of 6 or more. Lunch Mon–Fri, dinner daily. ♿ (West Anchorage)

EAGLE RIVER

GARCIA'S CANTINA & CAFE
11901 Business Blvd.
Eagle River
907/694-8600
$

Even people who don't like Mexican food flock here, in part because you can also get a great burger and because it's a very family-friendly place. When the place is packed, people are willing to wait quite a while for a table to open up. The food is American Mexican, with enchiladas, tacos, chimichangas, fajitas, and the like. A big seller is the pollo fundito, a deep-fried chicken chimi topped with flavored cream cheese and melted cheese. The kid's menu has both Mexican and

EAGLE RIVER

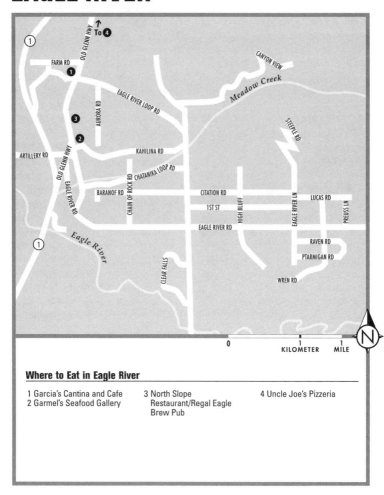

Where to Eat in Eagle River

1 Garcia's Cantina and Cafe
2 Garmel's Seafood Gallery

3 North Slope
Restaurant/Regal Eagle
Brew Pub

4 Uncle Joe's Pizzeria

"Yankee" foods, all served with free ice cream. (Don't insist that the kids clean their plates to get the ice cream, though—even the kid's portions are pretty sizable.) Full bar service. Open for lunch and dinner daily. &. (Eagle River)

GARMEL'S SEAFOOD GALLEY
11401 Old Glenn Hwy.

Eagle River
907/694-4732
$$
This small, homey restaurant with seashore decor reminded one New England expatriate of "beachfront restaurants I used to frequent . . . I could almost feel the sand between my toes." Garmel's emphasizes fresh Alaska seafood like halibut,

salmon, scallops, sole, and shrimp, plus regular visitors from other seas. You can order these items sautéed with olive oil and roasted garlic, charbroiled, and, yes, deep-fried—but the restaurant owner makes his batter with Chardonnay rather than beer and uses pure soybean oil for frying. It can be hard to get a seat on Friday or Saturday night, but the wait is worth it. Try the Seabed Salad, a huge platter of romaine, English cucumbers, and fresh vegetables topped with either shrimp, salmon, halibut, or crab. And if you have room, ask for the baked-on-the-premises New York–style cheesecake or a dessert called Utopia: a pecan cookie crust filled with glazed mandarin oranges, pineapple, and bananas and topped with whipped cream and blanched almonds. Hey, you had a healthy entrée, right? So live it up. Beer and wine available. Lunch, dinner Tue–Sun. ♿ (Eagle River)

NORTH SLOPE RESTAURANT/ REGAL EAGLE BREW PUB

11501 Old Glenn Hwy.
Eagle River
907/694-9120
$$
Steaks and seafood are the emphasis, especially halibut and salmon, in this family-oriented restaurant. Copper River Amber Ale, the pub's signature brew, is always on tap; five other kinds of brews change constantly. Full bar service available. Breakfast, lunch, and dinner daily. ♿ (Eagle River)

UNCLE JOE'S PIZZERIA
11823 Old Glenn Hwy.
Eagle River
609/696-4545
$/$$
Despite its name, Uncle Joe's sells more than pizza. You can get salads, ribs, wings, spaghetti, ravioli, subs, and gyros. A kid's menu offers smaller, but just as tasty, meals. The pizzas are hand-tossed, and Uncle Joe's sells plenty of them. Seating is limited, but takeout is available. Open for dinner nightly. ♿ (Eagle River)

Barb Willard/Alaskana Photo

5

SIGHTS AND ATTRACTIONS

Anchorage is still so young that it hasn't had much time to reflect on itself. The downtown area has some cherished "old" buildings, but this is a relative notion since the city was founded in 1915, and plenty of those original buildings were either tents or temporary. Still, residents are increasingly interested in the way the city came together—and visitors have always found Anchorage's brief history fascinating.

You can cover plenty of standard sights and attractions in a day or so of sightseeing—a plus for those whose vacation time is limited. As for the rest of Alaska, or even of Anchorage, it's merely a question of arranging it. How you do it is up to you: Hop on a tour bus, hire a seat on a flightseeing helicopter, show up during Fur Rendezvous and talk your way onto a snowshoe softball team. Or you can get gear and directions and set out on your own to discover, say, Crow Creek Mine or the Eagle River Nature Center.

Note: Anchorage doesn't have any entertainment centers, bells-and-whistles theme parks, or attractions that capitalize on Alaska's wild and woolly past. You won't find gold-rush reenactments or replicas of the original tent city. Nor will you find Six Flags Over Anchorage. The closest thing to a Lower 48-style "attraction" is the Alaska Native Heritage Center. Long-awaited, it finally opened in May 1999.

DOWNTOWN

ALASKA CENTER FOR THE PERFORMING ARTS
621 W. Sixth Ave.
Anchorage

907/263-2900
Yes, it's a rather unique looking building. Locals love to make fun of it. One politician said it looked as though it were made from three odd lots of Z-Brick. Another wag claimed that the lighted rings on the outside

were reminiscent of Texas strip clubs: "Those lights just scream, 'Girls! Girls! Girls!'" But what can you do? Inside, the three concert halls showcase local groups such the Anchorage Symphony Orchestra and the Anchorage Opera as well as visiting classical and popular music acts and Broadway musicals. The center is also the repository of some interesting artwork—some contemporary, some traditional—representing the various Alaska Native cultures. And the flowerbeds in adjacent Town Square Park are absolutely gorgeous, with mums so large and bright they seem radioactive (blame that endless summer sunshine) and flowering kale that looks good enough to eat. Guided tours Wed 1 p.m.; $1 donation requested. ♿ (Downtown)

ALASKA EXPERIENCE THEATER
705 W. Sixth Ave.
Anchorage
907/276-3730
Alaska the Greatland is a 40-minute Omnivision film shown on a three-story, 180-degree screen. The 70-millimeter film, with six-track sound, gives viewers the feeling of being right in the midst of the glaciers, mountains, wildlife, and villages of Alaska. *The Alaska Earthquake* is a multimedia exhibit explaining the Good Friday Earthquake of 1964, which measured 9.2 on the Richter scale and left an indelible mark on Alaska. The ground in the Safequake Theater rumbles and shakes beneath your feet, giving you the approximate effect of a 4.5 earthquake; science and history exhibits and giant murals complete the experience. Summer daily 9–9; winter daily noon–6. Theater $6.99 adults, $3.99 children 5–12; earthquake exhibit $4.99 adults, $3.99 children; combination ticket $9.99 adults, $6.99 children. ♿ (Downtown)

ALASKA PUBLIC LANDS INFORMATION CENTER
605 W. Fourth Ave.
Anchorage
907/271-2737
This is a good place to begin your travels since the staff can answer just about any question on Alaska. Each of the state's very different regions is represented in a setup that, viewed from above, would form something of a giant map, with each region correctly placed. Stuffed animals—the real ones, including caribou, bear, deer, birds, and Dall sheep—are displayed throughout the room. Interpretive exhibits offer loads of information about the state's geography, weather, flora and fauna, and peoples.

Some exhibits include short videos, such as *Katmai Eruption*, *Musk Ox from Nunivak*, *Reindeer Herding*, and *Blue Ice, Blue Water:*

Self-guided–tour maps are available at the blue kiosks along Fifth Avenue at D, E, and F Streets; along Fourth Avenue near D, E, and F Streets; on Third Avenue near F Street; and on Second Avenue near E and F Streets. They'll guide you to the oldest, most colorful, and most interesting buildings in the downtown area.

DOWNTOWN ANCHORAGE

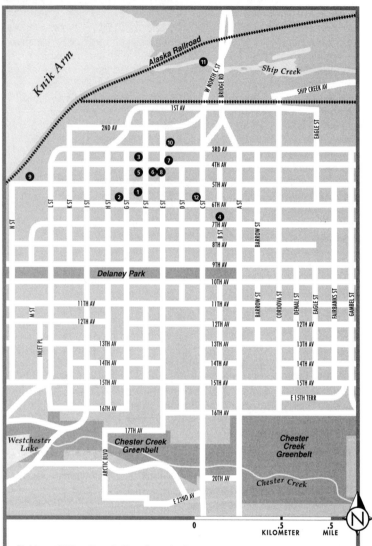

Knik Arm

Alaska Railroad

Ship Creek

SHIP CREEK AV

W NORTH C ST
BRIDGE RD

EAGLE ST

1ST AV
2ND AV
3RD AV
4TH AV
5TH AV
6TH AV
7TH AV
8TH AV
9TH AV
10TH AV
11TH AV
12TH AV
13TH AV
14TH AV
15TH AV
16TH AV
17TH AV
20TH AV
E 22ND AV
E 15TH TERR

L ST
K ST
I ST
H ST
G ST
F ST
E ST
D ST
C ST
A ST
N ST
M ST
INLET PL
B ST
BARROW ST
CORDOVA ST
DENALI ST
EAGLE ST
FAIRBANKS ST
GAMBELL ST

Delaney Park

Westchester Lake

Chester Creek Greenbelt

Chester Creek Greenbelt

Chester Creek

ARCTIC BLVD

0   .5   .5
     KILOMETER   MILE

N

Sights and Attractions in Downtown Anchorage

1 Alaska Center for the
  Performing Arts,
  Cineventures, Sky Song
2 Alaska Experience Theater
3 Alaska Public Lands
  Information Center

4 Anchorage Museum of
  History and Art
5 Fourth Avenue Theater
6 Log Cabin Visitor Center
7 Music in the Park
8 Old City Hall

9 Oscar Anderson House
10 Saturday Market
11 Ship Creek
12 Wolf Song of Alaska

Glaciers and Fjords. In addition, free nature films such as *The Day the Earth Shook*, *One Arctic Summer*, *A Gathering of Bears*, and *Alaska Rain Forest* are shown hourly in the adjacent theater. Be sure to take advantage of the free use of "Historic Alaska in Stereo View" stereoscopes, with such antique sights as "French Quarters, Dawson City," "City of Cold Feet, Alaska," "Our Alaskan Sisters up in the Klondike," and "Dr. Sheldon Jackson and Government Reindeer." You can also receive information about and make reservations for the Alaska Marine Highway, the state's ferry system. Open daily 9–5:30. Free. &. (Downtown)

ANCHORAGE FUR RENDEZVOUS
Greater Anchorage, Inc.
Anchorage
907/277-8615
Each year in mid-February, the city stages one of the larger winter carnivals in North America, the 10-day "Fur Rondy." Many events take place downtown. Among the numerous activities and sights are snow sculptures, Native arts and crafts, a melodrama, sled-dog races, snowshoe softball, a homebrew competition, and an outdoor carnival area. (Ever ridden the Scrambler at 10 below? It's a breathtaking experience!) Some events are free, with a nominal charge for others. (Downtown)

ANCHORAGE MUSEUM OF HISTORY AND ART
121 W. Seventh Ave.
Anchorage
907/343-4326
The museum's permanent collection features chronologically arranged art from the days of early explorers through current times. The Alaska Gallery depicts the state's history, ethnography, and aboriginal peoples, covering topics such as archeology, exploration, Russian settlements, the United States purchase, the gold rush, commercial whaling, World War II, and statehood. Take some time to appreciate Sydney Laurence's 6-by-12–foot painting of Mount McKinley.

Temporary exhibits, including traveling shows from the Lower 48, highlight art, history, archeology, and other subjects. The Children's Gallery features yearlong interactive exhibits that change each June (see Chapter 7, Kids' Stuff). The museum's library and archives—open mornings and afternoons by appointment—contain historical photos and reference works. The Museum Cafe offers coffee, light snacks, and a very inventive lunch menu (see Chapter 4, Where to Eat). In summer, the museum shows films about the art, history, and ethnography of Alaska. Summer daily 9–6; rest of year Tue–Sat 10–6, Sun 1–5. $5 adults, $4.50 seniors, youths under 18 free. (Downtown)

CINEVENTURES
Alaska Center for the Performing Arts
621 W. Sixth Ave.
Anchorage
907/263-2787
Two Imax-format films show every day, to the delight and awe of folks

TRIVIA

The city's drinking water comes from a glacier.

*Alaska Public Lands
Information Center, p. 87*

youths; all three films $19 adults,
$16.50 seniors, $15 youths. ♿
(Downtown)

FOURTH AVENUE THEATRE
630 W. Fourth Ave.
Anchorage
907/257-5600

This art-deco building was a real
hot spot in its heyday, when an
evening at the movies really meant
something. Construction of the
1,200-seat theater began in 1941 but
was delayed by World War II. Like
most single-screen, downtown
movie theaters in America, it slowly
withered and died with the advent
of multiplex cinemas with plenty of
parking. The Fourth Avenue last operated as a movie theater in 1990.
Currently it houses a gift shop and
live summer entertainment. Even if
you don't want to buy anything,
stroll in for a look at the gold-leaf
murals, the balcony, and the twin-
kling Big Dipper on the auditorium
ceiling, along with the photos of
earthquake-era Anchorage displayed in the basement. Summer
daily 8 a.m.–9 p.m.; winter daily
10–5. Free. (Downtown)

LOG CABIN VISITOR CENTER
Fourth Ave. and F St.
Anchorage
907/274-3531

Yep, it really is a log cabin—it even
has grass growing on the roof. (Look
for wild onions and Jacob's ladder
growing there, too.) The building's
quaintness, along with its abundant
flowers and foliage—from tuberous
begonias to flowering kale—make it
a good place to start that first roll of
film. Stop inside to pick up information about Anchorage sights, tours,
and lodgings. The staff will do its
best to answer any questions, and

who may never get much closer
than this to actual wilderness.
Alaska: Spirit of the Wild, narrated
by Charlton Heston, is an up-close
and personal look at nature: brown
bears fishing, bald eagles floating,
caribou stampeding, and glaciers
calving. The film points out the harsh
climate, surprising wildlife, and incredible scenery of Alaska, as well
as the spirit of the land. *Whales: An
Unforgettable Journey* looks at the
incredible lives of the largest mam-
mals that ever lived on Earth, including blue, humpback, orca and right
whales. The documentary also highlights other sea animals: penguins,
dolphins, seals, and manta rays.
May–Sept daily 9–9, every hour on
the hour. Single tickets $9.75 adults,
$8.75 seniors, $7.75 youths; combination tickets $14 adults, $12.50 seniors, $11 youths. One film in
combination with Sky Song, a film-
and-music presentation about the
northern lights (see listing on page
94), $12 adults, $10.50 seniors, $9

Flightseeing

From Anchorage, a small plane will take you just about anywhere. You can enjoy world-class fishing, buzz by Mount McKinley, learn about traditional Native cultures in towns like Kotzebue or Barrow, or simply gaze at some of the most beautiful scenery on Earth.

Private carriers operate from Anchorage International Airport, Lake Hood, and Merrill Field. Costs vary widely, depending on the length of the trip and what amenities (guide, lodging, meals, fishing equipment) are provided. There's a trip for every taste.

Companies like Ketchum Air Service (800/433-9114; in Anchorage, 907/243-5525; e-mail: info@ketchumair.com) and Rust's Flying Service (800/544-2299; in Anchorage, 907/243-1595; www.flyrusts.com; info@flyrusts.com) offer flightseeing, fly-in fishing, wildlife photography, "bear safaris," and glacier landings.

Get up-close and personal with Mount McKinley via the "Denali in a Day" trip from K2 Aviation. A van picks you up at your hotel and drives you to Talkeetna, where you'll have time for a walk around this friendly little burg (a guided walking tour can be arranged in advance). You'll then take a one-hour flightseeing tour of the Great One itself—Mount McKinley—including a flight along the stunning Ruth Glacier and through the world's deepest gorge. The total cost is $330 per person, with a two-person minimum. For reservations, call 800/764-2291.

ERA Aviation offers "Classic Flightseeing" in a restored DC-3 Skyliner, which features attendants clad in period costumes, original magazines from the 1940s, big-band music, and champagne service. Routes vary. The flight is $139 per person. For more information, call 800/866-8394 (in Anchorage, 907/266-8394).

since some of them speak foreign languages, they'll also do their best to understand everybody.

Stationed outside is a kiosk of free maps to start you on a self-guided downtown walking tour. Look outside, too, for the signs that tell you how far Anchorage is from everywhere else in the world; you may find your hometown listed. If you're here for the Iditarod (see Chapter 10, Sports and Recreation) or the Fur Rendezvous winter carnival (see page 89), duck inside the cabin to make sure you still have all your fingers and toes. Summer daily 7–7; winter daily 9–6. Free. ♿ (Downtown)

MUSIC IN THE PARK
Fourth Ave. and E St.
Anchorage
907/279-5650
This free summer concert series takes place from noon to 1 p.m. every Wednesday. Depending on the week, you'll hear bluegrass, folk, rock, a cappella, big-band, or South American music. You have to break for lunch anyway, so why not make it al fresco? (Hint: The hot-dog carts along Fourth Avenue often sell reindeer sausage—combine a local delicacy with local music for a uniquely Alaskan experience.) Also at this location, a free ice-carving demonstration starts at 10:30 a.m. every Friday in summer. The "rainy day" concert location is the Fourth Avenue Theatre, 630 W. Fourth Ave. ♿ (Downtown)

OLD CITY HALL
524 W. Fourth Ave.
Anchorage
907/276-4118
One of Anchorage's first concrete buildings, City Hall was constructed in 1936. Its lobby exhibits Early Anchorage, a series of historic photographic murals, dioramas, pioneer photos, and memorabilia that chronicle the city in its earliest incarnation. Mon–Fri 8–5. Free. (Downtown)

OSCAR ANDERSON HOUSE
420 M St.
Anchorage
907/274-2336
Anchorage's first permanent frame home was built in 1915, at a time when many locals were still living in tents. The exhibits in Anchorage's only historic-house museum depict the city's rough-and-tumble beginnings. Group tours can be arranged at any time during the year; Swedish Christmas tours run the first two weekends in December. Regular hours are June–mid-Sept Tue–Sat 11–4. $3 adults, $2 seniors, and $1 children 5 and up. (Downtown)

SATURDAY MARKET
Third Ave. and E St.
Anchorage
907/276-7207
An ordinary downtown parking lot transforms into an open-air bazaar every Saturday in summer. Enjoy music and other live entertainment as you browse among booths of Alaska-grown produce (check out those monster radishes!), handicrafts, gifts, food, and souvenirs. Some of the crafts and gifts are beautiful and classy, and others are,

Bald Eagle at Big Game Alaska, p. 95

Big Game Alaska

Snow sculpture at Fur Rendezvous, p. 89

well, unique. But, hey, who wouldn't like a moose-shaped candy dish that dispenses sweets from its backside? Be sure to show up early for the organic produce since locals are hungry for fresh foodstuffs after a long, gardenless winter—imported berries and lettuce simply aren't as good as those picked just hours before. Sat 10–6. Free. ♿ (Downtown)

SHIP CREEK
Ship Creek Ave.
Anchorage

According to the Alaska Department of Fish and Game, Ship Creek is the second-busiest salmon fishery in the state. Thousands of anglers try their luck each summer, particularly during the annual Ship Creek Salmon Derby in June. When the salmon run, you'll see countless kings and silvers returning to their ancestral homes to spawn. Photographers and fish fans love to watch them swim by. The best place to fish, or gawk, is the area near the Comfort Inn on Ship Creek Avenue. If you plan to fish, you'll need an Alaska fishing license, available at grocers, department stores, and most sporting goods emporia. The water, you'll notice, is a dirty brown; that's not pollution but silt washing in from nearby Cook Inlet. The fish are safe to eat, and if you've never had fresh-caught fish, you're in for a treat. Have an impromptu picnic on the shore with some of the best fish you ever ate. (Check department or grocery stores for disposable barbecue kits—charcoal and a heavy foil "grill." Pick up a lemon or some soy sauce, too.)

But be careful out there. The Ship Creek mud is incredibly sticky and slippery, and it regularly trips anglers who are rushing to shore with their catches. Some of the mud acts more like quicksand, actually, and people often need help from others to free their feet (and, often, their boots) from the gunk.

In addition, the water is truly ice-cold. A few years ago, a distracted fisherman took a wrong step and was quickly swept downstream into nearby Knik Arm. He was incredibly lucky: Two army fishing buddies, both of whom had been trained in water rescue, happened to be nearby and pulled him out. But in just a few minutes he had become hypothermic. So watch where you put your feet! (Downtown)

SKY SONG
Alaska Center for the
Performing Arts
621 W. Sixth Ave.
Anchorage
907/263-2935
www.AlaskaSkySong.com
You probably won't see the aurora borealis, or northern lights, if you're visiting in the summer. Get a vicarious glimpse—set to music!—at Sky Song, a slide show of more than 300 of Dave Parkhurst's photographs of the northern lights. Among the works you'll hear are Bach's "Adagio in G Minor" and "Sleepers Awake," Puccini's "Nessun Dorma," and Elgar's "Enigma Variations." The show lasts 35 minutes—and your feet won't get cold, the way they do when you're watching the real thing in the winter. If you like what you see, you can purchase a video version to take home. Open daily 9–9; show starts every hour on the hour. $6.95 adults, $5.95 seniors, $4 military personnel, $3.95 children. ♿ (Downtown)

WOLF SONG OF ALASKA
Sixth Ave. and C St.
Anchorage
907/274-9653
wolfsong@alaska.net
This nonprofit organization seeks to promote and understand the wolf and its natural history, relation to humans, and symbolic role in folklore, myth, legend, art, and religion. The downtown education center has wolf exhibits, dioramas, photographs, and art. Mon 11–6, Tue–Fri 10–7, Sat 10–6, Sun noon–5. Free. (Downtown)

SOUTH ANCHORAGE

ALASKA ZOO
4731 O'Malley Rd.

Anchorage Garden Tour

Anchorage's summer climate is not unlike that of England's. While the summer isn't long, it's intense because daylight lingers almost around the clock. Gardeners will seize every minute of summer and every scrap of dirt to produce flower gardens, vegetable gardens, color gardens, water gardens, wildflower gardens, and just about any other kind of garden you can imagine. On the last Sunday in July, a half-dozen or so selected gardens are open to the public for a free, self-guided tour sponsored by the Anchorage Garden Club. Watch the newspaper for directions and a map.

Anchorage
907/346-3242
You'll see more than 80 animals and birds in this 30-acre wooded setting with a network of trails. Alaskan animals are well represented, including moose, caribou, brown and black bears, wolves, a bald eagle, owls, trumpeter swans, lynx, and lemmings, plus freelance waterfowl that come in uninvited. Three Siberian tigers also live here; you may hear their distinctive coughing roar long before you reach them.

One of the zoo's most famous former residents was a polar bear named Binky, who became notorious nationwide after an Australian tourist hopped a couple of fences to get an up-close photo; Binky chomped on her leg and paraded around his pen with her running shoe dangling from his mouth. (Local T-shirt entrepreneurs had a field day with that one.) Binky and his buddy, Nuka, both died of viral infections in 1995. A new polar bear habitat was opened in 1999.

Another beloved zoo resident was Annabelle, "the painting pachyderm," who died in late 1997. The elephant used a brush and acrylics to create abstract paintings, although she also used the paintbrush to scratch bug bites. Her artwork has been sold at local galleries and is available in the zoo's gift shop. Other famous residents are Ahpun and Oreo—a polar bear and brown bear who were raised together as orphans, and who are still living together as pals.

If you're in Anchorage during the winter, by all means bundle up and come visit; some of the animals are at their friskiest and most visible when the weather turns cool. Summer daily 9–6; winter daily 10–5.

Anchorage CVB

Log Cabin Visitor Center, p. 90

$6 adults, $5 seniors, $4 youths, $3 ages 3–12 (children under 13 must be accompanied by adults). $50 annual pass (Jan–Dec). ♿ (South Anchorage)

BIG GAME ALASKA
Mile 79 Seward Hwy.
Portage
907/783-2025
Alaska's only drive-through wild-game park is home to moose, bison, caribou, Sitka black-tailed deer, elk, musk ox, owls, a black bear, and eagles. The animals are fenced in various areas; you can get out of your car and take pictures. Summer daily 8:30–7; winter daily 10–sunset. $5 adults; $3 seniors, military personnel (with ID), and children ages 4–15. ♿ (South Anchorage)

CROW CREEK MINE
Crow Creek Rd.
Girdwood
907/278-8060
This is the longest-running mining operation in southcentral Alaska.

GREATER ANCHORAGE

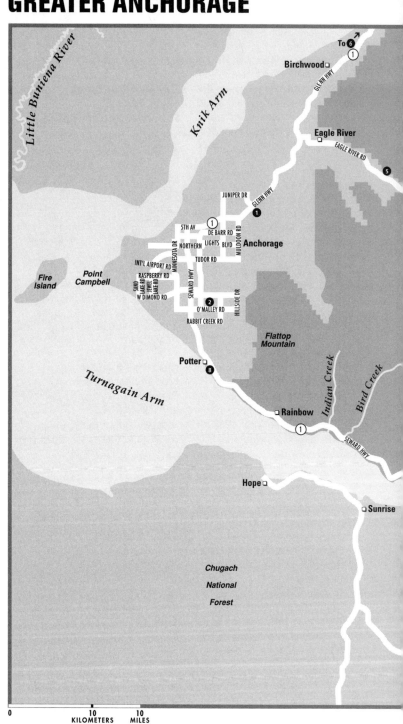

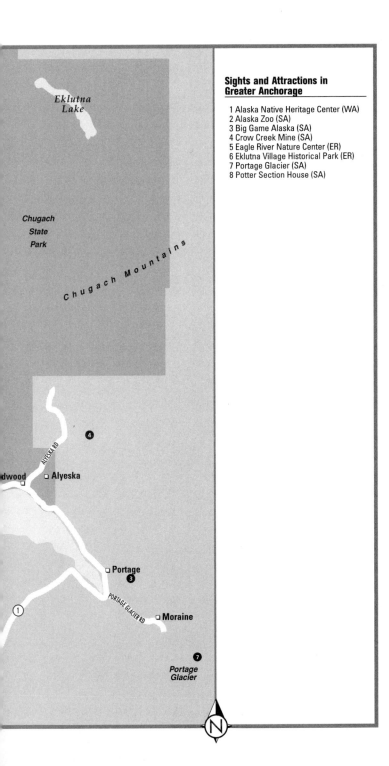

Sights and Attractions in Greater Anchorage

1 Alaska Native Heritage Center (WA)
2 Alaska Zoo (SA)
3 Big Game Alaska (SA)
4 Crow Creek Mine (SA)
5 Eagle River Nature Center (ER)
6 Eklutna Village Historical Park (ER)
7 Portage Glacier (SA)
8 Potter Section House (SA)

Eklutna Lake

Chugach State Park

Chugach Mountains

④

dwood ◻ Alyeska

◻ Portage ❸

PORTAGE GLACIER RD

① ◻ Moraine

❼
Portage Glacier

N

Gold was discovered in the mid-1890s at this site about 40 miles south of Anchorage. The mine was worked commercially for many years and, during its peak, produced more than 700 ounces of gold each month. Even so, it's believed that Crow Creek has more gold left than was ever taken away. Try your hand at finding it, with a lesson in gold-panning included in the admission fee. You're given a bag of "pay dirt," with at least one gold flake guaranteed, to get you started. The gold bug may bite, and it can be addictive. One 65-year-old Illinois woman harvested a half-ounce nugget and, according to mine-owner Cynthia Toohey, "The look on her face [was] a perfect example of why we don't want to turn commercial."

Even if you don't want to get down in the creek and dig, the beautifully landscaped mine is a scenic place to visit (weddings are regularly scheduled here) and is listed on the National Register of Historic Places. Eight of the original buildings are still standing, fully equipped. Original jewelry, made from Crow Creek gold, and other souvenir items are available in the gift shop. Mid-May–mid-Sept daily 9–6. $5 adults, $4 children, $3 browsers (i.e., non-panners). Self-contained campers can stay the night for $5. ♿ (South Anchorage)

PORTAGE GLACIER
Mile 78.9 Seward Hwy.
Portage
907/783-2326
The most visited sight in the state of Alaska, beating out even Mount McKinley, the glacier is nonetheless in retreat. If you want an up-close-and-personal look, take the tour boat that heads out toward the glacier's face. Walk along Portage Lake, too, for a close-up look at the icebergs that have calved from the glacier. The Begich, Boggs Visitor Center has displays on glaciers and how they have shaped the area and offers guided hikes, naturalist programs,

Eklutna Cemetery and St. Nicholas Russian Orthodox Church, p. 101

Eklutna Historical Park/Frank Flavin

Lake Hood is the world's largest and busiest seaplane base, with more than 800 takeoffs and landings on a peak summer day.

and an award-winning film, *Voices From the Ice*. The visitor center is in transition, adding more information about the Portage Valley and its flora, fauna, and ecosystem, and on how the new road to Whittier (see Chapter 13, Day Trips) may affect the Prince William Sound area. The renovations should be completed by Spring 2001. Visitors can also take self-guided hikes, including the pleasant and easy Byron Glacier Trail; watch for signs on the road in. Visitor center hours: Summer daily 9–6; winter Sat and Sun 10–4. Admission free; $1 for *Voices From the Ice*. & (South Anchorage)

POTTER SECTION HOUSE
Mile 115 Seward Hwy.
Anchorage
907/345-5014
This tiny frame building was home-sweet-home for an equally tiny crew of men who maintained the Alaska Railroad tracks in the old days. Marvel at the size of the rooms as compared to the length of the winters, and view an old-time snowblower and a working model railroad. Point out the outhouse to your kids—to show them how lucky they are to have indoor plumbing, especially in winter. The house also serves as Chugach State Park headquarters, where you can pick up some really useful material on the recreational

activities in this vast preserve (see Chapter 8, Parks and Gardens). Summer daily 8–4:30; rest of year Mon–Fri 8–4:30. Free. & (South Anchorage)

EAST ANCHORAGE

ALASKA NATIVE HERITAGE CENTER
8800 Native Heritage Center Dr.
Anchorage
907/330-8096
www.alaskanative.net
The center's mission is to celebrate, perpetuate, and share the cultures of the Aleut, Eskimo, and Indian peoples of Alaska. It consists of a "Welcome House" and five traditional village sites that represent the Eskimo (Yup'ik/Cup'ik, Inupiaq/ St. Lawrence Island Yup'ik), Aleut (Aleut/Alutiiq), and Indian (Athabaskan, Eyak, Tlingit, Haida, and Tshimshian) indigenous groups.

The Welcome House has interpretive displays such as "How the Athabaskan People Use Moose," "Dancing and Healing, Healing and Dancing," "Take the Best of Both Worlds," "Basketry Through Time," and "Fishing: How Families Work Together to Provide Food and Income." Visiting craftspeople create works of art on-site, including carvings, baskets, dolls, and jewelry, and answer questions about their traditional art forms. A 95-seat theater shows *Stories Given, Stories Shared*, a film that introduces the rudiments of Native culture to visitors. The "Gathering Place" is a performance area where singers and dancers perform each day. (Out of respect to the performers, please do not take pictures or make audio or visual recordings during the shows; an appropriate time for photos will be indicated afterward.)

Outdoors, follow a looping trail that takes you around a lake and to the five villages, each of which offers one permanent- and two or three temporary exhibits. Artists, performers, and "Native tradition bearers" are on hand to answer questions, to explain various aspects of Alaska Native life both past and present, and to show objects used in everyday life for thousands of years. May–Oct daily 9–9. $19.95 adults, $14.95 youths, children 6 and younger free. $59.95 family pass (2 adults, 2 children); $14.95 each additional adult, $12.95 each additional child. $49.95 individual season passes. ♿ (East Anchorage)

EAGLE RIVER

EAGLE RIVER NATURE CENTER
Mile 12 Eagle River Rd.
Eagle River
907/694-2108
This former homestead has been turned into a state park office. With indoor and outdoor spotting scopes you can scan the Eagle River Valley for moose, bears, eagles, beavers, sheep, and other animals (at least one pack of wolves lives in the area). The center's Close-Up Corner

Alaska Native Heritage Center, p. 99

is a cabin replica with animal pelts, bones, antlers, and hooves, along with information on the valley's wildlife. Interpretive displays explain geology, weather, flora and fauna, and other subjects. Outside, enjoy one of two easy hikes: the Rodak Nature Trail, which at only two-thirds of a mile is feasible even for little ones, and the Albert Loop Trail, a three-mile stroll among mixed forests of birch and spruce. Both trails are maintained, but watch for seasonal muddy spots—and make noise as you go because bears may be nearby. That's no joke: A man surprised a bear here recently and got swatted for his mistake. Twice-daily guided walks take place in summer, along with at least one Junior Naturalist program per month. Summer Tue–Sun 10–5; winter Thu–Sun 10–5. $3 parking. ♿ (Eagle River)

EKLUTNA VILLAGE HISTORICAL PARK

Eklutna exit on Glenn Hwy.
Eklutna
907/688-6026
Twenty-six miles north of Anchorage, the park includes two Russian Orthodox churches, one of which may be more than 150 years old. The St. Nicholas Russian Orthodox Church, built by Athabaskan Indians, is the oldest standing building in the Anchorage area and one of the oldest examples of Russian architecture in Alaska. Inside are icons shipped from Russia before the United States purchase in 1867 and an unusual candelabra that uses rifle shells to hold tapers!

The second church, dedicated in 1962, is known as the new St. Nicholas Russian Orthodox Church. It houses 200-year-old icons and two 250-year-old professional banners. Outside, the colorful burial ground mixes traditional Native and Russian Orthodox beliefs about souls in the afterlife. When an Orthodox Russian Athabascan is interred, a new blanket and the three-bar Orthodox cross are placed over the mound; 40 days later, a "spirit house" is erected over the grave and painted with the family's traditional colors. Small spirit houses are for children; a small house inside a large house means that a mother and child were buried together. Mid-May–mid-Sept daily 8–6. $3.50, children under 6 free. (Eagle River)

CITY TOURS

ALASKA SIGHTSEEING
CRUISE WEST
513 W. Fourth Ave.
Anchorage
907/276-1305 or 800/666-7375
This motorcoach tour of downtown highlights and explains area history, visits the Anchorage Museum of History and Fine Arts, and stops at the Alaska Aviation Heritage Museum (see Chapter 6, Museums and Galleries) at Lake Hood. The cost of the tour includes admission to both museums. You can combine the Anchorage tour with a visit to the Portage Valley, including a scenic bus tour along Turnagain Arm, a meal at the Westin Alyeska Prince Resort (plus optional tram ride to the top of Mount Alyeska), and a stop at the Begich, Boggs Visitor Center. City tour only, mid-May–mid-Sept daily 9 a.m.; $26 adults, $13 children. Combined tour, mid-May–mid-Sept Mon, Tue, Thu, and Sun 9 a.m.; $58 adults, $29 children. Note: A wheelchair-accessible minibus is available by advance reservation. &
(Downtown)

ANCHORAGE CITY TOUR
Gray Line of Alaska
745 W. Fourth Ave.
Anchorage
907/277-5581; 800/478-6388
This three-hour city tour includes a visit to the Anchorage Museum of History and Art. Gray Line also offers a seven-hour Portage Glacier cruise/tour: a trip along Turnagain Arm to Portage Glacier; a stop at the Begich, Boggs Visitor Center; and a one-hour cruise in the MV Ptarmigan along iceberg-dotted Portage Lake to within 300 yards of the Portage Glacier. City tour daily 8:30 a.m. and 3 p.m.; $25. Portage Glacier cruise/tour May 13–Sept 22 daily 9 a.m. and noon; $60. Some buses are accessible to the disabled. &
(Downtown)

ANCHORAGE CITY TROLLEY
TOURS

Top Ten Anchorage Photo Opportunities

by Jeff Schultz, operator of the Alaska Stock agency and official photographer for the Iditarod sled-dog race.

1. **Flattop overlook area:** A panoramic view of the Anchorage bowl with views of Mount McKinley and the Alaska Range on a clear day, and great up-close shots of the Chugach Range.

2. **Earthquake Park:** Great view of downtown, with the Chugach Mountains as a background. Also a good view of Mount McKinley.

3. **Captain Cook statue:** Nice view of Cook Inlet and possibly beluga whales.

4. **Potter Marsh:** Good place to photograph salmon and waterfowl in season, especially arctic terns in flight and feeding their young.

5. **Tract off Campbell Airstrip Road:** This is the place for landscape shots. It has good trails with views of the Chugach Mountains and Little Campbell Creek.

6. **Lake Hood:** Photograph floatplanes taking off or coming in for a landing.

7. **Point Woronzof:** Great sunsets and a view of Mount Susitna, also known as Sleeping Lady. It's a good spot to shoot freight barges coming into port.

8. **Tony Knowles Coastal Trail:** At Kincaid Park you'll often find moose grazing and get great shots of Cook Inlet. Farther along you'll get views of Anchorage, including Westchester Lagoon, where there are always waterfowl. Even farther you can get good views of the port of Anchorage.

9. **Arctic Valley Road:** Get views of Anchorage and Cook Inlet, especially at sunset, by stopping at turnouts along the road. There are also good views of Chugach State Park and the Chugach Mountains.

10. **Russian Jack Park:** Great shots of tree-covered trails, mushrooms on the forest floor, and possibly moose.

612 W. Fourth Ave.
Anchorage
907/276-5603
www.aktrolley.com
This one-hour tour in a red trolley car includes sights such as the railroad area, Earthquake Park (see Chapter 8, Parks and Gardens), Cook Inlet, the Anchorage Museum of History and Art, residential areas, and Lake Hood, the largest and busiest floatplane base in the world. Open daily 9–5, hourly departures. $10. (Downtown)

BEST OF ANCHORAGE TOUR
Princess Tours
Anchorage
907/550-7711
www.princesstours.com
This three-and-a-half-hour tour includes a visit to the Anchorage Museum of History and Art, a tour around South Anchorage with a stop at the Alaska Zoo, a view from the Hillside area high above the city, and a visit to the Potter Marsh bird and wildlife sanctuary. May 15–Sept 15 daily 8:30 a.m. and 2:30 p.m. $35 adults, $20 children. &. (Downtown)

ERA HELICOPTER FLIGHTSEEING TOURS
6160 Carl Brady Dr.
Anchorage
907/266-8351 or 800/843-1947
www.eraaviation.com
Era offers a pair of local tours: The Glacier Expedition is a two-hour flight above the town and into Chugach State Park (see Chapter 8, Parks and Gardens), where you can enjoy dramatic scenery, watch for wildlife, and land on a glacier. The Turnagain Tour is a 50-minute view of Anchorage from the mountains of Chugach State Park, with a look at both Knik and Turnagain Arms, and

a trip over Eagle Glacier. Glacier Expedition $279 per person; Turnagain Tour $179 per person. Era also offers tours out of the Valdez, Juneau, and Mount McKinley areas. (West Anchorage)

FOURTH AVENUE THEATRE TROLLEY
Fourth Avenue Theatre
630 W. Fourth Ave.
907/257-5635
These one-hour tours include stops at Ship Creek, Earthquake Park, the Alaska Aviation Heritage Museum, and the Anchorage Museum of History and Art. The company also offers a trolley shuttle to the Alaska Native Heritage Center, with a stop at Centennial Campground in Muldoon. Open daily 9–8. Regular tour departures at 10 minutes before the hour; $10. Shuttle trolley departures at 20 minutes after the hour; $2. (Downtown)

HISTORIC DOWNTOWN ANCHORAGE GUIDED WALKING TOURS
Old City Hall
524 W. Fourth Ave.
Anchorage
907/274-3600
This 90-minute tour, covering about two miles, tracks the history of the town's pioneers and encompasses some of its first buildings. It includes trivia, such as the fact that Club Paris, a beloved city steakhouse, was once a mortuary; the Wendler Building was built in 1948 as a ladies' club after a local bowling team went to a tournament in Texas; and the Anchorage Hotel had a dogsled kennel so that out-of-town visitors could "park" their transportation. The tour also explains the changes in the downtown

landscape after the Good Friday Earthquake of 1964. June–Aug Mon–Fri 1 p.m. $5 adults, $4 seniors, $1 children, under 5 free. Regular tour plus Oscar Anderson House tour $5.50 adults, $4.50 seniors, $1.50 children. (Downtown)

HORSE DRAWN CARRIAGE CO.
Fifth Ave. and K St.

Anchorage
907/688-6005
A team of mighty Percherons pull this lovely old-fashioned carriage on short or long rides around Anchorage. June-Aug daily 7:30 p.m.–midnight. Fares start at $5 per person. (Downtown)

Alaska Heritage Library & Museum

6

MUSEUMS AND GALLERIES

The Anchorage art world tends to be dominated by two genres: Alaska Native art and nature or animal art. Native art is being taken more seriously than ever before, and some artists are putting a modern spin on ancient techniques. Critter and nature art—bears, wolves, Mount McKinley, and the like—sells well in every possible medium, including on gold pans. A handful of contemporary artists ply their trades here, too, but you'll have to search harder to find their work.

One way to do that is to investigate First Friday, when a number of the city's galleries stay open late or stage special events (on the first Friday of each month). Some galleries make it a point to open shows on First Friday, so you may get wine, cheese, and other opening-night noshes during your travels. Watch for specific gallery information in the entertainment section of the Daily News *or the arts section of the* Anchorage Press.

Anchorage isn't exactly crammed with notable architecture. It's a relatively young town, and for many years the emphasis was on shelter, not design—what has been called "the architecture of expediency." (However, there's no truth to the rumor that Anchorage is an ancient Indian word meaning "strip mall.") Yet more and more spots around town are brightened by public art, from traditional Native designs to more avant-garde pieces that cause wildly diverse reactions among viewers.

ART MUSEUMS

ALASKA HERITAGE LIBRARY AND MUSEUM
National Bank of Alaska
Northern Lights Blvd. and C St.
Anchorage
907/265-2834
This small, often-overlooked treasure houses a lovely display of Native artifacts and baskets, plus rare books, photographs, and paintings by renowned northern artists such as Sydney Laurence, Eustace Ziegler, Fred Machetanz, Jules Dahlager, and Ted Lambert. It's a fascinating place. Mon–Fri noon–4. Free. & (West Anchorage)

ANCHORAGE MUSEUM OF HISTORY AND ART
121 W. Seventh Ave.
Anchorage
907/343-4326
This museum is an absolute must-see for Anchorage visitors since it shows history from the points of view of indigenous peoples as well as white settlers from the Russians on up. You'll find out about how aboriginal people got here, how they survived in such a rugged land, and how the lure of Last Frontier riches fur, whales, gold, oil—drew invaders and settlers from afar. Dioramas, artifacts, and photos (nuns on dogsleds?) illustrate this history. Allow plenty of time to view the museum's art collection, from explorer's sketches and Native artifacts to oil paintings by artists such as Sydney Laurence, Eustace Zeigler, and Ted Lambert. Modern Alaska artwork is also well-represented, including some marvelous Native masks, sculptures, and paintings.

Changing exhibits spotlight the art, history, and archaeology of the state, and traveling exhibits touch down regularly. The Children's Gallery features year-long interactive exhibits whose themes change each summer (see Chapter 7, Kids' Stuff). If you're interested in history, a library and archives offer opportunities for research; they're open mornings, and afternoons by appointment. Each summer you can watch films about Alaska and the popular Alaska Native Performance Series. Summer daily 9–6; rest of the year Tue–Sat 10–6, Sun 1–5. $5 adults, $4.50 seniors, youths under 18 free. (Downtown)

SCIENCE AND HISTORY MUSEUMS

ALASKA AVIATION HERITAGE MUSEUM
4721 Aircraft Dr.
Anchorage
907/248-5325
www.alaska.net/~aahm/
Aviation changed life in Alaska forever, and this museum shows you just how important small planes were—and continue to be—to the Last Frontier. View 22 vintage aircraft from the 1928–52 era, including the Fairchild American Pilgrim 100B, the 1929 Loening Commuter, and the 1928 Hamilton metal plane. Some are restored to mint condition; others look just as they did in the Bush. But the museum isn't just about a bunch of old planes—it's also about the adventures and exploits of the people who flew them, and about the communities that relied on them. On display are numerous old photos, models, aviation memorabilia, maps, newspaper stories, and vintage aviation apparel, plus a military aviation exhibit that includes Japanese arti-

Looking for Native Arts and Crafts?

Be aware that some of the "traditional" artworks in area gift shops were actually made as far away as Bali. To get the most authentic pieces possible, do a little homework.

First, look for a "Silver Hand" emblem; if you see it, the piece was made by an Alaska Native artist. However, not every single Native craftsperson uses the emblem, so if you see a piece you like, ask some questions. Who made the item and when? Where does he or she live? Is this person a true Alaska Native? (At least one Vietnamese carver is producing "traditional" pieces these days.)

Keep in mind, too, that things aren't always what they seem. What you think is ivory or whalebone might actually be plastic. Ask these questions or you might be fooled.

None of this makes any difference if all you want is a carved bear and you don't care who made it or how. But if you're looking for authenticity, be pleasantly insistent—and be prepared to spend some money since the better pieces aren't cheap.

facts from the World War II Aleutian Island Campaign. The theater shows a film about that campaign (when Japanese soldiers were present on American soil), documentaries about early Alaska air companies, and footage from private collections of the state's flying pioneers. Stand on the observation deck to watch takeoffs and landings from Lake Hood, the world's busiest floatplane base; or book your own sightseeing flight at the gift shop. May–Oct daily 9–6, rest of year Tue–Sat 10–4. $6 adults; $4.75 military, seniors, and AAA members; $3 youths; children under 12 free. & (West Anchorage)

ALASKA MUSEUM OF NATURAL HISTORY

11723 Old Glenn Hwy.
Eagle River
907/694-0819
This museum interprets the geology, biology, and archeology of the southcentral region of the state. You'll see an exhibit on the active volcanoes of the Cook Inlet region, some of which have erupted in the past few years and no doubt will again. Reproductions of the bones of "Lizzie," the oldest hadrosaur ever discovered in Alaska, are displayed in the dinosaur exhibit, along with a nodosaur (a type of armored dinosaur) skull, ammonites and other ancient invertebrates, and Alaska's only palm tree fossil. Other exhibits include rock and mineral collections, dioramas of Alaskan

wilderness and animals, and a depiction of an 11,000-year-old hunting camp. Mon–Sat 10–5. $3 adults, $2 seniors, $1 youths 5 and over. ♿ (Eagle River)

ALASKA TROOPER MUSEUM
Sixth Ave. between C and D Sts.
Anchorage
907/279-5050
One large room offers some pretty interesting pieces of the state's law enforcement past. Imagine policing more than half-a-million square miles of some of the most rugged territory in the world. You'll learn that the first law enforcement in the Last Frontier was actually the U.S. Marshal, who arrived in 1884. The troopers began as the Alaska Highway Patrol (1941–53), then became the Alaska Territorial Police (1953–59). After statehood, they were called the Alaska State Police (1959–67), and are now finally known as the Alaska State Troopers. You'll see badges, commendations, posters, an illegal bear trap, a pair of snowshoes ("walking a beat" in the Alaska bush means something entirely different than it does in Brooklyn), old firearms, a Motorola radio, antique leg irons, photographs, fur hats, and mukluks (don't you just love a man in uniform?), plus a re-created trooper office from 40 years ago. Also on display are two famous photos of Steve McQueen—mug shots, framed along with his fingerprints, from the late actor's 1972 arrest for having far too good a time (he was driving at high speeds up and down Fourth Avenue). Mon–Fri 10–5, Sat noon–4. Free. ♿ (Downtown)

ELMENDORF AIR FORCE BASE WILDLIFE MUSEUM

4803 Eighth St.
Anchorage
907/552-2282
This museum exhibits real Alaska wildlife mounted in re-creations of the animals' ecosystems. The museum also has a hands-on fur exhibit. Mon–Thu and Sat 3–4:45, Fri noon–5. Free. ♿ (East Anchorage)

FORT RICHARDSON ALASKA FISH AND WILDLIFE CENTER
Fort Richardson Army Base
Fifth St.
Anchorage
907/384-0431
Here you'll find more mounted exhibits of Alaska critters, notably black, grizzly, and polar bears; moose; caribou; birds; and various fish. Mon–Wed and Fri 9–11:30 and 1–4:30, Thu 1–3. Free. ♿ (East Anchorage)

THE IMAGINARIUM
725 W. Fifth Ave.
Anchorage
907/276-3179
This science discovery center offers hands-on fun for all ages, with exhibits on the physics of toys, marine life, wetlands, "brain games," and Alaska animals. One setup even lets you stand inside a giant bubble! The insect exhibit features live specimens of walking sticks, crickets, butterflies, Madagascar hissing roaches, and other bugs. The Mars Rock is a fiberglass cave that kids can crawl into and slide out of; nearby is the "Mission to Mars" exhibit, with Internet access so kids can explore information on past and current missions. The planetarium has one show on the planets, solar systems, and galaxies, and another on the aurora borealis. Mon–Sat 10–6, Sun noon–5. $5 adults,

$4 seniors and children ages 2–12. (Downtown)

OSCAR ANDERSON HOUSE
420 M St.
Anchorage
907/274-2336
In 1915 many residents of Anchorage were tent-dwellers. Oscar Anderson was one of the 18 men who lived in the very first tent pitched on the beach at Cook Inlet. He founded the Ship Creek Meat Company, the first wholesale and retail business of its kind in Anchorage, and became known as the man who supplied the two things residents needed the most: food and fuel. Anderson carried lumber from the beach up to a homesite at Fourth Avenue and M Street, and he built the first permanent frame house in town. It stands today as the city's only historic-house museum. The exhibits show the city's rough and dusty beginnings as a railroad boomtown. On the first two weekends in December, the house is open for Swedish Christmas tours; the rest of the year, group tours can be arranged. June–mid-Sept Tue–Sat 11–4. $3 adults, $3 seniors, $1 children. (Downtown)

GALLERIES

ALASKA GLASS STUDIO AND GALLERY
7924 King St.
Anchorage
907/349-8084
Local glass artist Cynthia England opened what she calls "the hottest spot in town" in summer 1999 to showcase her works in blown, slumped, fused, and stained glass. England's work is inspired by the extremes in the Alaska environment; living here, she says, is isolating yet "gives you a sense of independence in the creative process." You'll find bowls, platters, perfumers, ornaments, jewelry, sculptural glass, vases, and one-of-a-kind champagne flutes and wine goblets by

Decker/Morris Gallery, p. 110

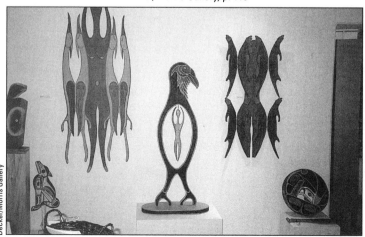

Decker/Morris Gallery

*Alaska Museum of Natural History,
ammonite display, p. 107*

England and 30 other renowned American glass artists. Daily glass-blowing demonstrations. Mon–Sat 11–7. ♿ (South Anchorage)

ARTIQUE LTD.
314 G St.
Anchorage
907/277-1663
Founded in 1971, this gallery specializes in fine arts and fine crafts, including original paintings, prints, ceramics, glass sculpture, jewelry, fish platters, clocks, and art gifts by Alaska's most renowned artists, including Fred Machetanz, Barbara Lavallee, and Byron Birdsall. Summer Mon–Fri 10–8, Sat 10–6, Sun noon–5; rest of year Mon–Sat 10–6, Sun noon–5. (Downtown)

DECKER/MORRIS GALLERY
621 W. Sixth Ave.
Anchorage
907/272-1489
The gallery displays work by more than 100 contemporary Alaskan

artists in various media, including painting, sculpture, photography, printmaking, ceramics, jewelry, books, and site-specific installations. Father-and-daughter managers Don and Julie Decker encourage innovative, experimental, and avant-garde works, including contemporary Native art. Monthly solo exhibits highlight new work, as do several annual group exhibitions. Mon–Fri 10–6, Sat 11–5; Sun noon–5 in summer. (Downtown)

INTERNATIONAL GALLERY OF CONTEMPORARY ART
5841 Arctic Blvd.
Anchorage
907/258-0307
This labor-of-love gallery, which recently moved to a new location, has produced some of the city's nervier exhibitions—works with a "higher threshold of involvement," as one board member put it, and works that push beyond accepted views of art. The nonprofit International Gallery is dedicated to the exhibition of high-quality pieces that generally cannot find a place in local commercial galleries, and it encourages artists to take risks. And they do: one show involved flooding a room with water an inch deep. Tue 5:30–8:30, Sat and Sun noon–4. (West Anchorage)

KILLER DESIGNS STUDIO
608 W. Fourth Ave.
Anchorage
907/258-5933
A new gallery that is also a working studio for Tamara Johannes, Killer Designs focuses mostly on glass and wearable art. You'll see Johannes's glass beads, jewelry, and candle holders, but also her fiber work, such as a stitched mural, *Bears Are in My Blueberry Dreams.*

The gallery carries other works, including blown-glass ornaments and some very unusual nightlights, plus one-of-a-kind clothing, accessories, and beading supplies. (Downtown)

OUT NORTH CONTEMPORARY ART HOUSE
1325 Primrose St.
Anchorage
907/279-8200
www.outnorth.org
The Out North building is an alternative arts center with live-, media-, and visual-art programs. Its gallery hosts art-student shows as well as professional artists' exhibitions. The good-sized room has seen a variety of exhibitions, including digital photography by NEA fellowship–recipient Ken Gonzales-Day; works by feminist photographer Jill Posner; a kinetic installation by British artist Alan Turner; the *Generation X* body-art show by Renee Haag; Renee Westbrook's *Shrines to the Everyday*, an installation that revealed "the sacred in the ordinary"; and

---

Alaska Design Forum

The Alaska Design Forum, a nonprofit group of architects, artists, and designers, works to address the singular needs of Alaskan designers. Given the unique setting of the Last Frontier, the ADF aspires to "have people talk, think, and ultimately act to create a built environment that inspires the soul and protects the body."

Its lecture series is immensely popular with laypersons as well as design professionals. Recent speakers have included Andy Goldsworthy, Will Bruder, Peter Eisenman, Merrill Elam, James Burnett, Robert Magne, Mary-Ann Ray, Steven Ehrlich, James Murcutt, Antoine Predock, James Cutler, and Cornelia Oberlander.

The ADF sponsors competitions such as "Imagine Anchorage," which called for visions of what the town might be, and "Shelter," a one-day seminar to design and build a homeless shelter.

ADF also organizes workshops and programs on topics relevant to the north, a monthly discussion group on local issues, performances of avant-garde music and dance, artist-in-residence programs, and original art installations. Basic membership costs $40, with higher sponsorship levels available. Lectures cost $10 general admission, $7 ADF and Anchorage Museum members, and $5 for students and starving artists. For more information on the Alaska Design Forum, call 907/566-0256.

Disaster Blankets, Lillian Tyrrell's series of tapestries depicting the turmoil of recent history. Mon–Sat 3–6, and during any live performances. ♿ (East Anchorage)

PUBLIC ART

ALASKA CENTER FOR THE PERFORMING ARTS
621 W. Sixth Ave.
Anchorage
Visual Music is a kinetic sculpture by Eric Staller on the south, east, and north walls. Ed Carpenter's 26 untitled stained glass panels are installed in the south, east, and west windows. *Northern Domes*, three pairs of fused- and slumped-glass wall sconces, are lit from behind in the inner lobbies of the Atwood Concert Hall. Alaska Native masks by 18 different artists are set up throughout the lobbies of the three concert halls. The carpets and upholstery

Anchorage Museum of History and Art, p. 106

Paul Warchol/Anchorage Museum of History and Art

were designed by artists, too; watch for *Field of Poppies* underfoot and *Salmonberry* and *Forest Floor* on theater seats. ♿ (Downtown)

ANCHORAGE MUSEUM OF HISTORY AND ART
121 W. Seventh Ave.
Anchorage
Crystal Lattice, a painted aluminum sculpture by Robert Pfitzenmeier, stands on the southeast corner plaza. *Intruder*, above the main entrance, is a stone and marble mosaic by Ned Smyth. *Ice Walls*, a glass-block sculpture by Athena Tacha, sits in the atrium's reflecting pool. ♿ (Downtown)

CAPTAIN COOK STATUE
Third Ave. and L St.
Anchorage
Explorer James Cook, at your service and in bronze. You'll get a nice view of Cook Inlet while you pose for pictures next to the cap'n. The monument honors the 200th anniversary of Captain Cook's exploration of this area, on his third—and final—voyage. (Downtown)

DOWNTOWN PARKING GARAGE
Sixth Ave. between G and H Sts.
Anchorage
Quartet, an aluminum sculpture by William King, stands on the northeast corner. Elizabeth Mapelli's fused-glass mural, *All That Glitters Is Not Gold*, brightens the north exterior wall near the west entrance. *Hats for Anchorage*, by Anita Fisk, is a series of 12 cast bronze and aluminum works located throughout the building. (Downtown)

EGAN CONVENTION CENTER
555 W. Fifth Ave.
Anchorage

Beaded Sky Curtain, a suspended sculpture of tiny glass beads by Jeanne Leffingwell, is at the west end of the lobby. Melvin Olanna's *Eskimo Spirit Carvings* are five wood and whalebone sculptures in the east seating area. *Volcano Woman*, a carved red-cedar sculpture by John Hoover, is in the west seating area. And behind the convention center is Roger Barr's *Spirit Bridge*, a sculpture made of stainless steel and granite with water and a gas flame. ᷫ (Downtown)

FIFTH AVENUE GARAGE
Fifth Ave. and C St.
Anchorage
Bill FitzGibbons' neon sculpture, *Fifth Avenue Reflections*, appears on the southwest exterior wall and in three elevator cabs. (Downtown)

NESBITT STATE COURTHOUSE
825 W. Fourth Ave.
Anchorage
Master carver Lee Wallace, a Tshimshian and Haida Native from Ketchikan, took a year to complete these two 10-foot red cedar totem poles depicting the major figures of Taven and Eagle, powerful clan emblems. (Downtown)

SIXTH AVENUE TRANSIT SHELTER
Sixth Ave. between D and E Sts.
Anchorage
Elizabeth Mapelli's fused-glass panels, titled *Akai Shikaku*, are above the entrance. (Downtown)

SLED DOG STATUE
Fourth Ave. and D St.
Anchorage
This bronze statue by Jacques and Mary Regat commemorates the continuing Alaska tradition of dog-mushing. It's a good place for a souvenir photograph. Just for fun, see if you can spot the typo in the accompanying bronze plaque. (Downtown)

WHALE MURAL
Fifth Ave. and D St.
Anchorage
Created on the west wall of JCPenney, the giant mural of Alaskan sea life—notably humpback and beluga whales (shown actual size)—measures 400 feet long and five stories high. Single-name artist Wyland, who's known for creating more than 50 "Whaling Wall" murals nationally, painted this one in 1994. (Downtown)

David A. Predeger/Imaginarium

7

KIDS' STUFF

Anchorage is full of family-recreation opportunities such as hiking, skiing, skating, camping, and even dog-mushing. Youth sports leagues abound—the Alaskan Sled Dog and Racing Association accepts mushers as young as age four—and classes and camps are available in subjects like art, theater, song and dance, computer programming, nature, and sports.

Demographically, the city is younger than the rest of the United States, so you'll see plenty of families with kids. Feel free to ask parents for tips about family recreation. Most Alaskans are proud of their state and generous with advice. You probably won't get directions to someone's secret fishing hole, but you may get an invitation to climb Flattop.

ANIMALS AND THE GREAT OUTDOORS

ALASKA ZOO
4731 O'Malley Rd.
Anchorage
907/346-3242
The zoo has more than 80 animals and birds in a 30-acre wooded setting with a network of trails. Small children, especially city kids who aren't used to big trees and big plots of land, might have so much fun romping on the trails that they won't pay attention to the critters. Do make sure they notice the collection, however, which includes moose, caribou, brown and black bears, wolves, a bald eagle, owls, trumpeter swans, lynx, and lemmings. Non-Alaskan animals live here, too, including an elephant and three Siberian tigers. Annabelle, the zoo's first elephant (who died in 1997), was actually a painter! (Her abstract works are for sale in the zoo's gift shop.)

A new polar-bear habitat was

opened in 1999, to house the zoo's most interesting residents: Ahpun and Oreo, a polar bear and a brown bear that grew up together. The orphaned cubs were lonely, so zoo officials experimented with putting them in the same enclosure. After a day or so of mistrust, the bears became great pals and delighted watchers with their playful antics. Even now that they're adult bears, Ahpun and Oreo still get along famously. Summer daily 9–6; rest of the year daily 10–5. $6 adults, $5 seniors, $4 youths, $3 ages 3–12, under 3 free (children under 13 must be accompanied by an adult); $50 annual pass (Jan–Dec). ♿ (South Anchorage)

ALASKAN SLED DOG AND RACING ASSOCIATION
Tozier Track
3400 E. Tudor Rd.
Anchorage
907/562-2235
Kids and dogs are a natural combination, but in Alaska, they don't just play together—they work together. Kids as young as four can enroll in the one-dog class, and teenagers can race as many as seven dogs, in weekly sprints of one-half to 10 miles. Some kids have their eye on the Junior Iditarod, or even the real Iditarod; others just love to be in the outdoors with their canine buddies. This is a great chance for visitors, new residents, and their kids to meet some of the friendliest dogs in the world and to ask their owners questions about the sport of sled dog racing. Dress in layers and wear decent boots; if you or the kids get cold, you can duck inside the clubhouse to warm up or to buy some hot chocolate. Racing takes place Jan–early Mar (later if snow condi-

tions permit) Sat 11 a.m. (East Anchorage)

DELANEY PARK STRIP
Between 9th and 10th Aves.
and A and P Sts.
Anchorage
Originally a firebreak for the townsite of Anchorage, the strip later became the city's first airfield. Today it's a long and very kid-friendly strip of land that's right near downtown attractions and lodgings. You'll find fields and courts for baseball, basketball, kickball, volleyball, and tennis—all of them great places to let off a little steam in the middle of a day of sightseeing. You'll also find an old locomotive engine, playground equipment, a Veteran's Memorial, and the city rose garden. Get your lunch to go and have a picnic. (Downtown)

EAGLE RIVER NATURE CENTER
Mile 12 Eagle River Rd.
Eagle River
907/694-2108
The Nature Center is smack in the middle of real, live nature—we're talking forests where moose, bears, wolves, eagles, beavers, and sheep can be and frequently are seen by visitors. The area offers two possibilities for family hikes: the Rodak Nature Trail, which at only two thirds of a mile is feasible even for small fry, and the Albert Loop Trail, a three-mile stroll among mixed forests of birch and spruce. Both trails are maintained. However, be sure to talk, sing, or bang sticks together as you walk; make plenty of noise and you're less likely to surprise a brown bear. (Give this important chore to your kids—they love to bang sticks together.) Twice-daily guided walks take place during

summer, along with at least one Junior Naturalist program per month. Or you could do all your critter-searching by telescope; the center has two spotting scopes indoors and one outside. Kids enjoy the "Close-Up Corner," a cabin replica filled with animal pelts, bones, antlers, and hooves, along with information on area wildlife. Anyone who thinks a sheep's skull is too gross to handle can enjoy Alaskan nature videos instead. Summer Tue–Sun 10–5, rest of year Thu–Sun 10–5. $3 parking fee. ♿ (Eagle River)

KIDS' KINGDOM
David Green Park
36th Ave. between Latouche and
Lake Otis
Anchorage
Face it: Your kids are pretty good sports for putting up with you on vacation. They have to wait while you read every placard at the museum and take photo after photo of the same view. Give them a break at least once a day by letting them do

something they really want to do. A good place to start is Kids' Kingdom, a park built by neighborhood families in the summer of 1997. Watch your children romp on the playground equipment (you may want to unlimber that camera yet again) and enjoy a nice view of the Chugach Range to boot. The park is yet another nice spot for lunch on a sunny day. (East Anchorage)

STAR THE REINDEER
10th Ave. and I St.
Anchorage
Yep, it's a real reindeer, just like Rudolph. Actually, the reindeer is the wild caribou's domesticated cousin. Several different reindeer, all named Star, have lived in a pen at this corner for more than a quarter of a century. If your kids are interested in finding out more, consider a visit to the Reindeer Farm in Palmer (see Chapter 13, Day Trips), where you can hand-feed the animals and get a snapshot for next year's Christmas card. (Downtown)

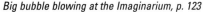
Big bubble blowing at the Imaginarium, p. 123

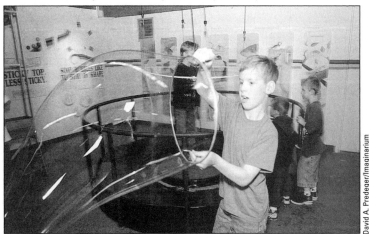

David A. Predeger/Imaginarium

STORYTIME IN THE GARDEN
Alaska Botanical Garden
Campbell Airstrip Rd.
(off Tudor Rd.)
Anchorage
907/265-3165

This is a summer tradition that delights parents and kids alike. Every Wednesday, storytellers hold forth at the Alaska Botanical Garden, a 110-acre site that's being developed as a mix of ornamental plantings and natural forest settings. Bring mosquito repellent, just in case. The free tale-telling begins at 6:30 p.m. (East Anchorage)

WOLF SONG OF ALASKA
Sixth Ave. and C St.
Anchorage
907/274-9653
wolfsong@alaska.net
www.wolfsongalaska.org/

Who's afraid of the big, bad wolf? Your kids won't be, once they've trooped through Wolf Song of Alaska. This nonprofit organization was formed to help people learn more about the misunderstood wolf, both as a living animal (Anchorage has wolves within its city limits) and as a symbol in stories and art through the ages. Wolf Song's education center has dioramas and photographs for an up-close and personal look at Canis lupis. Don't worry that your kids will get a "Disney-ized" view of wolf society. The center makes it quite clear that wolves do, in fact, eat other animals—even baby animals—but that they are part of the food chain. Your children will no doubt memorize and repeat such factoids as, "In chase, the wolf can achieve estimated speeds of between 28 and 40 miles per hour for up to 20 minutes" and, "The

wolf is opportunistic and will attempt to catch the easiest and most vulnerable animal." Mon–Fri 10–7, Sat 10–6, Sun noon–5. Free. (Downtown)

INDOOR FUN

ALASKA PUBLIC LANDS INFORMATION CENTER
605 W. Fourth Ave.
Anchorage
907/271-2737

Here you can experience great outdoors in an indoor setting: interpretive displays, free nature films, photos, and a collection of stuffed animals (real ones) that includes bears, Dall sheep, otter, caribou, deer, wolf, raven, musk ox, and birds. Ask at the front desk for a Scavenger Hunt sheet, which challenges children to answer questions and fill their sheets with animal stamps. (The sheet is available for three different age groups.) Many interpretive displays have interactive video screens and telephone receivers (kids love them—you may have trouble dragging them away). You can also view private screenings of films like *Katmai Eruption*, *Musk Ox from Nunivak*, *Reindeer Herding*, and *Blue Ice, Blue Water: Glaciers and Fjords*, or catch a bigger-screen nature film in the adjoining theater. Open daily 10–5:30. Free. ＆ (Downtown)

ALASKA ROCK GYM
4840 Fairbanks St.
Anchorage
907/562-7265

This indoor rock-climbing center has facilities and programs for all ages and several programs especially for young people. "Cling-On Kids," for

Reaching for the Sky

Some kids think June means summer vacation, but for Merrick Johnson it meant adventure: climbing Alaska's famous Mount McKinley. "I thought it would be cool," says Merrick, who lives in Anchorage.

"Cold" was more like it. The average June temperature up there is 10 to 15 below zero, with up to 60-mile-per-hour winds! But Merrick made it, and now she's famous: the youngest person ever to reach the top of this 20,320-foot mountain. She reached the summit on June 23, 1995, at the age of 12.

Merrick did a lot of workouts to get ready. With her mom, she climbed mountains near her home and did ice- and rock-climbing. A family friend made two sets of special climbing clothes to fit over Merrick's long underwear. They were just right for the weather, although Merrick's feet did get cold sometimes.

With seven other people, including her mom and a mountain guide, Merrick started on June 2. Because the climbers needed so much food and equipment, each day started with a "carry"—they'd move half the equipment up the mountain, then come back down for the rest of it. Each time, Merrick carried anywhere from 40 to 60 pounds of gear.

A day's work was five or six hours, plus four hours to set up camp. The climbers built snow walls around their tents to keep out the howl-

ages 6 to 12, takes place six days a week; you can drop in for $15, or pay for a sustained number of courses. Young people ages 13 and up can join beginner or intermediate groups that meet twice a week, or they can try a single session to see how they like rock climbing. And the "Teen Elite," a group of advanced climbers from 13 to 18, also meets twice a week. The drop-in fee for teen classes is $20. Individual lessons are also available. ♿ (West Anchorage)

CAPRI CINEMA
3425 E. Tudor Rd.
Anchorage
907/561-0064
This small theater shows mostly classic and repertory movies, a departure from its recent second-run programming. But plenty of "classic" films are family-oriented—in those days, movies were made for the masses, and everybody went to them. Some Hollywood flicks show up, too, most of them PG or PG-13. And the Capri popcorn is absolutely

ing winds. A few times they slept in snow caves. Their bathrooms were made of snow, too—Merrick was the "sanitary engineer" who dug the holes.

Meals were no-cook or quick foods like rice and beans, noodles, cheese, nuts, dried fruit, and chocolate. Merrick's favorite breakfast was mashed potatoes mixed with cheese and ramen noodles.

When bad weather forced them to stay in camp, they kept busy with chores like rebuilding the snow walls. And they "rescued" themselves. Climbers on McKinley wear long ropes in case someone falls. To practice, Merrick and the others jumped into crevasses—deep holes in the snow and ice—and then climbed back up the ropes.

Sounds dangerous? It was. Climbers have to be ready for anything: avalanches, blizzards, hidden crevasses. "It's a dangerous mountain," says Merrick. "If you don't watch every step and think ahead, you could die so easily."

She was glad to make the summit, but not only for herself. People in Alaska had promised to give money to the Anchorage Center for Families, based on how high Merrick climbed. More than $2,600 was donated.

And there's one more group Merrick wanted to help: girls everywhere. "I want to inspire girls to do what they dream," she says. "Go for it!"

the best in town because the theater uses real butter (spring for the extra butter, layered throughout). If you have a hankering for popcorn but no time for a movie, you can snack in the theater's adjacent Hollywood Canteen. $2.50 matinees, $5 evening shows. ♿ (East Anchorage)

CASTLE ON O'MALLEY
1520 O'Malley Rd.
Anchorage
907/344-2275
Downstairs at the Castle is an Alaska-themed miniature golf layout, with 18 holes set among waist-high mountains, an oil "pipeline," an erupting volcano, and a long narrow "lake" full of goldfish and golf balls that missed the last hole. Murals on the walls show the Alaska Railroad, bears pulling fish from streams, and a snowy wilderness with a built-in cabin of real logs. Other Alaska touches abound, including a crab pot, a dogsled, a cross-section of the real Alaska Pipeline, and an aquarium full of . . . trout! Upstairs is

a café that serves ice cream for the small fry and espresso for the adults. Open daily 2–10, Fri and Sat to midnight. $4.50 per game. (South Anchorage)

DISCOVERY ZONE
Northway Mall
3101 Penland Pkwy.
Anchorage
907/279-1234
Kids will love this indoor playground with tubes, tunnels, and slides. Mon–Fri 10–9, Sat 10–6, Sun 11–6. All-day admission $6.99 ages 3–12, $3.99 under age 3. (East Anchorage)

PLUCKING MONKEY TEA PUB
2700 Blueberry St.
Anchorage
907/279-5323
If your teenager wants to meet local kids, check out this spare, friendly little tea shop. You can sit and read, challenge someone to a chess game, sip interesting hot or cold beverages, and share your world views with others. The Plucking Monkey hosts local performers, mainly acoustic. Mostly, though, it's a place to hang out. Incidentally, the shop's name is a reference to the days when monkeys were trained to pick tea on plantations. (West Anchorage)

THE SPACE STATION
2710 Spenard Rd.
Anchorage
907/277-4027
Anchorage's largest arcade has easy games like Skee-Ball for the little kids and the latest video wizardry for everyone else. The atmosphere is family-oriented, although it's also a happening spot for young teens. For the pool sharks among you, Hawaiian Brian's Billiards is down-

Top Ten Family-Fun Opportunities in Anchorage

Some of the best things in life are free—and so are the fun activities on this list, courtesy of the staff at the Anchorage Department of Parks and Beautification.

1. Ice skating at Westchester Lagoon
2. Picking blueberries at Flattop
3. Scanning for belugas in Turnagain Arm
4. Smelling the flowers at the Anchorage Museum garden
5. Flying a kite on the Park Strip
6. Watching the Iditarod start
7. Bike riding on the Tony Knowles Coastal Trail
8. Cross-country skiing at Russian Jack Park
9. Listening to music in the Park summer concert series
10. Watching the northern lights

Oreo (left) and Ahpun romp at the Alaska Zoo, p. 114

place for stressed-out travelers to take their kids: Grab a favorite picture book and head for the pillow-strewn reading alcove, or flop into one of the low, funky chairs that look like flattened stick figures. After all, nothing soothes and refreshes like the hundredth rereading of *Officer Buckle and Gloria*. Every summer the library offers a special reading program, with games, activities, guest speakers, and prizes for kids who read. Mon–Thu 11–9, Fri and Sat 10–6, Sun noon–6 (closed Sun in summer). ♿ (West Anchorage)

MUSEUMS

ALASKA MUSEUM OF NATURAL HISTORY
Old Glenn Hwy.
Eagle River
907/694-0819
All kids love dinosaurs, but "Lizzie" has a special connection for kids: A nine-year-old Anchorage girl named Lizzie Williams helped excavate this fossilized hadrosaur, found during a camping trip near the Talkeetna Mountains. The dinosaur was named after Lizzie because she spent so much time helping chip the fossils out of solid rock. Reproductions of the hadrosaur's bones are on display, along with a nodosaur skull (also found in the Talkeetna Mountains), ammonites other ancient invertebrates and Alaska's only palm-tree fossil. Kids will be delighted (or alarmed!) to know that volcanoes in the Cook Inlet region have erupted in the past few years and no doubt will again. Other exhibits include rock and mineral collections, dioramas of Alaska wilderness and wild things, and a re-creation of an 11,000-year-old

stairs. Sun–Thu 10 a.m.–11 p.m, Fri and Sat 10 a.m.–1 a.m. ♿ (West Anchorage)

ULTRAZONE
1200 W. Northern Lights Blvd.
Anchorage
907/277-9663
Here you'll find entertainment for kids that's both high-tech (laser tag, networked computer games, a video arcade) and reassuringly low-tech (a pool, air hockey). Tue–Thu 3–10, Fri 3–midnight, Sat 11 a.m.–midnight, Sun 11–10. $7.50 for laser tag; other attractions vary. Ultrazone also offers a smaller laser-tag arena at Dimond Center, Fri 4–9, Sat and Sun noon–9; $5. ♿ (West Anchorage)

Z. J. LOUSSAC LIBRARY
3600 Denali St.
Anchorage
907/343-2975
The main city library has regular story hours and special events for kids and parents. It's also a great

Read All About It

You'll find a wide selection of Alaskan children's books in area stores. Be sure to skim before you buy since quality can vary widely. Here is a list of some good Alaska-themed children's books:

• **A Caribou Journey,** *by Debbie Miller; illustrations by Jon Van Zyle (Little, Brown): This book dramatizes the lives and migrations of caribou. Although it's nonfiction, it reads like a storybook.*

• **A Distant Enemy,** *by Deb Vanasse (Lodestar Books): Compelling young-adult novel about a half-Eskimo boy in a southwestern Alaska village and his anger toward the white father who deserted him.*

• **Flight of the Golden Plover,** *by Debbie Miller; illustrations by Daniel Van Zyle (Alaska Northwest Books): Another nature book that reads like good fiction. This one tells the amazing story of a bird that flies from Hawaii to Alaska and back each year.*

• **Go Home, River,** *by James Magdanz; illustrations by Dianne Widom (Alaska Northwest Books): This is a lovely, understated book about an Eskimo boy who takes a boat trip with his family.*

• **Children of the Gold Rush,** *by Jane G. Haigh and Claire Murphy (Alaska Northwest Books): This nonfiction book is full of fascinating true-life adventures and old-time photos of children who came to Alaska or were born here during the Gold Rush.*

• **Itchy Bears and Lucky Hares,** *by Susan Ewing; illustrations by Evon Zerbetz (Alaska Northwest Books): A whimsical book of rhymes about Alaskan critters.*

• **Kahtahah: A Tlingit Girl,** *by Frances Lackey Paul (Alaska Northwest Books): Precontact reminiscences from a little Tlingit girl.*

• **My Denali,** *by Kimberly and Hannah Corral; photos by Roy Corral (Alaska Northwest Books): Hannah is a 12-year-old who's been camping in Denali National Park with her parents since she was just two weeks old. With her mother—a science teacher—and her father—a noted photographer—she gives a kid's-eye view of the scenery and wildlife of one of North America's favorite outdoor playgrounds.*

hunting camp. Mon–Sat 10–5. $3 adults, $2 seniors, $1 youths, kids under 5 free. ♿ (Eagle River)

ANCHORAGE MUSEUM CHILDREN'S GALLERY
Anchorage Museum of History and Art
121 W. Seventh Ave.
Anchorage
907/343-4326

This made-for-kids wing features yearlong exhibits devoted to mind-stretching (but fun) topics like archaeological digs, time travel, and black holes. One year the gallery was turned into a jungle complete with a rainforest canopy, a rope bridge, and a driveable jeeplike vehicle. Last year the theme was "Aardvark to Zebra: Animals in Art," and exhibits showed animals in the zoo, on a farm, in their various natural environments, and, fancifully, on a carousel. Art enrichment activities happen in an adjacent room, where kids can use the things they've learned to create a souvenir to take home. The gallery is a great place for fun and learning, and it provides a chance for kids to do something just for them, rather than following mom and dad around all day. Each summer the museum also plans a series of conceptual art classes based on the gallery theme. Summer Sun–Fri 9–9, Sat 9–6; rest of the year Tue–Sat 10–6, Sun 1–5. $5 adults, $4.50 seniors, under 18 free. ♿ (Downtown)

THE IMAGINARIUM
725 W. Fifth Ave.
Anchorage
907/276-3179

Get an up-close look at the denizens of a tidal pool. Stand inside a giant soap bubble. Put on a "blubber mitt" and plunge your hands into ice water for a demonstration of how whales and walruses stay warm. This science discovery center is fun for adults, too, if kids don't mind showing them the ropes. You'll see exhibits on marine life and wetlands, play "brain games," check out Alaska animals, and learn the physics of toys. The insect exhibit has live specimens, including walking sticks, crickets, butterflies, and Madagascar hissing roaches. You won't want to miss the "Mars Rock," a fiberglass cave that kids can crawl into and slide out of, and the "Mission to Mars" exhibit, which explains our forays to the Red Planet and provides Internet access so that kids can get up-to-the-minute information on Sojourner discoveries. The planetarium has two shows: one on planets, solar systems, and galaxies, and another on the aurora borealis, or northern lights. (If you're here in summer, the planetarium is as close to the northern lights as you'll get.) And the Science Store gift shop is full of the kinds of toys that parents don't mind buying but kids still like playing with, despite the fact that they're ostensibly "educational." Mon–Sat 10–6, Sun noon–5. $5 adults, $4 seniors and children ages 2–12. (Downtown)

PERFORMING ARTS

ALASKA JUNIOR THEATRE
Alaska Center for the Performing Arts
621 W. Sixth Ave.
Anchorage
907/272-7546

Since 1981 Alaska Junior Theatre has been introducing young Alaskans to the arts. The organization stages three professional theater and/or musical productions each year at the Alaska Center for the Performing Arts. The best of the nation's professional theatrical and musical ensembles appear here, including the Paper Bag Players; Snowflake; Trout Fishing in America; Tears of Joy Puppet Theater; the Kennedy Center Theater for Young Audiences; the Potato People; the Street Sounds a cappella quintet; Theaterworks USA; Faustwork Mask Theater; and Sharon, Lois and Bram. Some productions are based on classic legends, fairy tales, or stories. More than 25,000 students are bussed in from around the city for a week of school shows; their teachers are given study guides and information to enhance the educational experience. The performances are also staged as a public family series, with season subscriptions available. (Downtown)

ALASKA THEATRE OF YOUTH
907/338-4901
www.aty.org

Shows feature resident actors and young performers and run during the fall and winter. Recent shows include *Frog & Toad, Frankenstein, The Cost of Living, Prodigy: Wolfgang Amadeus Mozart*, and *The Lion, The Witch and the Wardrobe*. In addition, ATY and the University of Alaska–Anchorage team up to present an intensive summer conservatory that covers all facets of theatrical production: set design and construction, lighting, sound, costuming, makeup, acting, singing, dancing, and even stage combat. Participants produce at least a half-dozen shows in which everyone gets involved. Both mainstage and conservatory productions are performed at the University of Alaska–Anchorage. & (East Anchorage)

ANCHORAGE CONCERT ASSOCIATION MAGIC MOMENTS SERIES
430 W. Seventh Ave.
Anchorage
907/272-1471

The Magic Moments series is designed for families. Its concerts, theatrical productions, and special events are perfect introductions to the magic of the performing arts. In recent years the series has hosted such performers as the Flying Karamazov Brothers, storytellers Jackie Torrence and David Holt, the Vienna Choir Boys, Mummenschanz, the Canadian Brass, the Preservation Hall Jazz Band, Victor Borge, the Peking Acrobats, Marcel Marceau, and the Ondekoza Drummers of Japan. All shows take place at the Alaska Center for the Performing Arts. & (Downtown)

ANCHORAGE SYMPHONY HALLOWEEN CONCERT
400 D St.
Anchorage
907/274-8668

Every Halloween night, the symphony presents its concert of "spooky" music, performed by orchestra musicians in costume at the Alaska Center for Performing Arts. The conductor might do something unexpected, too, such as rise out of the orchestra pit in Dracula's coffin or fly onstage as Batman. After the concert, the lobby is set up for trick-or-treating. This annual concert is always a big hit. ⚬ (Downtown)

STORES KIDS LOVE

BLAINE'S ART & GRAPHIC SUPPLY
2803 Spenard Rd.
Anchorage
907/561-5344

Art kits that let kids make jewelry, masks, greeting cards, and other projects are a good way to keep them entertained at night. The store also has modeling clay, paint sets, crayons, markers, chalks, and other art supplies. The pleasant staff is most helpful and encouraging. Each summer the store invites kids (and adults!) to its free Save Art Fair, featuring a sidewalk chalk contest, hands-on art projects, and the re-painting of its outdoor mural. (West Anchorage)

CHARLIE'S ALASKA TRAINS
410 G St.
Anchorage
907/278-7246

Kids love trains—they just do. So stop in for a train set or a single train car (all hand-painted by the owner), a whistle, a railroad spike, a video, a book, or another unique item from the city's largest vendor of Alaska Railroad souvenirs. (Downtown)

CLASSIC TOYS
341 E. Benson Blvd.
Anchorage
907/276-2732

"Classy toys" is more like it. This store has beautiful toys, dolls, stuffed animals, and educational games. It's a great place to get in touch with your inner child. (West Anchorage)

COLOR CREEK FIBER ART
6921 Brayton Dr.
Anchorage
907/344-7967
www.color-creek.com

Color Creek is a fiber-art studio open to the public; it's a warm, welcoming place that operates on one basic assumption: Everyone is creative. Color Creek provides materials and advice to anyone interested in doing work with fabric and/or beads. Kids

---

T i P

All three major grocery store chains—Carrs, Fred Meyer, and Safeway—give free cookies to kids. Head for the bakery if you stop for film or a cold drink.

(and grown-ups) can make batik banners; paint on silk; design and create beaded jewelry or amulet bags; learn the basics of bead-weaving; and paint, tie-dye, or otherwise embellish items such as T-shirts, sweatshirts, leggings, baby clothes, and hats. Why not create a memorable Alaska souvenir? A shirt the exact color of fireweed, a banner reflecting all the wildlife glimpsed during your stay, a hat with a whale, or a piece of jewelry that brings to mind the colors of an Alaskan sunset—the possibilities are limited only by your imagination. All can be done on your own, although children's art adventures are scheduled regularly. Tue–Fri noon–9, Sat 10–5. (South Anchorage)

HIPPETY HOP TOY SHOPPE
1120 E. Huffman Rd.
Anchorage
907/345-5311
This is a cozy toy store with a neighborhood feel and an emphasis on art

Alaska Sled Dog & Racing Association, p. 115

Tracy L. Barbutes/Alaska Sled Dog & Racing Association

and creativity kits. Specialty lines include Brio, Playmobil, Muffy Vander-Bear, Woodstock Percussion, and Breyer. Picture books, travel games, and coloring albums are also available. (South Anchorage)

NORTHWIND KITES
Fifth Avenue Mall
320 W. 5th Ave.
Anchorage
907/279-4386
Here you'll find beautiful sky-skimming kites and colorful windsocks (which make great souvenirs), plus a selection of old-time toys and puzzles. &. (Downtown)

OVER THE RAINBOW
1310 E. Dimond Blvd.
Anchorage
907/563-5483
This store carries specialty lines such as Brio, Breyer, Gund, Applause, and many craft, science, and puzzle toys. It's a fun place to browse, and the staff does not mind if adults get carried away. &. (South Anchorage)

PAINT YOUR POT
570 E. Benson Blvd.
Anchorage
907/272-6779
Kids absolutely must be accompanied by an adult (picture "bull in a china shop" otherwise), but this kind of thing should be family time anyway—together, you can produce lasting mementos of your vacation to Alaska. Choose from among 1,000 different pottery items, and let the staff offer advice on glazes, brushes, sponges, and stencils. Then have at it. Paint a fish platter, or jazz up a pottery moose, whale, bear, or salmon. Let the kids decorate soup mugs or cereal bowls with "Things

We Saw in Alaska." Splash local flowers like forget-me-nots or fire-weed onto a set of dinner plates. You need to allow three to four days for firing, so let this be one of the first places you visit. ⅋ (West Anchorage)

SANRIO SURPRISES
Dimond Center
800 E. Dimond Blvd.
Anchorage
907/522-6688
Come here for toys, gifts, and apparel from the various Sanrio lines, including Hello Kitty, Keroppi, and Pekkle. All of it is incredibly cute. Also downtown at Fifth Avenue Mall, 907/278-6688. ⅋ (South Anchorage)

RESTAURANTS KIDS LOVE

CHUCK E. CHEESE'S
308 E. Northern Lights Blvd.
Anchorage
907/274-9528
It's loud, it's hectic, and it's, uh, somewhat cheesy, but kids love this place. Tokens for games come with your pizza, but plan to buy some more and let your tots run around. You may even find yourself "borrow-ing" tokens—the noise of the games is irresistible. Lunch, dinner daily. ⅋ (West Anchorage)

COLD STONE CREAMERY
9001 Jewel Lake Rd.
Anchorage
907/248-2644
This is the ultimate ice cream parlor. Freshly made ice cream and yogurt are scooped onto a slab of chilled marble (the "cold stone") and kneaded with whatever "mix-ins" you choose. The choices are an astonishingly wide array of

syrups, candy chunks, nuts, bro-ken cookies, fresh fruit, cookie dough, gumballs, peanut butter, chocolate chips, and jimmies. Waffle cones, brownies, and cook-ies are made fresh daily. Having trouble making up your mind? The friendly staff will help you select from such tried-and-true combina-tions as Black Forest Brownie, Elena's Pina Colada, Hawaiian De-light, and Chocolate Chip Cookie Monster. ⅋ (West Anchorage)

ERIC'S
11541 Old Seward Hwy.
Anchorage
907/344-7512
Kids get a coloring menu and crayons to entertain them while their elders decide what to eat. The children's menu is reassuring, fea-turing time-tested goodies like burg-ers, barbecued ribs (a house specialty), chicken nuggets, halibut and chips (for the adventurous), and grilled cheese sandwiches (for the picky eater). Parents will be happy with the price: A full meal for less than $5. Older youngsters who think it isn't cool to order from the kiddie menu can select tasty favorites like fajitas, adult-portion barbecued ribs, and pasta dishes from the grown-up bill of fare. ⅋ (South Anchorage)

RED ROBIN BURGER & SPIRITS EMPORIUM

401 E. Dimond Blvd.
Anchorage
907/522-4321
Families flock to these extremely kid-friendly dining spots. They have a children's menu, the waitstaff is upbeat, and helium balloons and crayons are distributed freely. For more information on the grown-up menu, see Chapter 4, Where to Eat. Lunch, dinner daily; brunch Sun. Also at 3401 Penland Pkwy., 907/276-7788, and 4140 B St., 907/563-1515. & (South Anchorage)

THE ROYAL FORK
800 Northway Dr.
Anchorage
907/276-0089
This buffet-dining chain features plenty of choices so that even the pickiest eaters will find something they like. Kids especially enjoy comfort foods like fried chicken (enough drumsticks for everybody!), macaroni and cheese, mashed potatoes, and a dessert bar that includes make-your-own sundaes. Parents appreciate the high chairs on wheels (with diaper bag holders underneath) to help them roll little ones through the chow line more easily. Lunch, dinner daily. Also at 9220 Old Seward Hwy., 907/522-5600. & (East Anchorage)

SOURDOUGH MINING COMPANY
5200 Juneau St.
Anchorage
907/563-2272
Come here for ribs, chicken, burgers, and the like, including a make-your-own-sundae bar. Kids enjoy the Alaska-mining ambiance and the various taxidermied critters. Lunch, dinner daily; brunch Sun. & (South Anchorage)

TWIN DRAGON MONGOLIAN
BAR-B-QUE
612 E. 15th Ave.
Anchorage
907/276-7535
Kids love picking out their own food, and the Twin Dragon lets them. Parents report that their children will eat a surprising array of vegetables if they can choose which ones and how many. Here's how it works: You get a big shallow bowl and fill it with peppers, carrots, cabbage, sprouts, celery, and whatever other vegetables look good, along with slivers of beef, pork, or chicken if you like. Then you watch the cook work magic on a large, round stovetop, using only a couple of sticks to stir-fry one dinner after another. The best part is when he slings the food off the stove and, unerringly, into your bowl. In fact, the kids might want seconds just so they can watch this guy at work. Lunch, dinner daily. & (Downtown)

8

PARKS AND GARDENS

Anchorage has about 190 free public spaces, from flower-filled pocket parks and gracious greenbelts to thickly forested tracts that are, in effect, true wilderness in the middle of the city. Even in developed parks, the emphasis is usually on open space. Sports fields may abound, but bleachers and refreshment stands are few. Because "land" is the emphasis of our parkland, only those tracts with very specific draws are singled out in this chapter. The others will be finds that you stumble upon, driving by or through one of the city's paved trails.

ALASKA BOTANICAL GARDEN
Campbell Airstrip Rd. (off Tudor)
Anchorage
907/770-3692
www.alaska.net/~garden/
This garden is being carved out of a forest of spruce and birch, a five-phase project that calls for 10 percent of the 110-acre site to be developed in ornamental plantings. The rest will be preserved in its natural state. Easy trails lead visitors through the gardens; you may spot wildlife along the way. The Demonstration Garden blends introduced plants with the natural vegetation

and is creatively bordered with recycled materials. The Perennial Garden includes Alaskan native plants and hardy introductions. The Herb Garden showcases a variety of herbs in a classic setting. A pair of Alpine Gardens pay homage to alpine, or rock-garden, plants—sturdy, beautiful plants that do well at high altitudes and in colder climates. (The Alaska Rock Garden Society is hard at work to make the Alpine Gardens a success, in part because the North American Rock Garden Society annual conference will take place in Anchorage in

The summertime Music in the Park series presents a wide variety of musical styles, from bluegrass to klezmer to classic rock. The concerts take place Wednesday and Friday at noon on the corner of Fourth Avenue and E Street.

2002.) Strategically placed benches allow you to absorb the ABG's setting in a forest of birch and spruce. The weekly "Storytime in the Garden" family program brightens the summer months (see Chapter 7, Kids' Stuff). ᪻ (East Anchorage)

ANCHORAGE MEMORIAL PARK CEMETERY
Between Sixth and Ninth Aves. and Fairbanks and Cordova Sts.
907/343-6814
A National Historic Site, the Anchorage townsite's original graveyard, established in 1915, is still in use today. Its 22 acres are the final resting place for a number of famous Alaskans, including Dr. Joseph Romig, a medical missionary who traveled thousands of miles by dog team to care for the sick; Leopold David, the first mayor of Anchorage; Robert C. Reeve, a pioneer bush pilot and founder of Reeve Aleutian Airways, who was dubbed the "glacier pilot" due to

TRIVIA

The city Horticulture Section plants and maintains 461 flower beds and baskets around the city, using more than 76,000 annual flowers.

his habit of using glaciers as landing fields in remote areas; and artist Sydney Laurence, who's famous for painting Mt. McKinley so many times. Watch for graves marked by upright whalebones, an Eskimo tradition. May–Oct Mon–Fri 8–8, Sat–Sun 10–8; Nov–Apr daily 10–3. (Downtown)

CAMPBELL PARK
Lake Otis Pkwy. and Tudor Rd.
Anchorage
907/343-4355
This pleasant family recreation spot is located just south of one of the town's busier intersections, but you'd never know it once you get out of your car. The park offers a softball field, a tennis court, playground equipment, plenty of untrammeled green space for the kids to run in, and access to one of the city's multi-use trails. Additionally, Campbell Creek winds through the park. In many spots it's shallow enough for a nice wade. Pack a towel and a lunch, and stop off here to unwind from sightseeing. (East Anchorage)

CHUGACH STATE PARK
Potter Section House
Mile 115 Seward Hwy.
907/345-5014
One of the largest state parks in the country, these 495,000 acres provide

numerous recreational choices, from simple hikes to major backpacking treks. You can raft, canoe, fish, bicycle, climb, pick berries, and traverse glaciers. However, it's generally up to you to find a way to do these things because the park doesn't offer prepackaged tours or adventures at the entrance.

In fact, it doesn't even have an "entrance" per se. Because the park is so vast, it has access points in some pretty far-flung areas: the Hillside area, Eagle River Valley, and Indian Valley and Bird Creek trailheads (outside of Anchorage at Seward Highway Miles 103 and 101). The size can be puzzling to visitors. Just remember that everything is bigger in Alaska.

Orient yourself by stopping at park headquarters, just outside town at the Potter Section House, where the friendly park rangers can explain it all. Hours are 8 to 4:30 daily in summer, weekdays the rest of the year.

The park contains three campgrounds (Eklutna Lake, Eagle River, and Bird Creek) that cost $10 to $15 per night to use. You can also buy an annual pass, good for any state park facility, for $200 ($75 for residents). Those using the picnic areas and trails at Eklutna and Eagle River will be assessed $5 per day for parking; an annual pass is $25.

Year-round gold-panning is allowed within park boundaries, except in Eagle River, Ship Creek, Bird Creek, and Indian Creek; in those streams, which support salmon, you can only pan between May 16 and July 14, you have to work below the high-water line, and you can use only a pan and a shovel. But who knows? You may find that this vacation will pay for itself.

And when nature calls—well, don't bury it deep. Because the ground here is so cold, only the top five or six inches will, uh, compost. Be sure to dig your temporary potty at least 100 feet from streams or lakes. Don't forget to bury your pet's waste, too. (South Anchorage; Eagle River)

Potter Section House, Chugach State Park

Anchorage CVB

Bear Alert!

Technically, you could see a bear anywhere in Anchorage, including downtown. Not likely, but it could happen. Your chances of a bear encounter increase significantly when you walk in a remote area in Chugach State Park, or even in a city greenbelt. Observe some basic precautions, and you'll probably be all right.

First, check the trailhead for postings about bear activity. By all means, take warning signs seriously.

Look for signs such as droppings or tracks. Chat loudly, sing, whack trees with a stick as you pass—whatever it takes to let nearby bruins know you're in the neighborhood.

If you're camping, be sure not to pitch your tent near a trail, salmon stream, discarded garbage, firepit, or animal carcass. Find a quiet, open area where you can see critters and, more importantly, they can see you.

Do not—repeat, do not—cook near your tent. Move at least 100 feet downwind and try not to cook or carry anything stinky, including bacon or peanut butter. (Bears have an excellent sense of smell.) Cache your food high up in a tree, if possible. If not, hang it off a bridge or rock face, or store it well off the trail and downwind of your campsite.

You may find yourself face to face with a curious, startled, or hostile animal. Unfortunately, there is no foolproof way of dealing with bears. What scares 99 bears might make the 100th laugh hysterically and charge anyway. But biologists have determined some basics that apply most of the time.

If you see a bear some distance away, turn around and go back the way you came. Or circle as far around as you can, keeping an eye on the animal. End of story.

DELANEY PARK STRIP
9th and 10th Aves.
between A and P Sts.
Anchorage
907/343-4355

Originally a firebreak for the townsite of Anchorage, this area later became the city's first airfield. Now it's a series of fields and courts for baseball, basketball, volleyball, and

But what if the animal does see you? Let your mantra be, "Stay calm." Seldom do bears attack humans. More likely, the animal will stand on its hind legs or move toward you for a closer look. Your reaction should be to seem as human as possible. Don't scream, squeal, run, or otherwise sound or act like prey. Stand tall (some people hold their backpacks over their heads to add height), wave your arms, and talk in a loud but steady voice.

It's best to stand right where you are. If you feel you must move, back up slowly and diagonally. If the bear moves, too, stop and stand still, repeating the arm-waving, loud-talking behavior.

Should the animal charge, change your mantra to, "He's bluffing." According to biologists, almost all charges are bluffs. Don't even think of running away since that may trigger the animal's chase instinct— and bears can move incredibly fast. Stay right where you are. The bear may come within a few feet and then leave.

And if it doesn't leave? Play dead. Drop down flat on your stomach or curl up in a fetal position (which you may want to do anyway!). Lock your hands behind your neck and lie very still. The bear may give you an experimental slap or even take a nibble. Even if it hurts like hell, don't move. It's likely that the animal will take off once it thinks you're a goner.

However, if the attack continues for a while after you've stopped moving, fight back as hard as you can. Experts say that predatory bruins are often young animals that don't know how to behave around humans yet. Rocks, tree branches, or even a good punch in the nose can drive these "teenagers" away. That's a good reason to hike in a group: If you're being mauled, a bunch of friends armed with sticks and stones can save you.

tennis. In this area you'll also see an old locomotive engine, playground equipment, a veteran's memorial, and the city rose garden. A small but intense group of croquet players meets here in summer. This is a great spot for a picnic, or for kids to let off steam. The Centennial Rose Garden is a particular treat: A hedge of rugosa and hardy hybrids form an almost solid perimeter ringing an inside area of tender roses that volunteers take indoors to winter. Some roses are as small as Susan B. Anthony dollars, while others are the size of softballs. You're surrounded by a constant hum of happy bees and the tantalizing smell of sweet and spice that ebbs and flows with the breeze. Benches encourage you to take time to smell the roses. (Downtown)

EARTHQUAKE PARK
Northern Lights Blvd.
Anchorage
907/343-4355
The 1964 Good Friday earthquark was the strongest ever in North America, measuring 9.2 on the Richter scale. This park marks the area where the large slabs of land slid into Cook Inlet. An interpretive display informs visitors about the quake and also about the area's geology, flora, and fauna. Looking at the photos, and then at the land nearby, may make you nervous

enough to want to drive away quickly, afraid that another Big One will hit. (And it will, someday: Alaska is the most seismic state in the union, and scientists say that the question of another devastating earthquake is not "if" but "when.") But resist the impulse to flee too quickly—you'll miss a nice view. (West Anchorage)

ELDERBERRY PARK
Fifth Ave. and M St.
Anchorage
907/343-4355
This little park is as cute as a bug in lace pants. It features play equipment, access to the Coastal Trail, and a lovely view of Cook Inlet. Its location makes it a nice respite from sightseeing; grab a sandwich to go and eat it here. And keep an eye on the Inlet—you may spy a beluga whale out there during the summertime. (Downtown)

FAR NORTH BICENTENNIAL PARK
Between Tudor and Abbott Rds.

Eagle River Visitors Center, Chugach State Park, p. 130

Anchorage CVB

Those beautiful mountain streams look so inviting. But the clearest, swiftest creek, or even snowmelt, may give you giardiasis, an intestinal misery that's also known as "beaver fever." Drink only the water you bring with you. If you must drink from a stream, boil the water for at least two full minutes, use a chemical treatment, or pass it through a filter with a less than five-micrometer pore size.

Anchorage
907/343-4355

This massive (4,011-acre) park is the city's largest piece of undeveloped land. It encompasses wetland, creeks, and spruce woods. During World War II the acreage was used by the military as a training area and auxiliary airfield. Many of the byways forged by tank drivers formed the makings for more than 20 miles of challenging cross-country ski trails. (Note: Some trails are also used by mushers, so don't turn that Walkman up too loud or you may find yourself tangled up with a line of grinning, yapping dawgs.) In summer the sharp-eyed may spy shell casings or the ghosts of old foxholes in the tall grasses.

The park hosts a number of critters, including black and grizzly bears, coyotes, moose, wolves, lynx, beavers, porcupines, several types of fish, and a number of birds. Yet plenty about the park remains unknown. For instance, one local mycologist counted 110 types of fungi, including one she'd never seen before. Recently two songbirds that winter in El Salvador—the hermit thrush and Swainson's thrush—were found to nest in the park. There's no guarantee you'll see any of these creatures, but be alert to the possibilities. It's also home to massive amounts of mosquitoes, who breed and sing happily in the boggy areas, so protect yourself with chemicals or clothing. You can access the park via Campbell Airstrip Road or more easily from Hillside Drive. (East Anchorage; South Anchorage)

KIDS' KINGDOM
David Green Park
36th Ave. between Latouche and Lake Otis
Anchorage
907/343-4355

A parent-built, kid-friendly playground was recently installed in this small neighborhood park. It's a good spot for a picnic (a McDonald's is down the street) or for a break from sightseeing. The playground makes a good reward for your kids for behaving themselves while mom and dad enjoyed all the stuff kids think is boring. (East Anchorage)

KINCAID PARK
West end of Raspberry Rd.
Anchorage
907/343-4355

This is a well-used but still wild parcel of more than 1,500 acres. It has 30 miles of varied-terrain trails that are great for skiing, hiking, orienteering, and jogging. Be very cautious about the numerous moose that frequent the area—walking, biking, or skiing into a thousand-pound ungulate is no joking matter. Bears have been seen here, too. While you're in the park, look for the Andrew Lekisch Memorial Garden, a tribute to a teenaged athlete who died in a fall on a mountain. The young man's mother maintains this lovely garden at the foot of Lekisch Trail. Terraced against the side of a small hill, it mixes carefully placed rocks with brightly colored flowers. A great way to access Kincaid is via the Coastal Trail—it's about 10 miles from downtown to Kincaid Park. (West Anchorage)

MANN LEISER MEMORIAL GREENHOUSES
Russian Jack Springs Park
5200 DeBarr Rd.
Anchorage
907/343-4355
The city maintains thousands of flowerbeds around town and grows trees and shrubs for landscaping. One of the facilities at Russian Jack is a tropical greenhouse with an aviary and fish pond. It's a popular site for school tours and weddings. In the winter you'll often find cabin-fevered residents savoring a remembrance of mild weather and getting a fix of greenery; the chirping birds and healthy plants are a real tonic in February. Open daily 8–3. Free. (East Anchorage)

RUSSIAN JACK SPRINGS PARK
5200 DeBarr Rd.
Anchorage
907/343-4355
This nearly 300-acre park contains a golf course, the city greenhouses (see previous entry), softball fields, tennis courts, a sheltered picnic area, play equipment, and ski trails. It also contains plenty of moose and the occasional bear, so make lots of noise as you walk, in order to warn off the wildlife. (Admit it, though: You could dine out on such a sighting for weeks, back home.) In the wintertime, you'll notice folks skiing during their lunch breaks as well as after work. (East Anchorage)

TOWN SQUARE PARK
Bounded by Fifth and Sixth Aves.
and E and F Sts.
Anchorage
907/343-4355
Next door to the Alaska Center for

Anchorage Trail Index

Paved bike trails/multi-use trails: 121 miles
Plowed winter walkways: 134 miles
Maintained ski trails: 108 miles
Dog-mushing trails: 37 miles
Non-paved hiking trails (summer): 90-plus miles
Lighted ski trails: 25 miles
Skijoring trails: 41 miles
Equestrian trails: 6 miles

the Performing Arts, this park is a good place to take five when you're tired. The benches and the fountain may be cement, but the stunning flower plantings blaze with color, causing tourists to burn up rolls and rolls of film. Locals are puzzled, sometimes wondering aloud whether these visitors don't have chrysanthemums at home. But they probably don't, at least not like ours—the Alaskan summer sun creates outsized flowers with gorgeously colored blooms. And city crews scrupulously maintain them so that they never seem to fade. If it's a nice day, forget about a restaurant lunch—grab some take-out from a downtown eatery and dine al fresco. Watch out for skateboarders, though. (Downtown)

UNIVERSITY OF ALASKA–ANCHORAGE
3211 Providence Dr.
Anchorage
907/786-1800

The concrete planters along the 36th Avenue meridian in front of UAA are spilling over with blooms by early summer. But they're the merest hint of the floral delights all around the sprawling campus. Some 40 annual and 20 perennial beds, and numerous trees and shrubs, are maintained each year. One particularly nice area begins at the campus greenhouse—which, by the way,

pours out 12,000 plants each year for those annual beds. Enter off Northern Lights Boulevard, at the sign for the King Career Center; if you hit UAA Drive, you've passed it. Park your car (you don't need a permit in summer) and walk east. Depending on when you visit, you'll see daffodils, crocuses, poppies, Asiatic lilies, multicolored columbine, yellow roses, purple or pink campanula, and outrageous seas of tulips.

On the southwest side of the Business Education Building is a many-tiered plot of annuals—a "replacement garden" that lends fill-in plants to other campus spots and is also a place to try out new varieties. It's bursting with nonstop begonias, pansies, flowering cabbage, dianthus, lobelia, marigolds, geraniums, purple kohlrabi, or whatever else the horticulturists are trying that year.

The Sally Monserud Building is corsaged with tulips, spirea, and strawberry plants; a particularly unusual berry variety, called "pink panda," has shocking-pink petals instead of the usual sedate white blossoms.

Outside the Lucy Cuddy Center, you'll see a triangular bed of flowering kale and cabbage in green and purple hues. West of the Cuddy Center is the UAA Geological Rock Garden, with small and large specimens of "popcorn rock," chert concretion, zinc-lead-silver ore, glacial "erratics" (rocks left by receding glaciers), and petrified wood with bits of coal flaking off and glinting crystals inside small cavities. The rocks range in age from 30 million to 340 million years.

Seven kinds of lilacs are grown in hedges along the Auto/Diesel Technology Building. An herb bed can be found outside the Gordon Hartlieb Building, with coriander, sage, caraway, mints, hyssop, garlic, sorrel, fennel, St. John's wort, comfrey, rue, thyme, lamb's ear, chives, and horseradish. (Culinary arts students come here to forage for ingredients for their latest creations.)

Other plants to be glimpsed during your stroll: lilies; foxglove in various hues; rhododendron; bleeding hearts; blue poppies (meconopsis); lilies of the valley; a relatively rare azalea (hard to grow in Alaska); and pink, white, and red roses, from hardy rosa rugosa to fragrant hybrid Therese Bugnet and the interesting pink-green foliage of rosa rubifolia. And, of course (this being Alaska), fireweed.

In addition to the usual spruce and birch trees, here are a few species to watch for on campus: a mountain ash/chokecherry cross called Ivan's Beauty, bristlecone pine, Siberian pear (its wicked thorns keep moose from browsing it too closely), Himalayan little-leaf linden, Bali cherry, burr oaks, a hazelnut/filbert cross dubbed a "hazelbert," and a weeping Siberian pea.

Note: Summer is a quiet time on campus, and the wide walkways and large patches of soft green grass are good places for your kids to shake loose a few ya-yas. Let 'em romp—within eyesight, of course—as you admire the garden spots. (East Anchorage)

One People

9

SHOPPING

Increasingly, Anchorage is gaining the kinds of stores that are common in the Lower 48. Their openings here, though, are front-page news (sometimes jostling for space with articles on things like bear attacks), and enormous crowds show up on opening day for retailers like The Gap, the Body Shop, and even K-Mart.

One of the best things about shopping in Anchorage, though, can be summed up in three words: No sales tax! That means considerable savings no matter what you buy—a full-length fur coat, a unique Alaskan parka, a mountain-climbing harness designed especially for women, an incredible piece of Native art, or some exquisite modern jewelry made by an artist whose studio you visited. And if you're wondering how to get all your purchases home, plenty of storekeepers are happy to pack and ship.

If possible, shop when things are quiet. A manager surrounded by swarms of in-a-hurry cruise passengers won't have time to chat, but when things calm down you may learn something interesting. Wouldn't it be great to know the name of the village where a doll or a coat was made, or the reason an artist painted a particular picture?

APPAREL

ALASKA FUR FACTORY
408 W. Fourth Ave.
Anchorage
907/276-3252
Here you'll find parkas, jackets, full-length coats, slippers, and other fur

and leather goods. And remember, no matter where you shop for fur, there's no sales tax in Anchorage. (Downtown)

ALASKA FUR GALLERY
428 W. Fourth Ave.
Anchorage

907/274-3877
It's the usual fur suspects, plus a surprise in the front window: a fur jockstrap. (Hey, it's cold here in the winter!) (Downtown)

CLASSIC WOMAN
3030 Denali St.
Anchorage
907/563-5228
The store sells stylish and beautiful clothing for women sizes 14 to 24. (West Anchorage)

DAVID GREEN MASTER FURRIER
130 W. Fourth Ave.
Anchorage
907/277-9595
David Green has been in business since 1922. The shop's motto is, "If you don't know furs, know your furrier." (Downtown)

DENALI WEAR
416 G St.
Anchorage
907/278-9327
Local artist Tracy Anna Bader works in Polartec fleece, a lightweight but extremely warm fabric, as well as velvet, wool, and ski fabrics. From accessory coats to decorative vests, her creations are done in brilliant colors and with a real sense of style. Her hats, particularly the berets, are very popular among young people; surprise your kids or grandkids. (Downtown)

JCPENNEY
Fifth Ave. and D St.
Anchorage
907/279-5656
In addition to the usual clothing, this durable department store has a large selection of Alaska souvenirs, including videos, stuffed animals, and non-tacky sweatshirts and T-shirts that you and your relatives would probably actually wear. (Downtown)

LAURA WRIGHT ALASKAN PARKYS
343 W. Fifth Ave.
Anchorage
907/274-4215
If you want a parka (which some Alaska Natives pronounce "parky") that is both authentic and beautiful, here's the place to get it. The shop also has a nice selection of locally sewn clothing for the popular American Girl dolls, including traditional kuspuks (see "Shopper's Glossary" sidebar). (Downtown)

THE LOOK/KOOL SHOES
570 E. Benson Blvd.
Anchorage
907/278-5665
Here you'll find lingerie, women's and men's clothes, ladies' formal wear, dancewear, Gothic styles, and adult novelties. And the shoes really are Kool: John Fluevog, Candies, Skechers, Steve Madden, Muro,

Looking for an unusual souvenir? Treat your grandkids, or yourself, to an Eskimo yo-yo. Instead of a disc, it's two soft spheres at opposite ends of a string. The idea is to get one sphere spinning, and then start the other one spinning in the opposite direction. An Eskimo yo-yo is traditionally made of fur, but they're now made out of cloth as well.

Laura Wright Alaskan Parkys

Vans, Airwalk, London Underground, and other memorable brands. (West Anchorage)

NORDSTROM
603 D St.
Anchorage
907/279-7622
This department store has a strong emphasis on customer service that many people believe offsets its fairly high prices. (Downtown)

ONE PEOPLE
400 D St.
Anchorage
907/274-4063
One People sells clothing, jewelry, gifts, toys, and housewares made by international village cooperatives. Russian and Alaska Native items are included. (Downtown)

PIA'S SCANDINAVIAN SWEATERS
345 E St.
Anchorage
907/277-7964
Come here for absolutely gorgeous Scandinavian woolens, including socks, hats, mittens, Icelandic coats, vests, and lobbens (pressed-wool boots), in beautiful, intricate colors and patterns. A new line of Polartec fleece "sweaters" are almost indistinguishable from the knitted wool ones. The store has a nice selection of children's hats to make playing outdoors both comfortable and stylish. Pick up some fun stuff, too, like straw Christmas tree ornaments, "Uff da!" coffee mugs, or T-shirts that state, "Not only am I perfect, I'm Norwegian, too." (Downtown)

THE RAGE
423 G St.
Anchorage
907/274-7243
The Rage sells vintage clothing—the good stuff. (Downtown)

SUBTERRANEA
608 W. Fourth Ave.
Anchorage
907/277-9700

This tiny and intriguing store, which bills itself as "an antidote for civilization," carries Doc Martens, ultramodern clothing, T-shirts with strong social statements, and jewelry that will scare your parents. (Downtown)

ARTS, CRAFTS, AND GIFTS

ALASKA FUR EXCHANGE
4417 Old Seward Hwy.
Anchorage
907/563-3877
This place carries ivory, whalebone, soapstone, and horn carvings; dolls; fur parkas; mukluks; skin masks; hats; jewelry; and other Native arts and crafts. The shop also claims to be Alaska's largest fur-pelt dealer. (East Anchorage)

ALASKA NATIVE MEDICAL CENTER CRAFT SHOP
4315 Diplomacy Dr.
Anchorage
907/729-1122
You'll find a varying selection of baskets, dolls, carvings, beaded items, and Eskimo yo-yos made by artisans from all over the state. The selection varies because it depends on who's brought what into town. But it's a great source for authentic crafts made by real Alaska Natives, as opposed to some of the ersatz "Native" art sold around town. (East Anchorage)

ALASKAN IVORY OUTLET
319 W. Fifth Ave.
Anchorage
907/274-7748
Carvings, scrimshaw, whalebone sculpture, jewelry, artifacts, and bulk walrus and mammoth ivory are sold here. (Downtown)

ALEKSANDR BARANOV RUSSIAN GIFT SHOP
321 W. Fifth Ave.
Anchorage
907/274-9090
This shop offers samovars, dolls (including matrushka nesting toys), boxes, paintings, porcelain, and other Russian items. Check out the matrushka dolls—some start the size of a bowling pin and end in teensy little carvings smaller than a shirt button. (Downtown)

ANCHORAGE MUSEUM GIFT SHOP
121 W. Seventh Ave.
Anchorage
907/343-4326
The shop sells a respected collection of Alaska Native art, plus art books, jewelry, gifts, and cards. (Downtown)

ARTIQUE LTD.
314 G St.
Anchorage
907/277-1663
In addition to fine art, this gallery carries fine crafts such as fish platters, glassware, books, soft sculptures, and jewelry. Look for brightly painted ceramics by local artists Steve and Romney Ortland. (Downtown)

BELL'S NURSERY & GIFTS
Specking Ave. off New Seward Hwy.
Anchorage
907/345-4476
Bell's has Russian gifts such as icons, painted boxes, and matrushka dolls, along with candles, greeting cards, Dept. 56 Christmas collectibles, soaps, small gifts, and a good selection of crystal, flatware, dinnerware, and household

Where the Trail Is Always Cold

Two well-known mystery writers live in Anchorage. Watch for signed copies of their books in local bookstores.

Dana Stabenow writes the popular Kate Shugak series (A Fatal Thaw, Dead in the Water, Play with Fire, Breakup, *and* Hunter's Moon, *among others) and is introducing a somewhat darker series with a new character, Liam Campbell; the first title is* Out for Blood. *Stabenow is also the author of several science-fiction books:* Second Star, A Handful of Stars, *and* Red Planet Run. *Check out her home page at www.alaskana.com/stabenow/.*

Sue Henry's first book, Murder on the Iditarod Trail, *was made into a TV movie,* The Cold Heart of a Killer, *starring Kate Jackson. Henry has also written* Termination Dust, Sleeping Lady, *and* Death Takes Passage.

Both authors are members of Alaska Sisters in Crime, the local chapter of a national group that promotes mysteries written by women. Alaska SinC will host Left Coast Crime, a national mystery conference, February 15–18, 2001. To find out more about Alaska Sisters in Crime, visit the Web site at www.aonline.com~ /aksinc, or e-mail aksinc@sinbad.net. For information on Left Coast Crime, check out www.lcc2001.com.

linens. Enjoy an espresso in the greenhouse, which is particularly popular in the middle of winter. Also in West Anchorage, 7653 Cranberry Rd., 907/243-1020. (South Anchorage)

CHILKAT ART CO.
413 D St.
Anchorage
907/272-6261
This is another place for Native art and Alaskan carved ivory, soapstone, whalebone, antlers, and scrimshaw. (Downtown)

DECKER/MORRIS GALLERY
621 W. Sixth Ave.
Anchorage
907/272-1489
The gallery sells handcrafted jewelry, ceramics, and gift items along with fine art. (Downtown)

ELAINE S. BAKER & ASSOCIATES
Hotel Captain Cook
939 W. Fifth Ave.
Anchorage
907/272-0433
Here you'll find Russian boxes, Alaskan dolls, collectibles, furs, art

jewelry, Limoges and Fabergé items, and fine art. (Downtown)

FLYPAPER
341 E. Benson Blvd.
Anchorage
907/276-6095
Wonderfully eclectic and sometimes beautiful cards—you'll spend a long time browsing and laughing—plus specialty candles, soaps, jewelry, and other gift items. Check out the collection of clever, sardonic fridge magnets displayed on an antique meat-roaster. (West Anchorage)

HIGH GEAR
Sears Mall
Northern Lights Blvd.
and Seward Hwy.
Anchorage
907/349-9292
High Gear sells fun and funky gifts and a terrific selection of cards, some of which would make your mother blush. (West Anchorage)

KATHERINE THE GREAT
Fifth Avenue Mall

Molly Willson Perry

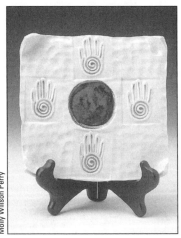

Molly Willson Perry

320 W. Fifth Ave.
Anchorage
907/272-5283
Stop by for Russian dolls, icons, and gifts. (Downtown)

KOBUK COFFEE CO.
504 W. Fifth Ave.
Anchorage
907/272-3626
Kobuk sells specialty teas and coffees; fancy and unusual candies; beautiful teapots and other china items; and small, pleasing items for the home. This shop smells just plain wonderful, and there's always a tea-of-the-day in the teapot. (Downtown)

MOLLY WILLSON PERRY
706 W. Fourth Ave.
Anchorage
907/258-2270
In her working studio Perry produces "anthropic art," jewelry, and sculptural wall hangings that reflect her dual degrees in anthropology and art. The jewelry is high-fired porcelain, and the wall hangings are based on pressed aluminum. Some works are fun and whimsical, others are spiritual. (Downtown)

THE MUSEUM STORE/THE NATURE SOURCE
Fifth Avenue Mall
320 W. Fifth Ave.
Anchorage
907/258-3373
These conjoined shops sell unusual, exotic, and just plain fun gifts for the person who has everything. Check out stuff like antique jewelry, rain sticks, reproductions of famous stained-glass works, lachrymatories (teardrop collectors), rocks and fossils, fine-art ties, artifact replicas, gargoyles, nature-themed toys, and

even blown-glass hard candy (with the helpful sticker "Do Not Eat"). (Downtown)

OOMINGMAK MUSK OX PRODUCERS CO-OP
604 H St.
Anchorage
907/272-9225
Oomingmak is an Eskimo word meaning "the bearded one." It refers to the musk ox, a prehistoric remnant of the last great ice age. This shop sells warm garments made of qiviut (kiv-ee-yute), the soft underfur of the musk ox. They're knitted by Natives from western Alaska. Be prepared for sticker shock, though, since the cloud-soft warmth of qiviut doesn't come cheaply. Still, it's a unique gift and useful in cold climates. And if you'd like to see a real, live musk ox, visit the Palmer Musk Ox Farm (see Chapter 13, Day Trips). (Downtown)

PACK RAT MALL
8200 Homer Dr.
Anchorage
907/522-5272
Need a scented candle, a Star Wars action figure, or a Beanie Baby? You'll find these, and more, at this co-op collection of stalls that offer toys, gifts, collectibles, and crafts. (South Anchorage)

SEQUELS
University Center
3901 Old Seward Hwy.
Anchorage
907/561-7898
Sequels sells handcrafted jewelry—the store is famous among art-earring aficionados—plus art glass, wind chimes, and other unique gifts. (West Anchorage)

VILLAGE GIFTS
3030 Denali St.
Anchorage
907/561-0767
You'll find crafts, gifts, and collectibles, many handmade by a number of local artisans who share studio space. (West Anchorage)

WHITTLEWINDS
Sears Mall
600 E. Northern Lights Blvd.
Anchorage
907/278-9434
Whittlewinds specializes in handmade pottery, hardwood jewelry boxes, wind chimes, wooden kaleidoscopes, candles, wind socks, and other gift items. (West Anchorage)

BOOKS AND MAGAZINES

BARNES & NOBLE
200 E. Northern Lights Blvd.
Anchorage

907/279-7323

This great big chain store manages to be both large and cozy at the same time. It stocks between 150,000 and 175,000 books and regularly hosts signings (many by local authors), book-club meetings, and other special events. The store has a café if all those words make you thirsty. (West Anchorage)

BORDERS BOOKS & MUSIC
1100 E. Dimond Blvd.
Anchorage
907/344-4099

This store has more than 200,000 book, music, and video titles, plus over 3,000 international periodicals. The store also presents regular readings, author signings, children's programs, video screenings, and other special events. Its café frequently features live music. (South Anchorage)

COOK INLET BOOK CO.
415 W. Fifth Ave.
Anchorage

907/258-4544

Convenient to downtown hotels, this shop houses an extensive collection of Alaskana in addition to popular and classic books. The store hosts frequent author events, including a series of summer book signings by local writers, so get that souvenir novel or guidebook personalized while you're in town. (Downtown)

CYRANO'S BOOKSTORE
413 D St.
Anchorage
907/274-2599

At this small, funky place people are as likely to talk about books as they are to buy them. The attached theater hosts poetry readings and live music, and it's also home to Eccentric Theatre Company, which produces some risk-taking entertainment (see Chapter 11, Performing Arts). (Downtown)

GULLIVER'S USED BOOKS
Northway Mall
3101 Penland Pkwy.

A Taste of Alaska

Alaska grub makes a great gift for the folks back home. Check local grocery stores and souvenir shops for these items:

- **pilot bread:** *A large, flat cracker that keeps almost indefinitely. It's very popular in the Bush as a base for everything from peanut butter and jelly to dried fish and seal oil.*
- **salmon jerky:** *Seasoned dried fish.*
- **reindeer sausage:** *Yep, it's Rudolph, with beef and/or pork in the mix, too.*
- **birch syrup:** *A lighter, more delicate flavor than maple.*
- **fireweed honey:** *Serve it with Russian tea.*

One People, p. 141

inventory to help you find what you need. (West Anchorage)

TWICE TOLD TALES
5121 Arctic Blvd.
Anchorage
907/561-3828
This independently owned store sells both new and used books. (South Anchorage)

HOUSEWARES

HABITAT HOUSEWARES
University Center
3901 Old Seward Hwy.
Anchorage
907/561-1856
Come here for cool dishes, cooking utensils, and fancy appliances, as well as some neat locally made stuff: funky birdhouses and Andy Kirsch's unusual aluminum clocks and modernistic wood-and-metal furniture. Also downtown, at Fifth Avenue Mall, 907/276-1856. (West Anchorage)

METRO HOME FURNISHINGS
570 E. Benson Blvd.
Anchorage
907/279-4455
This is the place for beautiful linens, dishes, candles, lamps, gourmet mixes, cookware, gift items, and furniture. (West Anchorage)

MUSIC STORES

CAMELOT MUSIC AND VIDEO
Fifth Avenue Mall
320 W. Fifth Ave.
Anchorage
907/272-1956
The store offers a good selection of both CDs and laser discs, along with

Anchorage
907/278-0084
Gulliver's sells used books of every stripe, including a decent selection of Alaskana. The prices are right, too. Check out the bargain racks for paperbacks to read on the plane. (East Anchorage)

METRO MUSIC & BOOKS
530 E. Benson Blvd.
Anchorage
907/279-8622
This locally owned shop makes up for its smaller-than-superstore size with atmosphere, courtesy, and a real love of words and music. (West Anchorage)

TITLE WAVE USED BOOKS
1068 W. Fireweed Ln.
Anchorage
907/278-9283
More than 100,000 books fill this 11,000-square-foot shop. Don't be overwhelmed, though—the friendly clerks will check the computerized

Shopper's Glossary

• **baleen (bay-leen):** *A hard, shiny material found in the upper jaws of some whales, this material was once used in corsets. Today baleen is often used as an accent for baskets or carvings—sometimes you'll see an entire basket made from it. Some people refer to baleen as "nature's plastic" for its flexibility and longevity.*

• **billiken (bill-eh-ken):** *A pointy-headed little creature with a benevolent smile, the billiken is a good-luck charm and a very popular souvenir. Although it is often carved by Natives, it is not a traditional Eskimo item. The billiken was patented in 1908 by a woman in the Lower 48.*

• **kuspuk (kuss-puck):** *Originally an Eskimo woman's parka, this definition has stretched to include a garment that looks like a dress with a hood. Kuspuks are usually made from very bright cotton prints. Some people wear them over slacks or jeans, and little girls often wear them as dresses.*

• **mukluk (muck-luck):** *Lightweight skin boots that will probably be the warmest footwear you'll ever own. If you're lucky enough to find traditional mukluks, they'll be made of moosehide and trimmed with fur and beads (Athabaskan), or of bearded-seal soles with caribou uppers (Eskimo).*

• **oosik (oo-sick):** *You'll hear a lot of jokes about this one—an oosik is a walrus penis bone. You can buy them in gift shops, either plain or carved. Good luck explaining it to your grandchildren.*

• **qiviut (kiv-ee-yute):** *The soft underfur of the shaggy old musk ox, finer than cashmere and eight times warmer than wool. It's collected and woven into some of the softest, coziest scarves and hats you'll ever touch. Qiviut is expensive but, in cold climes, worth it.*

• **ulu (oo-loo):** *A fan-shaped "woman's knife" formerly made of stone with a bone handle but now often assembled from an old saw blade with a wood handle. The ones in the stores are much sleeker, of course. Souvenir shops carry them, and lots of visitors find them surprisingly easy to use and very handy in the kitchen.*

video games and movies on tape. (Downtown)

MAMMOTH MUSIC
300 E. Dimond Blvd.
Anchorage
907/344-6155
The friendly and knowledgeable staff here will introduce you to music you never thought possible. Ask about recordings from local bands, too. The shop has thousands of used CDs for as low as $4. Also in West Anchorage, at 2906 Spenard Rd., 907/258-3555. (South Anchorage)

OUTDOOR WEAR/GEAR

ALASKA MOUNTAINEERING AND HIKING
2633 Spenard Rd.
Anchorage
907/272-1811
Not surprisingly, this store sells mountaineering and backpacking gear, sea kayaks, hiking boots, and Gore-Tex clothing and outerwear. Check the store bulletin board, too, for used equipment and information on local outdoors events. In summer the shop rents sea kayaks. (West Anchorage)

BOARDERLINE SNOWBOARD
Dimond Center
800 E. Dimond Blvd.
Anchorage
907/349-9931
Boarderline is the place to talk about snowboarding with someone who speaks your language. The shop sells boards and the protective gear you'll need to ride them, along with clothing that's just plain cool—either on or off the slopes. (South Anchorage)

EDDIE BAUER
Fifth Avenue Mall
320 W. Fifth Ave.
Anchorage
907/279-6606
This well-known chain sells outdoor gear, travel clothing, and accessories. (Downtown)

GARY KING SPORTING GOODS
202 E. Northern Lights Blvd.
Anchorage
907/272-5401
This locally owned and operated shop has been outfitting Alaskans for skiing, fishing, hunting, climbing, hiking, cycling, and just about every other conceivable sport for more than 35 years. The store has a family feel because King family members work there. (West Anchorage)

PETER GLENN SKI & SPORTS
1520 O'Malley Rd.
Anchorage
907/349-2929
Peter Glenn sells sporting equipment, gear, and clothing for skiers, snowboarders, in-line skaters, swimmers, hikers, and travelers. You can even buy a pair of shoes designed to help you "surf" down stair railings. Honest. (South Anchorage)

PLAY IT AGAIN SPORTS
2636 Spenard Rd.
Anchorage
907/278-7529
Used sporting equipment can be had here at sometimes considerable discounts. (West Anchorage)

REI
1200 W. Northern Lights Blvd.
Anchorage
907/272-4565
A department store for the outdoorsy, this local branch of the Seattle-based

Recreational Equipment, Inc. can help you outfit yourself for just about any adventure you can imagine. The store presents frequent classes, workshops, and lectures on all subjects recreational; most of the programs are free. (West Anchorage)

SKINNY RAVEN SPORTS
800 H St.
Anchorage
907/274-7222
Come here for running shoes, clothes, and accessories for all kinds of Alaskan running conditions. Skinny Raven carries children's gear, too. (Downtown)

THE SPORT SHOP
570 E. Benson Blvd.
Anchorage
907/272-7755
This store specializes in active- and outdoor gear for women, including hiking boots, swimwear, bike clothes, running gear, snowshoes, plus backpacks, sleeping bags, and climbing gear designed for female

Bell's Nursery & Gifts, p. 142

Bell's Nursery & Gifts

bodies. You can also rent backpacks, sleeping bags, and snowshoes. (West Anchorage)

THRIFT SHOPS

Don't laugh—you may find exactly the right memento of your visit in a secondhand store, whether it be a pair of manly Carhartt coveralls, a copy of the book Tisha, *or a dogsled tapestry. Thrift shops are also great places to buy "trashable" clothes if you decide to do something strenuous and potentially messy, like fishing or camping.*

THE BISHOP'S ATTIC
1100 Gambell St.
Anchorage
907/279-6328
Run by the Archdiocese of Anchorage, this downtown thrift shop has some real finds mixed in with the usual clothing, books, appliances, and such. (Downtown)

SALVATION ARMY THRIFT STORE
501 E. Dimond Blvd.
Anchorage
907/344-1053
It might be easy to overlook this shop, located right next to Value Village (see listing, below). Do stop in, though, for the shop's great pickings and very low prices. (South Anchorage)

VALUE VILLAGE
5437 E. Northern Lights Blvd.
Anchorage
907/337-2184
Also known as "the coolest garage sale in town," this thrift shop is run like a department store. Also in South Anchorage, 501 E. Dimond Blvd, 907/522-9090. (East Anchorage)

OTHER NOTABLE STORES

ALASKA KNIFE
3001 Tanglewood Dr.
Anchorage
907/243-6093

You'll find knives, knives, and more knives, from fine cutlery to serious hunting and survival tools. Shop here for your souvenir ulu (see "Shopper's Glossary" on page 148), or have the staff custom-make a knife specifically for your needs. (West Anchorage)

ALASKA WILD BERRY PRODUCTS
5225 Juneau St.
Anchorage
907/562-8858

How about some salmonberry jelly on your toast or lingonberry jam for those fresh-baked scones? Alaska Wild Berry makes preserves, candies, and teas with highbush cranberries, blueberries, rose hips, elderberries, black currants, and other local fruits. Get there early in the day to watch the cooks at work. Kids get a kick out of the chocolate waterfall, which splashes from a series of pans into a little mountain and pool. Alaska souvenirs are available here, too. A smaller outlet is downtown, in the Fifth Avenue Mall, 907/278-8858. (South Anchorage)

BOSCO'S COMICS, CARDS & GAMES
2606 Spenard Rd.
Anchorage
907/274-4112

Here you'll find a full line of mainstream and independent comics, along with sci-fi items and sports cards and memorabilia. Bosco's also has a good selection of Japanese animé tapes and manga (Japanese comics). And in case you don't already have enough T-shirts, the store stocks a huge inventory of shirts reflecting its many different products. Also in South Anchorage, at the Dimond Center mall, 907/349-3963; and in Eagle River, 11401 Old Glenn Hwy., 907/696-5166. (West Anchorage)

CHARLIE'S ALASKA TRAINS
410 G St.
Anchorage
907/278-7246

Got a train nut in your family? Stop in at this shop, which carries the largest line of Alaska Railroad souvenir items in the state: videos, books, T-shirts, spikes, lanterns, clocks, jackets, whistles, cups, and more. The owner hand-paints all train cars and does custom work as well. Trains from Z scale to G scale are available. (Downtown)

GREAT ALASKAN BOWL COMPANY
1038 W. Fourth Ave.
Anchorage
907/278-2695 or 800-770-4222
www.woodbowl.com

As the name suggests, this store has an enormous selection of bowls, all made in Alaska. Some of these wooden creations are "knotty but nice," while others are sleek and smooth, suitable for a dinner-party Caesar salad or for anything else you care to put in them. The shop also offers items such as birch steins, cutting boards, ulus, candles, baking mixes by Ah!Laska, chocolate-covered wild-berry candies, coffees, Alaskan herb teas, and Alaskan "snow soap." ♿ (Downtown)

GREAT HARVEST BREAD CO.
570 E. Benson Blvd.

Anchorage
907/274-3331

This place makes utterly delicious breads from flour that's ground fresh daily. If you're looking for picnic or in-room fare, make this one of your first stops. Most of the breads are no-fat and the rest are low-fat, yet they all taste great. The menu changes daily, but standard 2.2-pound loaves include honey white, honey–whole wheat, onion dill–rye, cinnamon-swirl, sunflower-millet, and tomato-basil. In the morning pick up some scones or breakfast rolls; if you've been very, very good, indulge in some of the wonderful cookies. Not sure what you want? They'll make it easy on you: As soon as you walk in the door, a counter person will ask, "May I offer you a slice of fresh bread?" Hard to refuse an offer like that. (West Anchorage)

IDITAROD GIFT SHOP
Northway Mall
3101 Penland Pkwy.
Anchorage
907/276-7533

Need a "Sled Dog Crossing" sign, mushing gear, shirts with images of the Last Great Race, a set of dog booties, a toy husky and dogsled, or an Iditarod video? It's all here, and then some. The store has a bunch of books on the history of the race and the people—and dogs—who run it. As they say, the greatest athletes in the world run naked, eat raw meat, and sleep in the snow (referring to the dogs, not the mushers, of course). Also downtown, at Fifth Avenue Mall, 907/276-2350. (East Anchorage)

THE MAPS PLACE
601 W. 36th Ave.

Anchorage
907/562-7277

Planning to trek around the state? Drop in for a map first. The store has maps of every conceivable place, both national and international. (West Anchorage)

THE McMAC SHOPPE
1083 W. 25th Ave.
Anchorage
907/276-0585

This tiny, friendly shop is full of Scottish, Irish, and Welsh imports, including sweaters, tweed hats, jewelry, china, Celtic gifts, and tartan fabric. (West Anchorage)

NATURAL PANTRY
601 E. Dimond Blvd.
Anchorage
907/522-4330

Forgot your herbal tea? Ran out of gorp fixings? This independently owned shop can help. A nice selection of healthy fare, including lots of bulk-buy goodies that let you tailor the trail mix to suit your own tastes. The store also offers vitamins, herbs, body-care products, and a takeout deli and bakery. (South Anchorage)

RAE'S HARNESS SHOP
401 W. International Airport Rd.
Anchorage
907/563-3411

This store has great stuff for your pets, including skijoring and dog-mushing equipment. Dogs on leashes (and not in heat) can shop with their owners—and get free treats! (West Anchorage)

SOURDOUGH NEWS & TOBACCO
735 W. Fourth Ave.
Anchorage
907/274-6397

Downtown's only newsstand sells

papers imported from the far reaches of Seattle and New York City, along with other periodicals and cigars, pipe tobacco, and domestic and imported cigarettes. (Downtown)

STEWART'S PHOTO SHOP
531 W. Fourth Ave.
Anchorage
907/272-8581
An Anchorage institution, this downtown shop has a friendly, knowledgeable staff who will sell you the right kind of film, camera, or other photographic equipment. The store also stocks bulk jade as well as finished jade items. (Downtown)

SHOPPING MALLS

Anchorage malls aren't quite as huge as the ones in the Lower 48, but they serve their purpose. They're particularly vital in winter, when cabin-fevered parents of small children appreciate an open space. And, of course, teen-mating rituals occur in Anchorage malls, just as they do in malls everywhere.

But some things do set our shopping centers apart. Your local galleria may not have drugstores that sell guns. Nor will it boast a shop called the Iditarod Checkpoint, which offers "Sled Dog

Crossing" signs and other collectibles having to do with the Last Great Race.

Mall souvenir stores sell marvelous remembrances of your trip north, as well as some goofy stuff that you'll probably buy just for the fascination factor. Moose-poop swizzle sticks and "Earthquake in a Can" spring to mind.

ANCHORAGE FIFTH AVENUE MALL
320 W. Fifth Ave.
Anchorage
907/258-5535
This downtown mall has some nifty shops, such as the Museum Store, the Nature Source, Iditarod Checkpoint, Katherine the Great, and the Body Shop. Mail your postcards at the postal service center, and if you're in a hurry for lunch—or traveling on a budget—check out the top-floor food court. (Downtown)

DIMOND CENTER
800 E. Dimond Blvd.
Anchorage
907/344-2581
This is the largest mall in Alaska, with more than 170 stores and attractions as well as business offices. In addition to gifts, clothing, and food emporia, the mall also has a post office, library, skating rink, bowling alley, fitness club, and nine-screen movie theater. (South Anchorage)

THE MALL AT SEARS
600 E. Northern Lights Blvd.
Anchorage
907/264-6695
Sears, obviously, anchors this mall. You can also go to the bank for extra cash or get your pictures developed in 59 minutes. At the Carrs Quality Center grocery store, you can stock up on traveling supplies—everything from sunscreen to Chinese takeout and fresh fruit. And Roscoe's Skyline Restaurant, one of the city's two soul-food eateries, recently relocated here. (West Anchorage)

NORTHWAY MALL
3101 Penland Pkwy.
Anchorage
907/276-5520
This small, serviceable mall has Lamonts and Office Max as anchors, as well as standouts like the Iditarod Gift Shop, Gulliver's Used Books, and slot-car racing at Chilly Willy's. It also has a bank and a grocery store, too. (East Anchorage)

UNIVERSITY CENTER
3901 Old Seward Hwy.
Anchorage
907/562-0347
Anchor stores here are the family-clothing store Lamonts and Safeway. The mall's other big attractions are Habitat Housewares and the University Cinemas, a six-plex movie theater. (West Anchorage)

Nikki Rooker/Powerline Trail

10

SPORTS AND RECREATION

Anchorage offers sports and recreation opportunities that people in other cities only dream of: mountains, forests, rivers, and lakes. Even developed areas of the city have plenty of "undiscovered country"—greenbelts and municipal parks with the stamp of wildness on them. Anchorage is the only big city in America with wolves living within its limits, to say nothing of moose, bears, lynx, and other critters.

Abundant snow allows for wintry pursuits like dogsledding, skijoring, snowshoeing, biathlon, skiing, and speed-skating. Mountain climbing, hiking, and backpacking opportunities draw visitors from all over the world—as does the chance to catch a 70-pound king salmon or a 300-plus-pound halibut.

To be sure, some residents and visitors prefer tamer acitivities like soccer, bicycling, tennis, and swimming. But, somehow, even ordinary sporting pursuits are different here. Where else do golfers regularly have to yield to moose on the greens?

SPECTATOR SPORTS

Baseball

Two city teams—the **Anchorage Glacier Pilots** (907/274-3627) and the **Anchorage Bucs** (907/561-2827)—take on teams from Palmer, Fairbanks, Kenai, and Hawaii. The baseball is semi-pro, the playing field is real grass, the grandstand is made of wood, and the tickets are cheap (six dollars or less). After games, spectators can come down on the field to greet

Women-Only Adventures

Women who are interested in the outdoors can find female-only adventures with several specialty outfitters, including the following:

Alaska Women of the Wilderness *has numerous classes and trips for women of all ages. Options include rock climbing, kayaking, Elderhostel and girls' camps, glacier excursions, hikes, and more—including a trek to Nepal. Custom trips and programs can also be arranged. For more information contact 907/688-2226 or akwow@alaska.net.*

Equinox Wilderness Expeditions *plans women's backcountry trips to places like Tongass National Forest, Wrangell–St. Elias National Park, the Alaska Maritime National Wildlife Refuge, and the Arctic National Wildlife Refuge. Custom trips can also be arranged to places such as the Brooks Range, Denali National Park, Kachemak Bay, and the Round Island State Game Sanctuary. For more information contact 907/274-9087, equinox@alaska.net, or www.equinoxexpeditions.com.*

Women's flyfishing classes and trips are offered by registered guide **Cecilia "Pudge" Kleinkauf**. *She offers fly-tying classes and float-tubing in town, as well as weekend outings and camping trips at locations such as Kodiak Island and the Brooks River. Contact Kleinkauf at www.halcyon.com/wffn/, ckleinkauf@micronet.net, or 907/274-7113.*

players and get autographs. (Hang on to those signatures—former players include Tom Seaver, Mark McGwire, and Randy Johnson.) All in all, you'll have a great evening watching America's favorite pastime. The season runs from the beginning of June through the end of July. All games are played at Mulcahy Field at East 16th Avenue and Cordova Street.

Basketball

The University of Alaska fields teams in basketball, gymnastics, hockey, skiing (both Alpine and Nordic), cross-country, and volleyball. Every Thanksgiving weekend, the UAA men's basketball team hosts the **Carrs Great**

Alaska Shootout, one of only two NCAA preseason college basketball tournaments. Eight teams compete for the trophy, and top-notch talent flies north, including such teams as Purdue, Duke, Seton Hall, Michigan State, and UCLA. The annual UAA women's basketball tournament, the **Northern Lights Invitational**, recently merged with the Shootout. In this contest, four women's teams compete for top honors. Recent visitors include teams from Tennessee, Pepperdine, Texas A&M, and Wisconsin. The Shootout takes place at Sullivan Arena, 1600 Gambell Street.

Hockey

Among university teams, the biggest draw is the **UAA Seawolves** hockey team (907/786-1293), a Division I team in the Western Collegiate Hockey Association. Home games are played at Sullivan Arena, 1600 Gambell Street. Most other sporting events take place at the UAA Sports Center, east of the intersection of 36th Avenue and Lake Otis Parkway.

The Anchorage Aces, 907/258-2237, play professional hockey (West Coast Hockey League) from October through April for a total of 64 games. Half those games are on the road, and the other half are played at Sullivan Arena. The atmosphere is both hockey-mad and family-friendly—you can take your best college buddy, a date, or your small children. Ticket prices of $8 to $12 make the games even more attractive, as do special promotions like prize giveaways.

Sled-Dog Racing

During the annual Iditarod in March, tough racers and even tougher dogs mush through some of the most rugged and beautiful country on Earth. Beginning in Anchorage and ending in Nome, this 1,150-mile, 10-to-17-day trip is followed by fans all over the world, through news reports, the Iditarod home page, and even by telephone—the folks staffing the lines at headquarters frequently get international calls.

The Iditarod is a commemoration of the serum run of 1925, when relays of dog mushers raced diphtheria serum to Nome. The first race took place in 1973, and the contest has evolved from a let's-go-camping lark into an international sporting event, with mushers showing up from Australia and England. Some racers are professional mushers with major kennels, while

If you catch a fish, you can take home more than a proud photograph. Local companies will pack the fish in ice and ship it home for you by express delivery. You can also get your catch smoked or cured into kippers or lox. Look in the Yellow Pages under "Fish & Seafood" and "Fish Smoking & Curing."

Anchorage actually adds snow to the street twice a year, for the Iditarod start and the Fur Rendezvous World Championship Sled Dog Race.

others are folks living out their fantasies with borrowed dogs and plenty of enthusiasm.

The race's ceremonial start takes place on the first Saturday in March in downtown Anchorage. (The mushers go only as far as Eagle River; the actual start of the race takes place the following day in Wasilla.) Because it's an exciting and accessible event, it draws thousands of locals and visitors; if you're among them, bring plenty of film, dress in layers to stay warm, and show up early to get a good spot along Fourth Avenue.

The scene is unlike anything you could imagine. Trucks and vans disgorge sleds, dogs, and gear bags. Mushers greet fans and try to calm their excited teams. Celebrity racers such as Martin Buser, DeeDee Jonrowe, Rick Swenson, and Jeff King are besieged by well-wishers. And everywhere, of course, are the dogs: howling, sniffing, pacing, tangling lines, wagging tails, and smiling at everyone.

If you're in the mood for a real adventure, check out the Iditarider program. The winning bidders in a special telephone auction get to ride in a musher's sled for the first eight to nine miles. The bidding begins the first Monday of November and ends on the last Friday in January at 5 p.m.

Kayaking on Alaskan rapids

Alaska Division of Tourism

Alaska Standard Time (note: Alaska Standard Time is four hours behind Eastern Standard Time). For information, call 800/566-SLED.

Or consider becoming an Iditarod volunteer. Numerous people from the Lower 48 and other countries come to help out, whether at a remote checkpoint or at race headquarters, located in the Regal Alaskan, one of the city's nicest hotels. To find out more about volunteer opportunities, contact the **Iditarod Trail Committee**, P.O. Box 980900, Wasilla, AK 99687-0800, 907/376-5155, iditarod@iditarod.com. For more information on the race itself or the Iditarider program, visit www.iditarod.com.

RECREATION

Alpine Skiing

Located 40 miles south of Anchorage, **Alyeska Resort**, 1000 Arlberg Drive, Girdwood, 907/754-1111, www.alyeskaresort.com, is the lowest-elevation ski area in North America, which means you can come here straight from the airport and strap on your skis—none of that pesky breathlessness that comes from traveling up into the hills. Of course, you may feel a bit giddy at the 3,939-foot summit, but that's because of the gorgeous view (*Condé Nast Traveler* named it the best view from any ski site in North America). Alyeska has nine lifts, including a 60-passenger aerial tram in addition to the usual chairs, quads, and ponies. A total of 62 runs are available; 71 percent of the terrain is considered intermediate, with 12 percent beginner and 17 percent advanced. More than 2,000 feet of lighted vertical terrain lets you ski well past sundown. Cross-country trails are also maintained, and Alyeska is probably one of the few ski resorts in America at which Nordic skiers are warned to watch out for dogsled teams.

Alyeska Ski School, affiliated with the Professional Ski Instructors of America, offers lessons in Alpine, telemark, and cross-country skiing, along with snowboarding instruction. You heard that right—snowboarding is permitted, so by all means bring your kids. And if you forget to pack their snowboards, you can rent one (you can also rent skis and snowshoes). Other recreational activities that can be arranged through the resort are dogsledding, snowmachine touring, goldpanning, whitewater rafting, flightseeing, horseback riding, hiking, paragliding, skijoring, ice skating, glacier touring, fishing, and mountain biking. The resort also boasts the 300-room Westin

TRIVIA

The largest wild king salmon caught on the Kenai Peninsula weighed 97 pounds, four ounces. It was taken by Les Anderson on the Kenai River in 1985.

Alyeska Prince Hotel and a number of places to eat and drink, from quick-bite joints to a pair of Japanese restaurants to the ultra-classy Seven Glaciers Restaurant. A number of B&Bs operate in the area, too.

Hilltop Ski Area, 7015 Abbott Road, 907/346-1446, has nine different groomed sections, all of which are open to snowboarders. Additionally, Hilltop has a snowboard "terrain park" that includes a half-pipe, a tabletop, rail slides, and many natural bumps and slopes. Hilltop offers ski rentals, private lessons to all ages, group clinics, parent-and-child ski programs, school-break events, after-school skiing, and individual and team skiing and jumping through SPYDER (Sports Program for Youth Development, Education and Recreation). The area is generally open from November through April, but it may open sooner if snow falls early.

Curling

The "indoor sport with an outdoor attitude" has a lot of followers in Anchorage—enough, in fact, to have built their own club. Sir Walter Scott called curling "the manly Scottish exercise," but women play it, too. The season runs October through April for men's, women's, and co-ed leagues. The **Anchorage Curling Club** is located at 711 East Loop Road, 907/272-2825.

Fishing

Alaska has more than 100,000 lakes and more coastline than all of the Lower 48—and plenty of that water is in or near Anchorage. Most people think "salmon" when they think about fishing in Alaska, but you can also go after halibut, trout, grayling, pike, and other piscine pleasures.

Generally speaking, king-salmon season begins in spring and is finished by mid-summer. Sockeye-, pink-, and chum-salmon fishing comes next, followed by silver-salmon in late summer and fall. All five species are available in large numbers. However, limits or even temporary closures may be imposed in some areas if returning salmon numbers are low.

Anchorage may be the only city in the world that has a king-salmon fishery downtown—Ship Creek. Locals and excited tourists alike hook 40- and 50-pound kings here, in the shadow of hotels and office buildings.

Some people like to carry pepper spray to protect themselves against bears in the wild. You can buy the stuff at local sporting-goods and department stores. Make sure you know how to use it, however, so that you don't wind up squirting yourself. Keep in mind, too, that the spray isn't a completely foolproof deterrent. As one local joke goes, "It'll just make the bear think he's eating Cajun tonight."

Bicycling along Knik Arm

Silver- and king-salmon derbies at Ship Creek are wildly popular and offer cash prizes. Be sure to buy a derby ticket if you plan to fish.

The city also stocks half a dozen lakes—Cheney, Delong, Sand, Jewel, Taku, and Little Campbell—with trout and salmon. These aren't exactly trophy specimens, but visitors, especially kids, enjoy trying to limit-out on warm summer days. Campbell Creek is open to salmon fishing at selected times. Great fishing is also available in the nearby Mat-Su Valley and just a few hours away on the Kenai Peninsula, home of a world-class king-salmon fishery (see Chapter 13, Day Trips).

Halibut are available at different times in different areas outside Anchorage. "Barn-door" specimens can weigh upwards of several hundred pounds—fish so massive and strong that you have to shoot them before you can bring them onto the boat. (Honest!)

When fishing in salt water, use medium- to heavyweight tackle (line strength from 20 to 100 pounds). In most freshwater spots, use light to medium tackle (8 to 20 pounds). In crowded "combat fishing" areas, use 20- to 40-pound tackle that will help you control the fish more quickly.

You can purchase a nonresident sport-fishing license for 1, 3, 14, or 365 days, for fees ranging from $10 to $100. Licenses are sold at groceries, drugstores, sporting-goods shops, and other locations around town. If you're going after king salmon, you'll also need a king-salmon tag, good for 1, 3, or 365 days; fees range from $10 to $100.

For more information and fishing regulations, check out the **Alaska Department of Fish and Game** home page at www.state.ak.us/local/akpages/FISH.GAME/ or call 800/874-8202. Or you can write to the **Division of Sport Fish**, P.O. Box 25526, Juneau, AK 99802-5526 (specify regulations for Region II).

T I P

If you want a really adventurous ski experience, with a ski run ranging from 2,000 to 5,000 vertical feet, consider a trip with Chugach Powder Guides, a heliskiing outfit. For more information, call 907/783-4354.

Didn't bring any tackle or not sure where to go? You can buy a package from a professional service (look in the Yellow Pages under "Fishing Guides" or "Fishing Parties"). The company will provide everything from the boat to the bait, and guides will even thread those li'l fish eggs onto the hooks if you're squeamish about such things.

You can also hire a flying service to take you quickly to where the fish are biting. Companies like **Ketchum Air Service**, 800/433-9114 or 907/243-5525, info@ketchumair.com, and **Rust's Flying Service**, 800/544-2299 or 907/243-1595, info@flyrusts.com, offer guided and self-guided day fishing. The services do a lot of the work for you by providing transportation, tackle, hip boots, lunch, a fishing license, and boats for lake fishing. Costs vary widely, depending on the location of the trip and amenities.

Watch for the "Fishing Report" every Friday in the *Anchorage Daily News*. The report includes a feature story and information on conditions and closings in local, area, and remote fisheries. The "Sunday Outdoors" section offers tips, in-depth features, and columns on the pleasures of fishing.

Golf

Golf is as popular here as it is in the rest of the country—maybe even more so. One local course reports 37,000 rounds played during the summer, more than some courses see all year. Fortunately, Alaska gets so much daylight in summer that everyone will get a turn. (Keep in mind, though, that a late spring or early winter may shorten the playing season.) For their part, visitors get to say that they've played golf in Alaska. With any luck, a moose will wander across the course, and they'll get to tell everyone back home about that, too.

If luck is with you, and clouds are not, you'll get an absolutely gorgeous view of Mount McKinley, the highest peak in North America, from the **Anchorage Golf Course**, 3651 O'Malley Road, 907/522-3363. The mountain happens to be 135 air miles from Anchorage, but you'll swear it's just an easy drive away. Speaking of driving: If you whack a ball too hard, walking into the trees to find it will make you feel like you're in the middle of the wilderness. The 18-hole course is beautiful, if hilly, and par 72. Daily opening and closing times vary but can be as early as 5 a.m. and as late as 11 p.m.

HIKING TRAILS

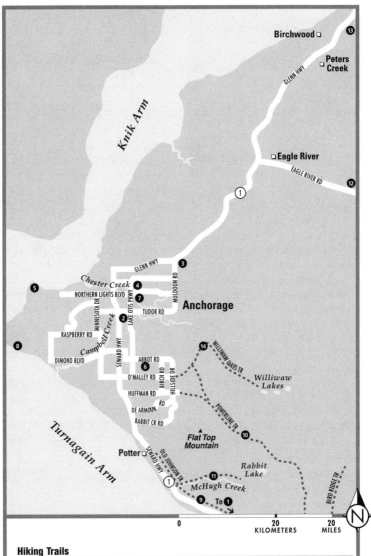

Hiking Trails

1 Bird Ridge
2 Campbell Creek Greenbelt
3 Centennial Park
4 Chester Creek Greenbelt
5 Coastal Trail

6 Far North Bicentennial Park
7 Goose Lake
8 Kincaid Park
9 Old Johnson Trail
10 Powerline Trail

11 Rabbit and McHugh Lakes
12 Rodak Nature Trail/Albert Loop Trail
13 Thunderbird Falls Trail
14 Williwaw Lakes

Alyeska Resort, p. 159

(depending on the daylight) mid-May through mid-October. The fee is $27 for residents, $40 for non-residents. Acclaimed designer Robert Trent Jones created **Eagleglen** on Elmendorf Air Force Base, 907/552-3821, an 18-hole, par-72 course. It's largely a traditional design that one golf fan described as "architectural and mostly sculptured." You'll also get the chance to hit a couple of holes across Ship Creek, which means you can watch for salmon. The course is open May to mid-October daily from 5:15 a.m. to 9 p.m. (depending on weather). The fee is $32—$25 after 8 p.m.—with discounts for military personnel.

Moose Run Golf Course, 27000 Arctic Valley Road, 907/428-0056, is a serene, out-in-the-woods course with no highway or aircraft distractions. Heavily wooded, the course has a challenging layout, with a chance for skilled golfers to go for the big shot. It's nicely maintained and, incidentally, no more overrun with moose than any other course in Anchorage. Moose Run has 18 holes and is par 72. Hours are Monday through Friday 7 a.m. to 9 p.m., Saturday and Sunday 6 a.m. to 9 p.m. mid-May through September (depending on weather). The fee is $28—$20 after 5 p.m.—with discounts for military personnel.

Weather too bad to venture out of doors? Keep your swing limber on golf simulators at **Full Swing Golf of Alaska**, 9360 Old Seward Highway, 907/344-4653, featuring 21 world-renowned courses such as Pebble Beach, Bountiful, and Innisbrook; or at **Par T Golf**, 1307 East 74th Avenue, 907/344-5717, with eight famous simulated courses, including St. Andrew's, Coeur d'Alene, and Spyglass.

Hiking within Anchorage

Even if you're just meandering along in-town trails in Anchorage, you can quickly become lost if you walk off the path. Two rules, then: Stay on the pavement, and let someone know where you're going and when you should be back. Be good enough to let that person know when you have returned, too, so he or she doesn't send out a search party.

Okay, one more rule: Hike with other people if at all possible. There is safety in numbers. If you were to turn an ankle, you might wait a long, long time for someone to come along and help you—and there's no guarantee that anyone would.

It's also imperative that you dress for different kinds of weather. You'll need layers of clothing, sturdy shoes, and rain gear, even if it's sunny when you start out. A sudden rain shower could put you at risk for hypothermia, a life-threatening condition in which your body's core temperature drops precipitously. Carry snacks and plenty of water for each person. Never drink from a stream, or even from snowmelt, because giardia will certainly ruin a vacation.

Be prepared for animal confrontations, which can turn from a photo opportunity into a real problem. You're likely to see moose, which look goofy and gentle. But people have been injured and even killed by these animals, so give them a wide berth. You may also see bears, both within the city limits and in outlying areas. Bears will usually make an effort to avoid you, so give them plenty of chances—sing, talk loudly, bang sticks together, or wear

---

Multi-use Trails

A number of multi-use trails, some with facilities, are found in Far North Bicentennial, Centennial, Hillside, Kincaid, and Muldoon Parks. Look for the following maintained winter trails:

- **Abbott Road Trail:** *This eight-mile trail runs from Campbell Creek Park to Service High and DeArmoun Road.*
- **Baxter Road Trail:** *A two-mile skip along the east side of Baxter Road from Nunaka Valley Park to Tudor Road.*
- **Bragaw Road Trail:** *This one-and-a-half mile roadway leads from Clark Junior High to East High School.*
- **Lanie Fleischer Chester Creek Trail:** *A four-mile path from Westchester Lagoon to Goose Lake Park.*
- **Delaney Park Loop:** *This two-mile loop runs around the Park Strip between 9th and 10th Avenues and A and P Streets.*
- **Jewel Lake Trail:** *A three-mile path along Jewel Lake Road. South Anchorage Trail: This three-mile path leads from Campbell Creek Park to Johns Park.*
- **C Street Trail:** *A 2.5-mile trot along the west side of C Street from Dimond Boulevard to 36th Avenue.*
- **Campbell Creek Greenbelt/Taku Park:** *A three-mile path from Dimond Boulevard to the Old Seward Highway.*
- **Tony Knowles Coastal Trail:** *11 miles of multi-use trail from Second Avenue to Kincaid Park.*

Top Ten Reasons to Run the Iditarod
by Martin Buser, three-time winner of the Iditarod

1. Possibility of making $50,000 for 10 days of work.
2. Get to consume 6,000 calories a day and never gain a pound.
3. Roller-coaster ride down the Dalzell Gorge at no extra cost.
4. You can fall asleep in the middle of dinner for days after the race and no one thinks you're rude.
5. Chance to vacation with your 16 best friends—and they do all the driving.
6. Stay awake for 10 days straight for the first time since college.
7. Frozen poppyseed muffins—yum, yum.
8. See the yellow eyes of wolves watch as you pass by in the middle of the night.
9. Great opportunity to hallucinate without drugs.
10. Free face-lift, compliments of the blizzards of Norton Sound.

a "bear bell" on your pack. Avoid areas of dense vegetation, particularly during berry season in late summer—a bear may suddenly stand up after a snooze in the bushes. With these rules in mind, head for one of the following trails in-town:

- **Far North Bicentennial Park**, off Abbott Road, offers 18 miles of trails through wooded areas, with excellent views and wildlife photo opportunities. There are no rest facilities, and trails are not maintained.
- **Campbell Creek Greenbelt**, located at Lake Otis Parkway and Tudor Road, offers 18 acres of parkland with hiking trails along the creek. Watch for salmon spawning here in fall. Trails are maintained, but there are no rest facilities.
- **Centennial Park**, off Glenn Highway near Muldoon Road, has three miles of trails in a wooded area with some hilly terrain. A kilometer of ski trail is lighted at night.
- The **Chester Creek Greenbelt** consists of 13 miles of paved trail running from East Northern Lights Boulevard to Westchester Lagoon. The trail is suitable for hiking, but watch out for cyclists and in-line skaters (and skiers, in season).
- The **Coastal Trail**, 10 miles of paved trail along the coast, runs from downtown at Second Avenue to Kincaid Park in West Anchorage. The trail is excellent for biking and skiing, with scenic views. Rest facilities are available.

- **Goose Lake**, located off East Northern Lights Boulevard and UAA Drive, consists of 90 acres of parkland with views of the Chugach Mountains. The maintained trails are adjacent to Alaska Pacific University trails. Rest facilities are available.
- **Kincaid Park**, at the extreme west end of Raspberry Road, is a 1,400-acre park with additional access via the Tony Knowles Coastal Trail. The park includes 30 miles of varied-terrain trails. Its maintained trails are good for skiing, hiking, orienteering, and jogging.

Hiking Wilder Trails

Some of these trails are "wilder" in name only—i.e., not within the city. People with no experience, even children, can enjoy hiking in Alaska if they pick an easy route like Thunderbird Falls or the Rodak Nature Trail. Even so, the same safety precautions described previously apply.

You can travel up to 11 miles each way on the easy-to-moderate **Powerline Trail**, an old road bed. You'll experience an elevation gain of 1,300 feet. Access is at Glen Alps (take Upper Huffman to Toilsome Hill Road).

On the 13-mile (round trip) **Williwaw Lakes** hike, you'll view several alpine lakes in the shadow of Mount Williwaw (5,445 feet). The hike has relatively little elevation gain and wonderful scenery. Access is via Glen Alps (take Upper Huffman to Toilsome Hill Road) or Prospect Heights (take Upper O'Malley to Prospect Drive).

The trail at **Rabbit and McHugh Lakes** is set in alpine tundra, with the rugged Suicide Mountain peaks as a backdrop. The trail distance is seven miles each way, with a total elevation gain of 2,750 feet. It's a moderately difficult hike. Access is via the McHugh Creek Trailhead (Mile 112 of the Seward Highway).

The **Old Johnson Trail** is nine miles each way, with minimal elevation gain but moderate difficulty. The trail provides wonderful views of Turnagain Arm (and, hopefully, beluga whales) along with Dall sheep and moose. Access is at the Potter Historic Site (Mile 115.5 of the Seward Highway), McHugh Creek Wayside (Mile 112 of the Seward Highway), Rainbow (Mile 108.5 of the Seward Highway), Windy Corner (Mile 106.5 of the Seward Highway), and Falls Creek (Mile 105.5 of the Seward Highway).

Bird Ridge, a steep, 1.5-mile trail, leads to a fabulous view of Turnagain Arm. Your legs may complain

Cross-country skiing

Anchorage CVB

but your eyes will thank you! Bring a camera for the view, the wildflowers, and (possibly) the Dall sheep. You can climb as high as 3,500 feet if you like. Access is at Mile 101.4 of the Seward Highway; look for the trail sign.

Just about anyone can hike **Thunderbird Falls Trail**, a one-mile trail over rolling terrain, and enjoy the 200-foot falls at the end. Access is via the Thunderbird Falls exit at Mile 25 of the Glenn Highway.

The **Rodak Nature Trail** runs just two-thirds of a mile along a graveled, wheelchair-accessible path. The salmon-rearing stream has a viewing deck. Nearby, **Albert Loop Trail** is a three-mile trip that's easy but sometimes muddy (watch for wildlife tracks!). Access to both trails is at the Eagle River Visitor Center.

Horseback Riding

Alaska Wilderness Outfitters, 7015 Abbott Road, 907/344-2434, offers guided trail rides for $30 to $35 per hour. Day rides through Johnson Pass for groups of five or more cost $150 (including lunch and beverages). **Snowy Mountain Ranch**, at Mile 2.7 of the Buffalo Mine Road, Palmer, 907/745-8270, offers guided trail rides costing $20 for the first hour, $15 for each additional hour. Overnight outings and guided wilderness trips for wildlife viewing are also available.

Hunting

Alaska is home to 14 species of big-game animals spread among 365,000,000 acres. Densities are much lower than hunters from the Lower 48 expect, however, and many species engage in vast migrations. So it's important to figure out the best time and place to find the animal you're after.

From Anchorage, hunting is available a short drive out of town. Some visitors prefer to charter flight services for fly-in hunting, either as a camping trip or at a hunting lodge. Generally speaking, day or weekend hunts aren't feasible, due to unpredictable weather and animal behavior. Try to allow at least five days for your trip, preferably longer. The more time you have, the better you'll be able to deal with the variables.

A non-resident hunting license costs $85; non resident aliens must pay

$300. Depending on the species you're after, you may also need to buy a tag. For more information on hunting, check out the **Alaska Department of Fish and Game** Web page at www.state.ak.us/local/akpages/FISH.GAME/. The site offers tips on animals, restrictions, rifles, ammunition, clothing, camping gear, and other essentials. For information on licenses by mail, write to the **Alaska Department of Revenue, Division of Fish and Game Licensing**, P.O. Box 25525, Juneau, AK 99802-5525.

Ice Skating

The city hot-mops four lakes—Goose, Cheney, Spenard, and Jewel—all winter long. The most popular skating, however, takes place at **Westchester Lagoon**, near 13th Avenue and U Street, where hundreds of folks show up every winter weekend for a community skating party. No matter how cold it gets, you'll see people of all ages, including plenty of families, skating on the large open area and along a network of meandering trails cut through the snow. Warming barrels are provided, and local radio stations broadcast live from the site. The espresso trucks sell plenty of coffee and hot chocolate, too.

If you're interested in speed, the **Alaska Speedskating Club** and the city maintain a speedskating oval at Wendler Middle School, 2905 Lake Otis Parkway, from December through March. The facilities are occasionally reserved for club practices but are usually available for public use free of charge.

Finally, you can enjoy indoor skating at **Ben Boeke Indoor Ice Arenas**, 334 East 16th Avenue, 907/274-5715; **Dempsey-Anderson Ice Arena**, 1741 West Northern Lights Boulevard, 907/277-7571; and Dimond Ice Chalet, Dimond Center, 800 East Dimond Boulevard, 907/344-1212.

Women's Nautilus Club

Tired of exercising with men in the room? You won't have to worry about it at Women's Nautilus Club, 1920 West Dimond Boulevard, 907/349-7878. The club has numerous treadmills, stairsteppers, recumbent bikes, and Nordic Tracks, along with a free-weight room, aerobics classes, saunas, steam rooms, and an espresso bar. At each fitness station, you can plug in headphones to listen to radio or TV programs. There's another Women's Nautilus Club in West Anchorage, at 207 East Northern Lights Boulevard, 907/278-2211.

Mountain Climbing

The Chugach Range offers numerous recreational opportunities, from family climbs to complicated ascents. Remember all the dangers and safety precautions noted in the "Hiking" section? They apply here, too—and then some since whenever you climb something there's the danger of falling. Even experienced alpinists have been unpleasantly surprised by slippery, slithery scree and rocks underfoot (called "Chugach crud"). Watch where you put your feet, and, by all means, climb with at least one other person.

Wear or bring layers of clothing to deal with temperature changes, and make sure your outer layer is extremely waterproof. The weather here can get pretty ugly pretty quickly, and you don't want to get caught short. Remember, too, to bring some high-energy snacks (chocolate, nuts, dried fruits, bagels, and the like) and a large bottle of water for each climber. There are no services at any of these mountains, and dehydration and low blood sugar will make your descent a lot more perilous.

Below are a few popular, easy-to-moderate climbs. You must first hike into some of these mountains, so get yourself a book like *55 Ways to the Wilderness in Southcentral Alaska* or *Walk-About Guide to Alaska: Volume One*. Such books offer very specific instructions on how to find your way and also tell you what it is you're seeing (Knik Arm versus Turnagain Arm, the names of nearby mountains, etc.).

Little kids climb **Flattop** with their families all the time, but it's still no mountain for sissies. The 1,550 feet of elevation gain include some steep areas and rock scrambling. For a three-and-a-half–mile round trip, your reward is a terrific view of Anchorage, plus bragging rights about climbing a mountain in Alaska. Access is at Glen Alps—take Upper Huffman to Toilsome Hill Road and follow the well-defined trail.

McHugh Peak offers mostly hiking, but some rock scrambling as well, for a 4,201-foot elevation gain. Round trip, the climb is about seven miles. Don't forget your camera and your binoculars. Access is at McHugh Creek Wayside, Mile 112 of the Seward Highway.

Wolverine Peak includes 3,380 feet of elevation gain in a 10.5-mile round trip. You'll get terrific views of the city, Cook Inlet, and the Alaska Range. Don't forget your camera! Access is at Prospect Heights (take Upper O'Malley to Prospect Drive). Follow the trail east from the parking area, turn left on the powerline, continue to the South Fork of Campbell Creek, and, 1.1 miles later, follow a trail that goes off to the right and uphill.

The Ramp and **The Wedge** offer an 11-mile round trip that's doable by kids, since much of the "climb" is actually a hike in a brush-free and beautiful valley. The trip entails some rock scrambling and a stream crossing that can usually be accomplished on rocks. Watch for Dall sheep. Access is at Glen Alps (take Upper Huffman to Toilsome Hill Road). Follow the lower of two trails for half a mile to the advisory sign (avalanche, fire) near the powerline, turn right on the powerline, continue for about two miles, then turn left on the old jeep trail.

> Skijoring, an unusual sport that combines Nordic skiing and dog mush-
> ing, can be enjoyed at Centennial Park, Connors Lake, Far North Bicen-
> tennial Park, the Chester Creek Trail, and the Coastal Trail.

Rendezvous Peak, also climbable by kids and the inexperienced, is a
4,050-foot peak whose climb begins at the 2,550-foot mark. You'll get marvelous views of Mount McKinley (when it's out), Cook Inlet, Turnagain Arm,
the Ship Creek and Eagle River Valleys, and the city of Anchorage. It's great
fun to slide or roll part of the way down on the tundra-covered slopes. Access is at the Arctic Valley exit off Glenn Highway, about seven miles northeast of Anchorage. Proceed up the road to the civilian ski area. Note: This
peak is located on Fort Richardson, and therefore access may occasionally
be restricted or denied.

Mushing

Hourly to overnight mushing trips are available through **Birch Trails Adventures**, 22719 Robinson Road, Chugiak, 907/688-5713, thamill@micronet.net.
You'll have the chance to mush your own team, so be sure your companions bring a camera! Snacks are provided for short trips; meals and gear
provided for overnighters. Prices vary depending on the length of the trip.

Chugach Express, Girdwood, 907/783-2266, offers tours ranging from 20
minutes to two hours, available November through April, with a chance to
drive. Hot drinks and blankets are provided. Prices vary.

A family-run business north of Eagle River, **Mush-A-Dog Team**, 17620
Birchwood Loop, Chugiak, 907/688-1391, offers winter and summer mushing. In winter you'll enjoy a 20- to 30-minute ride followed by hot chocolate
or cider. In summer dogs pull carts on a track system, and you get a course
on the Gold Rush era along with panning for gold. Prices vary.

Redington Sled Dog Rides, Mile 12.5 of the Knik Road, Wasilla, 907/376-
6730, offers short day trips as well as overnighters with Raymie Redington, a
veteran Iditarod racer. Warm gear is provided if you don't have your own.
Prices vary.

Nordic Skiing

Groomed cross-country trails are maintained all winter long, with parallel
tracks set to one side. Skate skiers, runners, walkers, skijorers, and other
outdoor enthusiasts also use the trails. **Beach Lake Trail** has 10 miles of

groomed cross-country trails, two miles of which are lighted. **Campbell Creek Greenbelt** has three miles of trails stretching from Victor Road to Old Seward Highway. **Chester Creek Greenbelt/Goose Lake**, a ski/running trail, stretches about six miles from Goose Lake (off Northern Lights Boulevard and UAA Drive) to Westchester Lagoon (off Minnesota and Hillcrest Drives). Edmunds Lake Trail offers 7.5 miles of ungroomed trail in Eagle River. **Kincaid Park** offers 30 miles of maintained cross-country trails, 16 of them illuminated until 11 p.m. Note: Gates into Kincaid close at 9 every evening. **Russian Jack Springs Park** contains more than three miles of trails, some lighted, connecting to Chester Creek Trail.

The **Nordic Ski Association** is involved in a number of volunteer and service activities around Anchorage. It also hosts ski tours, including the extremely popular Ski Trains, and sponsors a hotline so skiers can check trail conditions. For more information about the club, call 907-276-7609. For trail information, dial 907/248-6667. Trail conditions are also updated weekly and published in the *Anchorage Daily News*.

Alaska Dance Theatre/Cathy Hart Photography

11

PERFORMING ARTS

Yes, the performing arts do exist in Anchorage—theater, opera, dance, and classical and other types of music. In fact, these art forms are more accessible here than they are in many big cities: It's easy to get tickets, people feel safe walking back to their cars at night, and the city's casual dress code lets you attend a show or concert without worrying about whether you packed the "right" clothes for the occasion.

The scene continues to offer a mix of durable fare like Oklahoma *and* The King and I *with riskier, in-your-face productions like* How I Learned to Drive *and* Pounding Nails in the Floor with My Forehead. *Lately, companies and presenters have leaned toward the tried and true, possibly due to reduced funding for the arts. Even so, risks are still being taken and the result is often pleasing, if uncomfortable for certain segments of the audience.*

THEATER

ANCHORAGE COMMUNITY THEATRE
Alaska Pacific University
Grant Hall Theater
University Dr.
Anchorage
907/344-4713
Anchorage's oldest theater company was founded in 1945 as the Anchorage Little Theatre when a group

of theater buffs got together to create some live entertainment. By 1953 three local arts leaders changed the name to Anchorage Community Theatre, with an eye toward creating a training ground for performers. It wasn't all local talent, though—performers included Boris Karloff in *Arsenic and Old Lace*, Will Rogers Jr. in *Ah, Wilderness*, Theresa Wright in *The Dark at the Top of the Stairs*, and Lee Sullivan in *Brigadoon*. In

Ernst Schneider/Alaska Division of Tourism

Alaska Center for the Performing Arts

Alaska Center for the Performing Arts
621 W. Sixth Ave.
Anchorage
907/272-1471
These shows tend to be big-budget dazzlers such as *Tommy, Evita, Cats, Grease,* and *The Phantom of the Opera.* However, the association has also branched out into such lesser known shows as *Jelly Roll* and *Crazy for You.* (Downtown)

ECCENTRIC THEATRE CO.
Cyrano's Off Center Playhouse
Fourth Ave. and D St.
Anchorage
907/274-2599
A relatively recent addition to the Anchorage theater scene, Eccentric Theatre Co. is the very ambitious resident company of Cyrano's Off Center Playhouse. ECT doesn't shrink from darker, thought-provoking pieces such as *Metamorphosis, American Buffalo, Oleanna, Glengarry Glen Ross, How I Learned to Drive,* and *A Delicate Balance.* But it also does justice to shows such as *Mass Appeal, Dancing at Lughnasa, The Faith Healer,* and *The Fourposter.* Recent shows include *Moonlight,* the latest Harold Pinter play; *Having Our Say,* adapted from the best-selling book by the Delaney sisters; *Women of Will,* a show about Shakespeare's female characters; *Three Sisters,* the Lanford Wilson translation of Chekhov's work; *Libby,* developed from diaries and letters written by an Alaskan woman in 1879; and *Syd,* an original work by area-playwright Eric Wallace about the life and times of painter Sydney Laurence, who painted numerous awe-inspiring canvases of Mount McKinley (catch his work at the Anchorage Museum

fact, it was Karloff who really gave ACT a jump-start: He donated his professional fee to the fledgling organization. Nowadays, the talent is all homegrown, and the bill of fare tends to focus on crowd-pleasers like *The King and I, The Sound of Music, The Music Man, Oklahoma!,* and *Little Women.*

In the mid-1990s, the company became even sturdier under the guidance of artistic director Theresa Pond, a spirited young woman who could stretch a dollar beyond all reason, breathe new life into hoary old stage chestnuts like *A Christmas Carol,* and inspire even the youngest thespian into giving his all. After several years, Pond departed for grad school, leaving ACT in the hands of its previous artistic director—her father, Robert Pond. The company also conducts a thriving children's theater program and a summer theater camp. (East Anchorage)

BROADWAY & BEYOND
Anchorage Concert Association

of History and Art). The theater sometimes leases its stage for live theatrical or musical performances. It's a small place, lending a great degree of intimacy to shows—that's a good thing, generally, but if you don't want to sit too close to the action, it's best to get there early. ♿ (Downtown)

OUT NORTH CONTEMPORARY ART HOUSE
1325 Primrose St.
Anchorage

907/279-8200
www.outnorth.org
This nonprofit organization promotes a culturally diverse slate of performers. Recent shows include the Pomo Afro Homos, a gay African-American theater ensemble; Nuyorican Poets Cafe Live, performance poetry from New York's Lower East Side; the world premiere of *June Bride*, Sara Felder's compelling comic monologue (with juggling) about your average Jewish lesbian wedding; the British music-hall drag

---

It's Probably Happening at Cyrano's

In its first decade of operation, Cyrano's Off Center Playhouse, Fourth Avenue and D Street, 907/274-2599, made a major impact on the Anchorage arts scene. Also known as Cyrano's Books, it's in the same building with Bistro Bergerac (see Chapter 4, Where to Eat) and with a small cinema. The complex, in the heart of downtown, has hosted some of the city's best theater. Recognition came in the form of the 1997 Governor's Arts Award.

Owners Sandy and Jerry Harper are the nucleus of Eccentric Theatre Company, the resident ensemble at Cyrano's. Jerry Harper acts in or directs a number of ETC productions. The small theater frequently hosts productions by local directors and nationally known writers. Sometimes a local writer puts a play onstage, such as Syd, *the story of acclaimed artist Sydney Laurence, or* Johnny's Girl, *an autobiographical story about growing up in Anchorage with no mother and a criminal father.*

The tiny, intimate theater is a chameleon. It can be a chilly northern palace for a puppet production of The Snow Queen *or, with the addition of hundreds of pounds of sand, a blazing beach for* Seascape. *It can morph from an upper-class English drawing room into a Hoboken convent. If it needs to be a dockside bar, an Irish farmhouse, or a Maryland kitchen, it can be those things, too.*

Anchorage Symphony's Colorful History

The Anchorage Little Symphony premiered in 1946, providing background music for a production of A Christmas Carol. Now known as the Anchorage Symphony Orchestra, the organization has had a colorful past. Charter member and conductor Peter Britch also ran a bulldozer business, was a trapper, and built his own home.

When the Cold War brought an increased military presence to Alaska, performers rejoiced—at least some of those soldiers had to be musicians! And right they were. In 1949 four of the five woodwind players were from Fort Richardson. To keep the sound full and rich, the symphony had to request that base commanders not schedule maneuvers during concert weeks.

The municipal auditorium burned down in 1953, taking with it instruments, sheet music, and risers. It was rebuilt, however, and the symphony kept building, too. By 1960 the symphony had 45 musicians. During a performance with the Anchorage Civic Ballet, the musicians overflowed the orchestra pit and had to be placed in the aisles.

After the Good Friday Earthquake on March 27, 1964, musicians were expected to show up on time for rehearsal. They did, although in a

---

troupe Bloolips in *The Island of Lost Shoes*; a one-woman show called *Dona Rosita's Travelin' Jalapeno Kitchen*; and *Sugar Tit*, an exploration of African-American lives in music and dance.

Out North works to develop local talent with its annual "Under 30" performance competition. It also opens its stage to such works-in-progress as *Superbeast*, a solo performance by Alaska Native Donny Lee; and *No More*, Jill Bess's theater piece about rape and sexual abuse. Recently the organization has begun hosting live concerts by bands such as Sadhappy. Additionally, the Out

North gallery space has hosted installations such as *The Boy in the Boat*, kinetic sculptures by British artist Alan Turner; and *The Bone-Grass Boy: The Secret Banks of the Conejos River*, Ken Gonzales-Day's computer-enhanced historic-photo story based on Native American and Mexican-American cultures. Out North has also created ONSTAGE (Out North Student Theater Artists Gaining Experience), a creative-writing and performance project for at-risk teens. (East Anchorage)

UNIVERSITY OF ALASKA–ANCHORAGE

different place since their regular performance hall was so badly damaged. The next concert took place on April 28, with proceeds donated to the Salvation Army's earthquake relief efforts. The symphony received a telegram from Leonard Bernstein that read, "Bravo for your gallantry. Best wishes for a splendid concert tonight and warm greetings to you all."

In 1974 the orchestra received an NEA grant to travel to Kenai, Homer, and Kodiak. During the Kenai concert, the full orchestra sat on-stage waiting for an audience. But by 8:10 p.m., the only people seated were the bus driver, a musician's wife, and one Kenai family. When the music started, one of the family members stood up and said, "Excuse me, but this isn't the wrestling match, is it?" However, the bus driver and the wife did enjoy the show.

The current maestro, Randall Craig Fleischer, took over in the fall of 1999, after being an associate conductor at the National Symphony Orchestra in Washington, D.C. As a composer, Fleischer is interested in the fusion of rock and classical music. He has also co-authored several instructional works for children in collaboration with comedian Heidi Joyce. No word yet, however, on whether he plans to run a bulldozer, build his own home, or operate a trapline.

MAINSTAGE AND SECOND STAGE PRODUCTIONS
UAA Arts Building
Alumni Drive
Anchorage
907/786-1792

University theater majors get to do some of their "homework" on stage, in Mainstage and Second Stage productions. Second Stage shows are often one-act play festivals presented several times during the year. At least four Mainstage productions are performed annually; in recent years, shows have included *The Dragon*, a Russian allegory about totalitarian governments; *Five Women Wearing the Same Dress*, a comedy about bridesmaids; *A Piece of My Heart*, a drama about the women who served in Vietnam; *The Death of Von Richthofen as Witnessed from Earth*, a moody piece about the real-life Red Baron; *Arcadia*, the alternately romantic and mysterious drama by Tom Stoppard; and *Inspecting Carol*, a riotous satire about funding for the arts.

The department has also been involved in various community-oriented activities, such as the Canada Celebrates the Arts festival, the UAA/ATY Summer Theatre Conservatory for youth, and the Alaska

Native Plays Contest. Theater professor Michael Hood directed a version of *True West* with actors from Yuzho-Sakhalinsk, Russia, and the department also sent *A Piece of My Heart* to a Russian theater festival. & (East Anchorage)

VALLEY PERFORMING ARTS
Fred and Sara Machetanz Theatre
251 W. Swanson (off the
Parks Hwy.)
Wasilla
907/373-9500
www.akcache.com/vpa
Valley Performing Arts began with a 1976 production of *Harvey* in a former church building on the Alaska State Fairgrounds in Palmer. (Loyal theatergoers remember those days well—the church had no bathrooms!) In the summer of 1993, VPA converted their shop and storage building into a theater, and three years later they moved that building to its present location in Wasilla.

This nonprofit company produces six to seven shows each year, including new works by Alaskan playwrights whenever possible; recent offerings have included *Arcadia*, *The Master Builder*, *How to Eat Like a Child*, *Jake's Women*, and *How to Succeed in Business without Really Trying*. A typical season features a family play and at least one major musical. The company also sponsors Camp VPA, a summer theater program for kids.

CLASSICAL MUSIC AND OPERA

ALASKA AIRLINES AUTUMN/ WINTER CLASSICS
Alaska Pacific University
Grant Hall Theatre

University Dr.
Anchorage
907/747-6774
These two concert sets are offshoots of the world-famous Sitka Summer Music Festival. Founded in 1972, that festival has featured cellists Gregor Piatigorsky and Stephen Kates, violinist Christiaan Bor, and pianist Jerome Lowenthal, along with violinist and festival-founder Paul Rosenthal. It has also inspired some performers to begin special events of their own, including the Boston Chamber Music Society, the Seattle Chamber Music Festival, and the Barge Music Series. The Autumn/Winter Classics are six concerts in September and two in February. More than 75 musicians from all over the world have performed here. (East Anchorage)

ALASKA CHAMBER SINGERS
907/333-3500
www.alaska.net/~akcs/
This 40-voice ensemble performs both a cappella and accompanied, with an emphasis on classical works. The singers were featured in a 1996 broadcast of *A Prairie Home Companion* on National Public Radio, as well as in a 1997 series of concerts at the Kennedy Center in Washington, D.C. The ensemble performed the world premiere of *Shadows and Light: Reminiscences of Alaska,* a work based on the poetry of Robert Service. The ACS was the first American chorale to perform in Magadan, Russia, as part of a cultural exchange. It also collaborated with the Kamchatka Choir and the National Symphony Orchestra in Petropavlovsk-Kamchatsky in a performance of Prokofiev's *Alexander Nevsky*. Each year the

Anchorage Opera's 1997 production of Orpheus in the Underworld, *p. 180*

ACS performs winter and spring concerts at the Alaska Center for the Performing Arts, in addition to appearing at other special events. Visit the group's home page (see listing) and listen to "The Alaska Flag Song." (Zone varies with venue.)

ALASKA CHILDREN'S CHOIR
907/562-7006
This 160-voice ensemble celebrated its 20th anniversary in 1998. The choir has traveled far and wide, performing in Canada, England, Wales, Norway, Sweden, Denmark, Italy, Austria, and Germany. In addition to two major concerts of secular and sacred music each year at the Alaska Center for the Performing Arts, the choir collaborates with other local arts groups. Recent examples include *Tosca* and *Hansel and Gretel*, with the Anchorage Opera; *Benedicite* with the Alaska Chamber Singers; and *Carmina Burana* with the Anchorage Concert Chorus. (Zone varies with venue.)

ANCHORAGE CIVIC ORCHESTRA
(no phone)
This community-based orchestra consists of performers who play for the sheer joy of it. Some are young, some are old; some are professionals, some not. The 45-person orchestra presents a concert in November, a family show in February, and a spring concert in April, at the Alaska Center for the Performing Arts and a local high school. (Zone varies with venue.)

ANCHORAGE CONCERT ASSOCIATION
Alaska Center for the Performing Arts
621 W. Sixth St.
Anchorage
907/272-1471
This nonprofit corporation began almost 50 years ago as a strictly classical program. Over the years the ACA has expanded to include entertainment in a half-dozen different genres, from family fare to Broadway. Most of these internationally

acclaimed artists and attractions would never make it to Anchorage otherwise. Recent offerings include flutist James Galway, the New England Ragtime Ensemble, Tibetan Monks, Nuevo Caribe, Quartetto Gelato, the Mendelssohn String Quartet, the Moscow Men's Chorus, the Whirling Dervishes, the Musicians and Dancers of Bali, the Labeque Sisters, Denyce Graves, and the St. Petersburg Ice Ballet's *Romeo and Juliet.* Season tickets are available. ♿ (Downtown)

ANCHORAGE CONCERT CHORUS
Alaska Center for the Performing Arts
621 W. Sixth St.
Anchorage
907/274-7464
In 1947 members of church choirs around town came together to perform the *Messiah.* Fifty years later, the chorus is 160 voices strong and frequently collaborates with other groups, including the Anchorage Symphony Orchestra, the Alaska Dance Theatre, and the Alaska Chil-

XSIGHT! Performance Group at the Out North Contemporary Art House, p. 175

William Frederking/XSIGHT! Performance Company

dren's Choir. The chorus has traveled to Australia, New Zealand, Great Britain, Germany, Austria, Hungary, Czechoslovakia, Russia, Canada, and the Lower 48 (including Lincoln Center and Carnegie Hall). A typical season includes two pops concerts (holiday and family), a classical concert, and a major choral piece. ♿ (Downtown)

ANCHORAGE FESTIVAL OF MUSIC
Alaska Center for the Performing Arts
621 W. Sixth St.
Anchorage
907/276-2465
The annual Summer Series is a mix of instrumental and choral performances with professional workshops and master classes. The 1999 program included Verdi's *Requiem,* a program of chamber music called "Vivaldi & Vienna"; a chamber and choral affair featuring the San Jose Symphonic Choir; and "Instrumental Interludes," a mix of Alaskan musicians and visiting guest artists. Concerts take place at the Alaska Center for the Performing Arts; other programs are held at the University of Alaska–Anchorage. ♿ (Downtown)

ANCHORAGE OPERA
Alaska Center for the Performing Arts
621 W. Sixth St.
Anchorage
907/279-2557
The only professional opera company in the Last Frontier has been around for more than 35 years. Each season encompasses three fully staged productions, one of which is comic or lighthearted. Recent shows have included *Faust, Fidelio,* the *Merry Widow, Orpheus in the Underworld, Aida, La Sonnambula, Cosi*

Certain Anchorage arts groups sponsor pre-performance lectures to give audiences a better understanding of what they're about to see. The Anchorage Opera, the Anchorage Festival of Music, the Anchorage Symphony, the Anchorage Concert Chorus, and the Anchorage Concert Association (except for the Broadway & Beyond series) provide these lectures one hour before show time. The symphony lecture is interpreted in American Sign Language.

Fan Tutte, Carmen, and a double bill of *I Pagliacci* and *Gianni Schicchi*. Executive Director Peter Brown vows to keep producing operas that have never before been seen in Alaska, from Baroque and classical to modern works. ♿ (Downtown)

ANCHORAGE SYMPHONY ORCHESTRA
Alaska Center for the Performing Arts
621 W. Sixth St.
Anchorage
907/274-8668

Since its inception 50 years ago, the symphony has gone from a small volunteer group to a full-fledged orchestra that offers classic concerts, chamber ensembles, and music for families. Recent concert themes include "Power Play" (Mozart's Concerto for Piano no. 23 in A Major and Mahler's Symphony no. 1, *Titan*), "Heart Strings" (the *Marriage of Figaro* Overture, Prokofiev's *Romeo and Juliet* Suite, and *West Side Story* Symphonic Dances), "World Series" (Two World Symphony and New World Symphony), and "Great Opera-tunity" (excerpts from *La Boheme* and the *Ring* plus Polovetsian Dances from *Prince Igor*). During its October through May season, the orchestra also presents Ensemble Evenings, chamber-music favorites performed by orchestral ensembles. ♿ (Downtown)

UNIVERSITY OF ALASKA–ANCHORAGE RECITAL SERIES
UAA Arts Building
Alumni Drive
Anchorage
907/786-1595

The university's music department offers an ongoing recital series, with on-campus performances by both faculty members and visiting artists. Alaska Pro Musica, a faculty trio, has performed throughout the state, in the Lower 48, and in South America. The music department also sponsors Jazz Week each April. (East Anchorage)

DANCE

ALASKA DANCE THEATRE
2602 Gambell St.
Anchorage
907/277-9591

This nonprofit dance school is ballet-based but offers modern, jazz, and creative dance as well. Each winter the company stages Mobius, a concert of jazz, modern, and ballet works by ADT dancers and guest

Buying Tickets

The occasional independent show will vend its tickets through book-stores or specialty shops, but CarrsTix, 907/263-2787, handles just about everything on local stages. It has a total of 13 outlets: one in each Carrs Quality Center store in town, one at the University of Alaska, and one at the Alaska Center for the Performing Arts. Call from 10 a.m. to 9 p.m. Monday through Saturday, or drop in at a Carrs Quality Center any time. The UAA outlet, in the Campus Center, is open from 10 a.m. to 8 p.m. daily. You'll pay an outlet fee of one or two dollars on most tickets. For a calendar of upcoming events, check out www.carrstix.com.

artists from national troupes. Alaska Dance Theatre also runs rehearsals for the annual production of *The Nutcracker*, staged with a mix of local dancers and a guest ensemble. (West Anchorage)

DANCE SPECTRUM ALASKA
1300 E. 68th Ave.
Anchorage
907/344-9545
This eclectic semiprofessional troupe consists of local performers from teens on up. Dance Spectrum features modern, jazz, tap, ballet, and theatrical dance forms. Guest artists from New York and Los Angeles travel here for residencies. The troupe performs each spring at the Alaska Center for the Performing Arts. ♿ (South Anchorage)

DISCOVER DANCE
Anchorage Concert Association
Alaska Center for the
Performing Arts
621 W. Sixth St.
Anchorage

907/272-1471
In recent years the association has brought in Les Ballets Jazz de Montreal, Stomp, the Martha Graham Dance Company, the Dance Theatre of Harlem, Jam on the Groove, Tangeruos Dance Company, the Joffrey Ballet, Manhattan Tap, the Urban Bush Women, Jose Limon Dance Company, Tap Dogs, and Ballet Stars of Moscow and Kiev. All productions are staged at the Alaska Center for the Performing Arts. ♿ (Downtown)

UNIVERSITY OF ALASKA–ANCHORAGE
DANCE AND THEATER PROGRAMS
UAA Arts Building
Alumni Drive
Anchorage
907/786-1792
This integrated dance program and theater department embraces the idea that "actors need kinesthetic awareness and dancers need performance sensitivity." Such interdis-

ciplinary study, practice, and performance allow theater and dance students to learn from one another. Student-choreographed work now appears in the theater department's one-act play festivals. Additionally, the UAA Dance Ensemble performs in "Expanding the Stage," a November program showcasing new works in theater and dance. All performances take place on campus. (East Anchorage)

PERFORMANCE VENUES

ALASKA CENTER FOR THE PERFORMING ARTS
621 W. Sixth Ave.
Anchorage
907/263-2900
This odd-looking building—Alaskans make fun of it even as they stand in line for a show—is the venue for most local arts groups, as well as for visiting classical and popular music acts and Broadway musicals. The centerpiece is the Evangeline Atwood Theatre, which seats just under 2,100 people and is an acoustical delight. When it comes to sound, this house has no bad seats, whether you're listening to the Anchorage Opera or to Ani DiFranco. The other theaters are the Discovery, seating about 700, and the Sydney Laurence Theatre, seating approximately 350. During intermission, roam around and look at the interesting artwork, particularly the Native masks. Guided tours Wed 1 p.m.; $1 donation requested. &
(Downtown)

EGAN CENTER
555 W. Fifth Ave.
Anchorage
907/263-2800
This downtown convention center is the site for both trade shows and arts-and-crafts shows, such as the Crafts Emporium and the Alaska Federation of Natives Convention crafts show. Several halls are very popular for concerts, providing cabaret seating (tables and chairs, with alcohol available) and festival-style events for up to 2,800 people. Egan has hosted a wide range of rock, country, and comedy events, including Presidents of the United States of America, Tim McGraw, Great White, Violent Femmes, Gallagher, LL Cool J, Bob Goldthwait, Slayer, Ronnie Milsap, Marilyn Manson, Dishwalla, Bryan White, Southern Culture on the Skids, Primus, Joe Diffie, Social Distortion, and Aaron Tippin. & (Downtown)

SULLIVAN ARENA
1600 Gambell St.
Anchorage
907/279-0618
The city-owned arena is the home ice for the UAA Seawolves and the Anchorage Aces hockey teams. In the past it's hosted everything from truck pulls to professional wrestling, from the Harlem Globetrotters to the World Figure Skating Champions tour. It's the scene of annual trade events like the RV show (March), the Sportsman's Show (April), the Woman's Show (May), the Make It Alaskan Festival (October), the Winter Sports and Recreation Show (October), and the Holiday Food and Gift Show (November). The Sullivan, which seats more than 8,700 people, is also the venue for large-scale pop concerts. (West Anchorage)

Jeff Stevenson for Chilkoot Charlie's

12

NIGHTLIFE

Anchorage's nightlife scene is a mix of homegrown bands and imported ensembles of various stripes—everyone from Neil Diamond to Marilyn Manson. You can line dance at a country bar, nod appreciatively to a blues or jazz combo, or fling yourself around on a crowded rock 'n' roll dance floor. Country is a big seller; recent visitors include Vince Gill, Reba McEntire, Brooks & Dunn, Pam Tillis, and Toby Keith. "Dinosaur rock," metal acts, and '80s bands do well, plus the occasional rap performer, too. Loyal fans flock to see Ozzy Osbourne, Aerosmith, The Temptations, Foreigner, Jethro Tull, White Zombie, Chicago, Snoop Doggy Dogg, Metallica, and MC Hammer.

Folk has always sold well. Bill Morrissey, Tom Paxton, Jerry Douglas, Peter Rowan, and Dar Williams draw respectable crowds, as do Celtic acts like Dougie MacLean, Men of Worth, Cathie Ryan, and Kevin Burke. Jazz and blues performers like Mose Allison, Scott Cossu, George Winston, and Kirk Whalum also do well here.

Stand-up comics used to perform here regularly, but the trend toward mainstage comedy has faded, just as it has in the Lower 48. The University of Alaska–Anchorage books a couple of acts a year, and sometimes an independent promoter will book a nationally known headliner. But the only consistent comedy fix in town is the series of satirical musical revues at the Fly by Night Club. Wildly popular with tourists and locals alike, they play five nights a week for much of the year.

184

DANCE CLUBS

CHILKOOT CHARLIE'S
2435 Spenard Rd.
Anchorage
907/272-1010

You need to go to this place at least once, just to say you've been. The club's motto is, "We cheat the other guy and pass the savings along to you!" They offer live rock 'n' roll acts from here and away, plus swing-dance lessons, karaoke singing, and occasional live comedy, all played in a sawdust-floored, high-energy, just-got-paid atmosphere. There's also a swing bar, where martinis rule. Cover charge varies. (West Anchorage)

GASLIGHT LOUNGE
721 W. Fourth Ave.
Anchorage
907/277-0722

Weeknights this downtown bar is a casual socializing spot for friends. On Friday and Saturday nights, it's more of a pickup scene. The DJ plays rock, techno, and dance music Monday through Saturday. Wednesday night is ladies' night. No cover. (Downtown)

HOT RODS
4848 Old Seward Hwy.
Anchorage
907/562-5701

A DJ plays everything from '50s oldies to contemporary dance music. The pub also specializes in promotions like the Lock Party (singles get locks and keys and roam around trying to find their "mates"), Silly Games Night, karaoke, cribbage tournaments (yes, cribbage), and prize giveaways. If you don't feel like dancing, walk downstairs to the Anchorage Billiard Palace, where 16 antique tables await. There's full bar service there, too. (West Anchorage)

RUMRUNNERS OLD TOWNE BAR
330 E St.
Anchorage
907/278-4493

This small, oddly shaped room sports a nicely carved wood bar. The regulars here are extremely friendly to visitors, so if you have any questions about Alaska, ask them. Dance music—classic rock, Top 40, and '80s tunes—courtesy of a DJ, Fri and Sat; $2 cover. Karaoke Sun–Thu. (Downtown)

FOLK, ROCK, AND COUNTRY

A-K KORRAL SALOON
2421 E. Tudor Rd.
Anchorage
907/562-6552

This is a big, dark den of a place with plenty of space to dance and even enough room to get away from the noise and bustle. The atmosphere is friendly and comfortable, with no singles bar–type pressure. Live music Friday and Saturday nights. Recorded tunes for dance lessons Tue–Thur. (East Anchorage)

TRIVIA

Amy Ray of the Indigo Girls wrote the song "Cut It Out" after a visit to downtown bar Darwin's Theory. She was in Anchorage in 1995 for the Honor the Earth concert tour.

The Fancy Moose, p. 189

BUCKAROO CLUB
2811 Spenard Rd.
Anchorage
907/561-9251
This dancehall in Spenard offers live music Friday and Saturday nights. No cover. (West Anchorage)

LAST FRONTIER BAR
369 Muldoon Rd.
Anchorage
907/338-9922
Come here for country and country rock played by a DJ Thursday through Saturday, karaoke Sunday through Tuesday. Pool tournaments take place Sunday and Wednesday, and a dart tournament is on Saturday. Free dance lessons Wed. (East Anchorage)

LONG BRANCH SALOON
1737 E. Dimond Blvd.
Anchorage
907/349-4142
Munch a really terrific burger while you listen to new and classic rock from local bands, Tuesday through

Saturday. No cover charge. (South Anchorage)

TIMEOUT LOUNGE
4600 Old Seward Hwy.
Anchorage
907/562-2532
The Timeout Lounge is a good-natured joint offering country-western and country-rock music, usually live. (West Anchorage)

WHISTLING SWAN PRODUCTIONS
Whistling Swan Productions, a literal mom-and-pop promoting company, produces folk concerts, along with some special offerings, by the likes of Ani DiFranco, Dougie MacLean, Janis Ian, Holly Near, Bill Morrissey, Rosanne Cash, the Laura Love Band, Leo Kottke, Loudon Wainwright III, and Dar Williams. (Zone varies with venue.)

JAZZ AND BLUES

BLUES CENTRAL
Chef's Inn
Northern Lights and Arctic Blvds.
Anchorage
907/272-1341
Blues acts—both local and imported—play in a lounge atmosphere, with food service from sandwiches to full dinners. Devoted fans have heard the likes of Coco Montoya, Debbie Davies, Studebaker John and the Hots, Kenny Neal, Pat Boyack and the Prowlers, Too Slim and the Taildraggers, Little Charlie and the Nightcats, Tommy Castro, the Fabulous Thunderbirds, Omar and the Howlers, Guitar Shorty, and the Mike Welch Band. Blues Jam Sun. $3 cover Fri and Sat. (West Anchorage)

Fly by Night Club

Mr. Whitekeys, owner and operator of the Fly by Night Club, sums up his club's appeal in half a dozen words: "Spam, booze, and rhythm 'n' blues." You can buy that motto on a T-shirt at the club entrance, or you can sit through an evening at the nightspot and experience it for yourself.

Spam is a big part of the club's ambiance. Listed on the bill of fare are dubious entrées like Spam nachos, Spam bagels and cream cheese, Spam burgers, and, of course, the famous Spam du jour. If the idea of potted meat freezes your blood, look for other items on the menu. Any place that serves mango-chipotle barbecued ribs and halibut tacos with Thai chile sauce is worth checking out.

You can endear yourself to the club owner with a "traveling can" picture. That means a photo of yourself or a loved one holding a can of Spam at some exotic or unusual attraction. These pictures wind up in shows throughout the year: You'll see folks holding up Spam on the Great Wall of China; near the Sphinx; at the Pentagon; next to the tourist information sign for Intercourse, Pennsylvania; and underwater at the Great Barrier Reef.

Mr. Whitekeys and his house band, the Fabulous Spamtones, love playing R&B and rock 'n' roll. Several times a year the club also presents visiting blues and world-music performers. Most of the time, though, the nightspot's tiny stage hosts one of three comic musical revues. The Whale Fat Follies, Christmas in Spenard, and Springtime in Spenard feature satirical skits, bizarre musical numbers, and slide-shows that spotlight the foibles of Alaskans and Outsiders. If you don't have much tolerance for bad puns and low humor, better keep away. "We have our standards, and we won't raise them for anyone," vows Whitekeys.

The Fly by Night Club is located at 3300 Spenard Road, Anchorage, 907/276-SPAM. Tickets for the musical revues are $12 to $17; reservations are strongly recommended. The club is closed each year from January to sometime in March.

FLY BY NIGHT CLUB
3300 Spenard Rd.
Anchorage
907/279-7726

House band the Fabulous Spamtones will play blues or R&B on request, though the crowds tend to favor rock 'n' roll. The band's front man, Mr. Whitekeys, also owns the joint, and has booked nationally known blues and world-music acts over the years. He's also prone to give the stage over to local groups, including those that play tunes that are off the beaten path, musically speaking. The club is also home to several wildly popular poetry slams each year. No cover. Closed Jan–mid-March. (West Anchorage)

ROSCOE'S SKYLINE RESTAURANT
The Mall at Sears
Northern Lights Blvd. and Seward Hwy.
Anchorage
907/276-5879

This soul-food restaurant also serves up live music three nights a week. On "Soulful Sundays," the sound is soulful rhythm and blues. "Blue Monday" is mellow jazz. And "Jazzy Wednesday" is a more upbeat jazz sound. You can enjoy a full dinner or just sip iced tea, beer, or wine while you listen. No cover. (West Anchorage)

SULLIVAN'S STEAKHOUSE
320 W. Fifth Ave.
Anchorage
907/258-2882

This pricey chain steakhouse restaurant has live, upbeat jazz by local musicians Wednesday through Saturday. (Downtown)

PUBS AND BARS

CLUB OASIS
4801 Old Seward Hwy.
Anchorage
907/561-2470

This nothing-fancy joint offers live rock music, pool and pool tournaments, and promotions like half-price appetizers and ladies' night. (West Anchorage)

CUSACK'S BREWPUB
Northern Lights Hotel
598 W. Northern Lights Blvd.
Anchorage
907/278-2739

This casual, friendly pub features live music tending toward folk and blues on Friday and Saturday nights. During hockey season it's home base for the Anchorage Aces, so

If you're a fan of acoustic music, check out JoAnn & Monte's Alaska Show, a summertime staple in Anchorage. JoAnn and Monte have performed together and been married for 20 years, facts borne out by their easy, bantering stage rapport (the show is billed as "bad jokes and good music about a great land"). They sing songs about Alaska with a style that incorporates elements of folk, country, blues, jazz, pop, and rock. Their show runs daily from mid-May to early September at the Anchorage Sheraton.

you'll see players and fans after the games. Watch for local rugby players who come here on Sunday to catch foreign matches via satellite. The on-site brewery features 9 to 12 flavors at any given time, along with microbrews from elsewhere in Alaska and the Lower 48. Teetotalers might sample the unusual homemade root beer, made with Alaskan birch syrup. For those who don't fancy brews, Cusack's also has full bar service and plenty to eat because it's also a restaurant. See also Chapter 4, Where to Eat. (West Anchorage)

Humpy's Great Alaskan Alehouse

Humpy's Great Alaskan Alehouse, p. 191

DARWIN'S THEORY
426 G St.
Anchorage
907/277-5322
This tiny and immensely entertaining downtown institution is often packed with people who are ready for an institution. Eat lots of the free popcorn, and if they offer you a "Red Hot," prepare to yelp afterward— the drink is made with cinnamon schnapps and a touch of Tabasco. (Don't worry—the yelping is expected and appreciated.) This is a great place to meet the locals. (Downtown)

FANCY MOOSE
Regal Alaskan Hotel
4800 Spenard Rd.
Anchorage
907/243-2300
Come to this pleasant, cozy place for a drink or two while watching aircraft take off and land on adjacent Lake Hood. The food is pricey but good, the popcorn and the jukebox are free, and the waitstaff is friendly. Each waiter wears his hometown on his nametag—who knows, you might even see somebody from back

home. The Regal Alaskan is headquarters for the Iditarod sled-dog race, so if you show up in March, you'll meet some pretty interesting folks. See also Chapter 3, Where to Stay. (West Anchorage)

F STREET STATION
325 F St.
Anchorage
907/272-5196
This very centrally located downtown pub doesn't have any music at all, not even a jukebox. It's more of a conversation bar, where people meet after work and spend an evening chatting and sipping—and, at the oyster bar, slurping. Other fresh seafood specials are available nightly. The crowd tends to be professional and lawyerish, but tourists are welcomed. Help yourself to a slice of cheese, and then ask the bartender to explain why this cheese stands alone and under a glass cover. See also Chapter 4, Where to Eat. (Downtown)

Radio Days

A spin of the dial may have you convinced that Anchorage radio sta-tions play mostly Top 40 or oldies. Here are a few ways to break the musical mold.

To hear cutting-edge music, tune in to KRUA (88.1 FM), the University of Alaska–Anchorage station. It plays all kinds of music, but even the "alternative southern music" is stuff you simply won't find anywhere else. Shows like Girls of Ska (peppy horn-flavored dance music, hosted by female aficionados), Secret Eighties Man (music from—you guessed it—the 1980s), Jeffrey at the Drive-In (songs from movie soundtracks), The Current (British music), Vibes of the Time (reggae), and The Punk Show (pretty self-explanatory) can be as educational as they are listenable. As the on-air person-alities point out every so often, KRUA does occasionally play music that may be considered offensive, but not indecent. If you're a grownup, give the station a listen—you'll never be the same.

Interested in Latin music? Anchorage's public radio station, KSKA (91.1 FM), offers Hispanic programming. Mexican, Norteo, and Caribbean/tropical music, along with local news and a syndicated news feature program, play Sunday 8:30 p.m. to 1 a.m. and Monday 8:30 to midnight.

Although the mission of KNBA (90.3 FM) is to serve Native peo-ple in the southcentral area, a lot of non-Natives tune in, too. The station runs an unusual mix of cultural programming—storytelling, a "Native Word of the Day," talk shows, Native music—and alter-native sounds by artists like Lyle Lovett, Jewel, Ani DiFranco, Paul Simon, and Dan Bern. Local performers are likely to be played on KNBA, too. Weekends, the station offers even more specialized pro-gramming: blocks of old-time country, reggae, and Hawaiian music. The station is the first Native-owned urban public radio station in the United States.

GLACIER BREW HOUSE
737 W. Fifth Ave.
Anchorage
907/274-2739
There's a warm, comfortable atmosphere at this downtown brewpub, which offers brewery tours and beer samplings on request. It's particularly busy before and after hockey games and events at the nearby Alaska Center for the Performing Arts. Try the sandwiches and wood-fired pizzas or, if you're making an evening of it, the full dinners, which include wood-grilled seafood and rotisserie-grilled meats. See also Chapter 4, Where to Eat. & (Downtown)

HUMPY'S GREAT ALASKAN ALEHOUSE
610 W. Sixth Ave.
Anchorage
907/276-2337
This super-popular watering hole features 40-plus microbrews, tasty food (you can tell the folks back home about the halibut tacos), and live entertainment nightly. The music tends to be acoustic from 5 to 9:30 p.m., with either a duo or a band after that. Most nights you'll hear jazz, classic rock, or original local music. Because this downtown bar is right across from the Alaska Center for the Performing Arts, you'll see folks in tuxes and evening gowns bellying up to the bar right next to those in T-shirts and boots or flannels and Birken-

stocks. Humpy's is also within walking distance of downtown hotels, giving visitors easy access to local color. Enjoy the patio with its murals painted by area-artist Duke Russell. (Downtown)

MOOSE'S TOOTH
3300 Old Seward Hwy.
Anchorage
907/258-2537
This specialty pizza place has a microbrewery, so you can enjoy some quality suds during open-mike night on Monday. See also Chapter 4, Where to Eat. (West Anchorage)

PIONEER BAR
739 W. Fourth Ave.
Anchorage
907/276-7996
One of the city's older bars (circa 1952), the Pioneer still has its shuffleboard, dart board, and pool tables in place. An older crowd shows up during the day to play cribbage and drink coffee, but a younger group has adopted this old-Anchorage institution at night. The draw, apparently, is a good jukebox and "almost perfect bartenders" (as claimed by the neon sign in the window). (Downtown)

REGAL EAGLE BREW PUB
11501 Old Glenn Hwy.
Eagle River
907/694-9120
The first brewpub in the state of Alaska offers live music Friday and

If you've had too much to drink, don't get into your rental car. Many local bar managers will gladly pay for a cab.

Top Ten Bad Films and TV Shows about Alaska

Linda Billington, longtime film columnist for the Anchorage Daily News, *has made a hobby of collecting bad celluloid Alaskana. Here is Billington's list of dishonor, "ranged from worst to least worst."*

1. ***On Deadly Ground:*** Big-budget Hollywood Alaskana at its most inept. This 1994 outing features Steven Seagal defending Alaskan Natives against a nasty old oil company. The firm is headed by Michael Caine, giving his worst performance in years. ODG includes rampant inaccuracies, loopy dialogue, and an ennui-provoking monologue in which Seagal plays environmental Messiah.

2. ***Equalizer 2000:*** A low-budget 1986 *Road Warrior* ripoff (one of many), the film is obstensibly set on the post–nuclear winter North Slope, which resembles a Mojave Desert gravel pit. Who knows—with global warming, anything's possible.

3. ***Kodiak:*** In this blessedly short-run TV series that lived and died in 1974, Clint (Cheyenne) Walker played an Alaska state cop with a trusty Eskimo sidekick. The series managed but a handful of episodes, all of them howlingly terrible, showing the writers' ignorance of Alaskan geography, weather, and human nature.

4. ***The Hell Hounds of Alaska:*** This 1973 adventure shot in Yugoslavia features every cliché known to celluloid, including taboo Indian burial grounds, a stolen gold shipment, and a missing child.

Saturday, tending toward Alaska-style blues. Try your luck on the small dance floor, then cool down with any one of a half-dozen fresh brews, including the signature Copper River Amber Ale. No cover. (Eagle River)

SIMON & SEAFORT'S SALOON & GRILL
420 L St.
Anchorage
907/274-3502
The bar at this downtown seafood restaurant doesn't have music, but it's a very pleasant place in which to shoot the breeze with the locals. Simon's has the city's largest selec-

tion of single-malt scotches. And if the dynamic smells of prime rib and grilled seafood from the adjacent restaurant prove too tempting, a full meal can be served to you right at the bar. See also Chapter 4, Where to Eat. ઐ (Downtown)

SNOW GOOSE RESTAURANT AND BREWERY
Third Ave. and G St.
Anchorage
907/277-7727
This downtown brewpub serves six different fresh brews, along with a homemade root beer and unusual beers from Belgium. If you're interested in snacking, try the most pop-

5. *Klondike Fever:* Dialogue of surpassing banality, poor editing, and abysmal direction—and those are the good points of this 1980 "epic" about the year Jack London spent in Alaska and the Yukon during the gold rush.

6. *Higher Ground:* Try, pray, to envision John Denver as a disillusioned FBI agent who quits to become a bush pilot in Alaska. 'Nough said? For this 1988 TV movie, Denver sings the title song, too. All in all, it's a pretty rocky mountain high.

7. *Ice Palace:* Edna Ferber wrote the book about post-WWII entrepreneurs in Alaska. Despite some nice scenery, Richard Burton, Robert Ryan, Carolyn Jones, and other Hollywoodians can't overcome the melodrama, which they play to the hilt and beyond in this 1960 outing.

8. *Arctic Blue:* The most terrifying thing about this ecologist-versus-poachers tale from 1993 is the sight of outlaw-trapper Rutger Hauer lifting his naked, flabby avoirdupois out of a hot tub.

9. *The Alaskans:* This one-season 1959 Warner Brothers TV series had potential, including Roger Moore as a gambler in gold rush Alaska. But the recycled scripts never lived up to the promise.

10. *The Cold Heart of a Killer:* This less-than-scintillating 1996 made-for-TV movie could've been far worse. Kate Jackson makes a credible musher, and the sled-dog sequences, incorporating footage of the real Iditarod start in Anchorage, are decent.

ular appetizer: Thai oysters made with basil, fish sauce, and vinegar. The upstairs area is cigar-friendly, selling a good selection of them, and its outdoor deck serves up a nice view of Sleeping Lady and of Mount McKinley when it's out. See also Chapter 4, Where to Eat. (Downtown)

COFFEEHOUSES

BARNES & NOBLE CAFÉ
200 E. Northern Lights Blvd.
Anchorage
907/279-7323
The national bookstore chain offers coffee drinks, occasional live music, and a pleasant, literary atmosphere. See also Chapter 9, Shopping. (West Anchorage)

CAFÉ ESPRESSO AT BORDERS
1100 E. Dimond Blvd.
Anchorage
907/344-4099
The Borders café offers jazz, classical, folk, and pop acts—everything from violin to guitar to didgeridoo to "Yup'ik doo-wop." This is a good place to go on a first (or second, or third) date since you get the pleasure of musical entertainment without the pressure of a bar scene or the presence of alcohol. See also

Chapter 9, Shopping. (South Anchorage)

HOLY GROUNDS COFFEEHOUSE
New Directions Church
639 W. International Airport Rd.
Anchorage
907/561-3802
An "alternative Gen-X church" runs this coffeehouse on Thursday, Friday, and Sunday evenings. From time to time, Holy Grounds hosts concerts by alternative Christian rock bands such as Stavesacre, Skypark, and 5 O'Clock People. (West Anchorage)

JITTERS
11401 Old Glenn Hwy.
Eagle River
907/694-5487
This coffeehouse is decorated with antiques and old-time coffee memorabilia. In the wintertime, local bands perform from time to time. (Eagle River)

KALADI BROTHERS COFFEE CO.
6921 Brayton Dr.
Anchorage
907/344-6510
A variety of local musicians, mostly acoustic and folk, perform Friday and Saturday in this laid-back coffeehouse/art gallery. It's on a frontage road off the New Seward Highway; get very specific directions or you'll have to backtrack. (South Anchorage)

PLUCKING MONKEY TEA PUB
2700 Blueberry St.
Anchorage
907/279-5323
This tea shop, popular with young people, hosts a wide variety of local acts, mostly acoustic. (West Anchorage)

QUPQUGIAQ CAFÉ
640 W. 36th Ave.
Anchorage
907/563-5634
This is a friendly, offbeat place: It's a coffeehouse that presents varying types of live music, tending toward acoustic and folk, on Friday and Saturday, but it also provides space for community group meetings (from construction workers to Greenpeace) and classes (from Jewish mysticism to "A Course in Miracles"). The café also rents rooms upstairs (see Chapter 3, Where to Stay). The sandwiches, soups, and coffees are good, and it's the kind of café where you can comfortably linger with coffee and a book. (West Anchorage)

SLEEPY DOG COFFEE CO.
11517 Old Glenn Hwy.
Eagle River
907/694-6463
You'll hear occasional live music here, from folk to Renaissance and a cappella. (Eagle River)

SNOW CITY CAFE
1034 W. Fourth Ave.
Anchorage
907/272-2489
This laid-back downtown restaurant offers coffees, teas, juices, wine, beer, and mellow live music Friday and Saturday. But on Sunday's open-mike nights, the joint may be jumpin'. See also Chapter 4, Where to Eat. (Downtown)

SURF CITY
415 L St.
Anchorage
907/279-7877
This small, friendly Internet café has live music every Thursday night, mostly acoustic. (Downtown)

MOVIE HOUSES OF NOTE

CAPRI CINEMA
3425 E. Tudor Rd.
Anchorage
907/561-0064 or 907/275-3799
(show times)
Art cinema does exist in Alaska, in its own quirky way. Ask for directions to the Capri Cinema, and you'll be told it's "right across the street from the sled-dog track." And some winter evenings you'll see departing movie patrons standing around outside and looking up—that's because the northern lights are putting on their own show.

The farthest north art-movie house in America is a scrappy little 90-seater that's had a checkered past. In its 20-year history, the Capri has shown everything from G-rated cartoons to triple-X adult films. Until fairly recently, the theater concentrated solely on art and alternative movies, both domestic and foreign. Titles like *Nowhere*, *Doom Generation*, *Spanking the Monkey*, *The Substance of Fire*, *Love! Valour! Compassion!*, *Ridicule*, *Riff Raff*, *Trainspotting*, *Like It Is*, *Barcelona*, and *The Pillow Book* have all enjoyed successful runs.

In 1999, the Capri changed tacks and began presenting second-run Hollywood hits, with art-house fare brought in for special engagements. A film discussion group meets on the first and the third Monday of every month.

Adjacent to the Capri is the Hollywood Canteen, a combination snack emporium and espresso bar with the best popcorn in Anchorage—they use real butter! Some people come by just for popcorn and conversation, or to snack and read the magazines stacked by the front door. (East Anchorage)

Robert Angell/Alaska Division of Tourism

13

DAY TRIPS FROM ANCHORAGE

DAY TRIP: Girdwood/Portage

Distance from Anchorage: 40/54 miles; 60/75-minute drive

The Seward Highway is one of the most beautiful driving trips in America, hugging the north shore of Turnagain Arm out of Anchorage and serving up fabulous views of the Chugach and Kenai Mountains. At Mile 117, just outside of town, you'll see a boardwalk system in the **Potter Point State Game Refuge**, an extremely busy bird-watching spot; take your binoculars and watch for red-necked grebes, arctic terns, trumpeter swans, numerous ducks, and other water-loving birds.

Some people choose to begin bright and early in Portage and allow the rest of the day and evening for Girdwood. What you'll notice right away about Portage is that there is no "there" there—the town "died" after the 1964 Good Friday earthquake, which caused the land to drop 6 to 12 feet and to flood during high tides. A few remnants of old buildings mark the spot of the former townsite.

At Mile 78.9 is the access road to **Portage Glacier**, one of Alaska's most popular tourist attractions. As you drive in, watch for the **Williwaw Nature Trail** and the **Byron Glacier Trail**; both self-guided hikes will take you through moose, beaver, and spawning-salmon habitat. Bears are also a possibility, so talk loudly or sing as you go.

Portage Glacier has receded considerably in recent years, but it still calves off hunks of ice that float down Portage Lake. Those icebergs, which glow an eerie blue-green, come to rest just outside the **Begich, Boggs Visitor Center** (see Chapter 5, Sights and Attractions). The center has

TIP

Do not attempt to climb on icebergs floating in Portage Lake. The ice is extremely unstable and could roll over at any time.

displays on glaciers and the region's natural history, hikes and naturalist programs, and an hourly film, *Voices from the Ice*. It's open daily from 9 a.m. to 6 p.m. in the summer and on weekends from 10 a.m. to 4 p.m. in the winter. Be prepared for rain, and dress warmly because the wind off the glacier can be, well, icy.

Want to get closer to the source? **Gray Line of Alaska**, 907/783-2983, hosts the Portage Glacier Cruise to within 300 yards of the ice; with any luck, you'll see the glacier calve while you're there. Cruises depart daily at 10:30 a.m., noon, 1:30, 3, and 4 p.m.

When you're through exploring Portage, drive a dozen miles back toward Anchorage to Girdwood (Mile 90 of the Seward Highway). Technically a part of the Anchorage municipality, the town has a personality all its own. Many people identify it as the home of the **Alyeska Resort**, the state's largest ski area and a year-round attraction (see Chapter 10, Sports and Recreation). Skiing on the 3,939-foot mountain usually runs mid-November to mid-April; other winter fun includes Nordic skiing, heli-skiing, ice fishing, snowmachining and dogsled touring. In the summer, people go to Girdwood for glacier skiing, hiking, mountain biking, canoeing, rafting, and flightseeing.

Class V Whitewater Inc., 907/783-2004 (e-mail: classv@alaska.net), stages high-intensity raft runs and scenic float trips, and the company will also set you up with fishing, fly-in river trips, floatplane or helicopter fishing and rafting, and kayak instruction. Both **Alyeska Air Service**, 907/783-2163, and **Alpine Air Inc.**, 907/783-2360 (e-mail: alpinair@alaska.net), offer flightseeing over snowfields, glaciers, mountains, and Prince William Sound.

Don't miss the gold-panning at **Crow Creek Mine**, Crow Creek Road, 907/278-8060 (see Chapter 5, Sights and Attractions). An 1898 mining site with eight original buildings, it's a beautiful place to take pictures and a picnic, and to camp if you have a tent or a self-contained vehicle. You're guaranteed at least one genuine gold flake with each bag of "pay dirt." The mine is open May 15 through September 15.

And be sure to stop at the **Double Musky**, Crow Creek Highway, 907/783-2822, for dinner. It serves Cajun food that brings folks out from Anchorage on a regular basis. Not hungry enough for a big dinner? Try the **Chair 5 Restaurant**, Lindblad Avenue, 907/783-2500.

Getting There from Anchorage: Take the New Seward Highway south to Mile 90 (Girdwood) and Mile 78.9 (Portage).

ANCHORAGE REGION

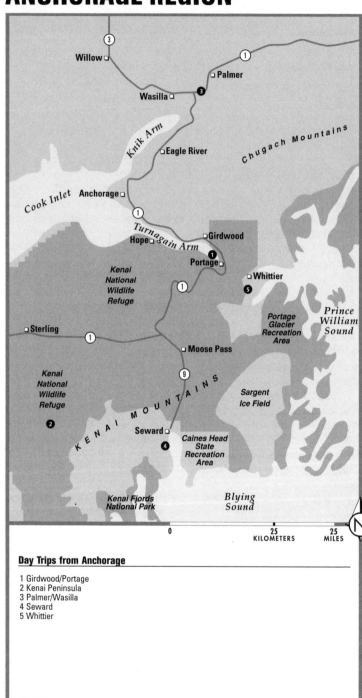

0　　　　　　　　　25
　　　　　　KILOMETERS

25
MILES

Day Trips from Anchorage

1 Girdwood/Portage
2 Kenai Peninsula
3 Palmer/Wasilla
4 Seward
5 Whittier

The Good Friday earthquake of 1964 made the land along Turnagain Arm sink. From about Mile 90 to Mile 74 of the Seward Highway, you'll notice the result: dead spruce trees whose root systems were slowly poisoned by the inrush of salt water. However, these "snags" make great vantage points for bald eagles and other birds, so keep your binoculars handy.

DAY TRIP: Whittier

Distance from Anchorage: 40-plus miles; approximately 55-minute drive, plus 12-mile (35-minute) train trip

During World War II, Whittier was chosen as a second supply route into Alaska, however, mountains blocked it from the rest of the state. No problem: The railroad blasted two tunnels through solid rock, a 3.5-mile project. In the town, the military built docks, housing, and roads. Until 1960, the town was an active army facility with a population of 1,200; nowadays, the population is just under 300.

Whether or not to build a road to Whittier has been an ongoing battle. In 1997, construction blasting began, then was halted by a court order, then began again with an eye toward opening for automobile traffic sometime in 2000. The locals worry about auto overload since the town has hardly any public parking, or public toilets. More of each are allegedly in the works, but you still might want to take the train. You can load on kayaks, camping gear, or any other big stuff you want. For reservations, call the **Alaska Railroad**, 800/544-0552 or 907/265-2494. Or check www.akrr.com.

Gold panning at Old Crow Creek Mine in Girdwood, p. 197

Ernst Schneider/Alaska Division of Tourism

Whittier is popular with kayakers and those interested in Prince William Sound sightseeing. Family-owned companies like **Lazy Otter Charters**, 800/587-6887 or 907/694-6887 (lazyottr@alaska.net), and **Honey Charters**, 907/344-3340 or 907/472-2493, offer cruises and kayaking drop-offs. If you've never kayaked but would like to learn how, or if you'd like to be led out and back by professionals, contact **Alaska Sea Kayakers/Nova**, 800/746-5753, or the **Prince William Sound Kayak Center**, 907/276-7235 or 907/472-2452 (in Whittier).

Phillips' Cruises & Tours, 800/544-0529 or 907/276-8023, has the 26 Glacier Cruise, a five-hour cruise in a high-speed catamaran with a money-back guarantee that you won't suffer from motion sickness. **Renown Charters & Tours**, 800/655-3806 or 907/272-1961 (e-mail: info@RenownCharters.com), offers the three-hour Seven Glacier Cruise around Prince William Sound in a heated 42-passenger vessel. **Major Marine Tours**, 800/764-7300 or 907/274-7300, does a six-hour cruise that includes a buffet dinner of salmon and chicken.

Alaska Deep Sea Adventures, 907/345-8478 or 907/472-3474 (e-mail: adsa@customcpu.com), will take you out for monster halibut and other Alaska fish, including salmon and rockfish; while you're out there, enjoy beautiful scenery and wildlife photo opportunities. The company also offers fall drop-off hunting.

Getting There from Anchorage: Take the Seward Highway south to Mile 80.3, the Alaska Railroad loading area.

DAY TRIP: Kenai Peninsula Fishing

Distance from Anchorage: 158 miles; 2.5-hour drive
The Kenai Peninsula covers 25,600 square miles, but only 15,600 of them are land. All that water is the reason the area is most often associated with sport fishing. Men and women come from all over the world to land world-class salmon and giant halibut.

Parts of the Kenai River and the Russian River may be plagued by "combat fishing"—men and women standing elbow-to-elbow, or boats lined up nearly bow to stern. Blame it on the red salmon, which makes people a little crazy. Generally speaking, the reds run in mid-June and again around the third week of July.

It's possible to fish without a guide for reds, kings, and other specimens since the **Department of Fish and Game** offers plenty of information on the best places to go. Check out their Web site at www.state.ak.us/local/akpages/FISH.GAME/, and augment that information with the "Fishing Report" found each Friday in the *Anchorage Daily News*. Once you get to the Kenai, ask around for local tips, particularly at tackle shops. It's vital to get the most up-to-the-minute information in case of sudden closures or changes in regulations.

T i P

Do not walk on Turnagain Arm mudflats. Some of that mud has the consistency of quicksand. If you get caught, rescue might not reach you before the tide does.

> **When driving on the Seward Highway, you must have your headlights on at all times.**

However, even Alaska residents will go out with a guide service because it's so convenient. The guides know where the fish are, they provide the gear if you need it, and they'll even clean and cut up your catch for you. Literally hundreds of guides can be found on the Kenai; ask around for those that are concerned about conservation since the fish habitat has taken a beating over the years.

What if you don't fish? Consider hiking, birdwatching, rafting, camping, flightseeing, or other recreational activities. Pick up information at the **Kenai Visitors and Cultural Center**, 11471 Kenai Spur Highway, Kenai, AK 99611, 907/283-1991. The center also has an on-site museum.

Note: If you have more than a day trip in mind, consider continuing on to **Homer** (226 miles from Anchorage), a funky little burg recently cited as one of *Utne Reader*'s "Most Enlightened Towns in America." It's a nice spot to spend a couple of days enjoying things artistic and outdoorsy.

Getting There from Anchorage: *Take Seward Highway south to Mile 37.7, and turn onto the Sterling Highway.*

DAY TRIP: Seward

Distance from Anchorage: 127 miles; 2.5-hour drive
Seward is a pretty, friendly town of about 2,900 souls. Located on Resurrection Bay, it has a relatively mild climate; as an ice-free harbor and the ocean terminus of the Alaska Railroad, Seward is an important link in the supply chain to interior Alaska.

The town got an important tourism boost with the opening of the Alaska SeaLife Center, 301 Railway Avenue, 800/224-2525 or 907/224-6300, and the Chugach Heritage Center, 501 Railway Avenue, 800/947-5065 or 907/224-5065. The **Alaska SeaLife Center** is a 115,000-square-foot educational and research facility with underwater views of Steller sea lions, a giant octopus, many types of fish, marine birds, and seals; outdoors, you can photograph the sea lions, seals, and birds, and watch river otters in the research area. Kids particularly enjoy the "Discovery Zone," which lets you get up-close and hands-on with sea stars, sea urchins, sea cucumbers, and other invertebrates. The center is open daily 9 a.m. to 9:30 p.m. in the summer, and 10 a.m. to 5 p.m. during the rest of the year. Admission is $12.50 for adults, $10 for kids over age four. More information can be found online at www.alaskasealife.org.

The **Chugach Heritage Center** gives visitors an introduction to the rich cultures of the area's Native people, through art demonstrations and a mix of singing, dancing, and storytelling called "So They Say." Hours are Tuesday through Sunday from 10 a.m. to 6 p.m. Admission is $8 for adults, $6.50 for kids; children under seven get in free when accompanied by a parent, and group discounts are available.

Get to know the city a little better through a self-guided historical walking tour; the pamphlet with directions is available for a one-dollar donation at the **Seward Chamber of Commerce**, Mile 2 of the Seward Highway.

Tour boat near Seward

Rex Melton/Alaska Division of Tourism

Be sure to visit the **Seward Museum**, Third and Jefferson, 907/224-3902, which has historical photos and exhibits on the Good Friday Earthquake, the Iditarod trail, the city's role in World War II, the paintings of Rockwell Kent (who spent time in Alaska), a selection of Native baskets, and many other items.

Seward is the gateway to the Kenai Fjords, so stop in at the **Kenai Fjords National Park Visitors Center** (in the Boat Harbor) for displays, a slide show, and information. What you see will probably convince you to take at least a partial-day cruise while you're there, for a look at scenery so beautiful that it strikes visitors mute: mountains, glaciers, and wildlife, including but not limited to whales, sea lions, eagles, puffins, and otters.

Among the companies who'd be glad to take you out and around are **Kenai Fjords Tours**, 800/478-8068 or 907/276-6249 or 907/224-8068 in Seward (e-mail: info@kenaifjords.com); **Renown Charters & Tours**, 800/655-3806 or 907/272-1961 (e-mail: info@RenownCharters.com); and **Major Marine Tours**, 800/764-7300 or 907/274-7300.

A number of charter companies will take you out to try your luck at salmon, halibut, Dolly Varden, flounder, lingcod, and other fish, including **The Fish House**, 800/257-7760 or 907/224-3674; **Bear Lake Air & Guide Service**

T I P

Since there are no gas stations between Mile 90 (the Girdwood turnoff) and just outside of Seward, Girdwood is the place to top off the tank.

800/224-5985 or 907/224-5985; **Crackerjack Fishing Charters**, 907/224-2606; **Puffin Family Charters**, 800-978-3346 (e-mail: pfcfshon@alaska.net); and **Dave & Marie's Excellent Adventures**, 800/422-2030 or 907/224-2030 (e-mail: dmea@arctic.net).

Note: Each year the Chamber of Commerce sponsors a **Silver Salmon Derby**, with $250,000 worth of cash and prizes, so be sure to buy a derby tag if you go fishing. You'll feel pretty darn silly if you catch a trophy-size silver and miss out on the cash because you didn't buy a tag.

Seward throws a huge party every Fourth of July, and the weekend's centerpiece event is the **Mount Marathon Race**, an event that begins downtown, proceeds to the 3,022-foot summit of Mount Marathon, and concludes back downtown. If you want to see the race—and it really has to be seen to be believed—reserve your accommodations *well* in advance.

On your way into or out of town, take time to look at **Exit Glacier** (turn at Mile 3 of the Seward Highway and drive nine miles to the ranger station). You can get a close-up view of the unusual formations of the bluish glacial ice. Keep back, though, since rocks and ice may fall without warning. You can also take a walk on a three-quarter-mile loop trail or on a 3.5-mile trail that leads to the 300-square-mile **Harding Icefield**—that trail, however, is steep and rough-cut. Do not under any circumstances venture onto the icefield itself, as you need special equipment and experience to travel safely.

Getting There from Anchorage: Take the Seward Highway to the very end. (That's why they call it the "Seward" Highway.)

DAY TRIP: Palmer/Wasilla

Distance from Anchorage: Just over 40 miles; 55-minute drive
Palmer was first established in 1916 as a railway station, but in 1935 it became one of America's stranger experiments: the **Matanuska Valley Colony**. More than 200 families, mostly from Michigan, Wisconsin, and Minnesota, came up to develop what the government considered the vast untapped agricultural potential of the area. Many failed and left, but some endured and their descendants live there still. The annual Colony Days celebration in June spotlights the history of the experiment.

You can see the modern version of agriculture each year at the **Alaska State Fair**, 907/745-4827, a 10-day celebration that runs through Labor Day

---

TRIVIA

Giant veggies abound at the Alaska State Fair each August. Here are some of the current record-holders: cabbage, 98 pounds; broccoli, 39.50 pounds; celery, 24.52 pounds; squash, 303.05 pounds; sunflower, 16.75 feet tall.

---

weekend. The giant-vegetable competition is a particular favorite among the tourists—where else can you snap photos of 90-pound cabbages and other amazing garden feats?

Palmer has a pair of really interesting animal farms. The **Musk Ox Farm**, Mile 50 of the Glenn Highway, 907/745-4151, raises these improbable Ice-Age beasts in the shadow of beautiful Pioneer Peak. The large, furry critters are combed for "qiviut," their cloud-soft and incredibly warm underfur, which makes equally soft and warm scarves, hats, and the like. The **Reindeer Farm**, Mile 12 of the Old Glenn Highway, 907/745-4000, is home to the caribou's domesticated cousins—pony-sized animals with large, branching antlers and friendly dispositions. Visitors are allowed to hand-feed them with "reindeer chow" and to walk among the animals, many of whom aren't averse to a scratch behind the ears. Bring your camera for the best Christmas-card picture ever.

Feeling lucky? Pan for gold at **Independence Mine State Historical Park**, Mile 49 of Fishhook-Willow Road, 907/745-2827, which highlights the history of gold-mining in Alaska with interpretive displays in original buildings, including a simulated mining tunnel complete with the voices of the men who "moil for gold." The park is also a beautiful place to hike. Nearby is the **Hatcher Pass Lodge**, 907/745-5897, which offers overnight cabins, meals, hiking, and groomed ski trails in the winter.

Wasilla has been a victim of unchecked sprawl, both in housing for commuters and retail operations to serve those new residents. However, it's worth a visit for several reasons. Valley Performing Arts (see Chapter 11, Performing Arts) produces six to seven shows each year at the **Fred and Sara Machetanz Theatre**, 251 West Swanson, 907/373-9500, from Broadway shows such as *Arcadia* and *Lettice and Lovage* to fun family fare like *Annie* and *Cinderella Meets the Wolfman*.

The **Iditarod Trail Sled Dog Race** maintains a small but nifty free museum, Mile 2.2 of Knik Rd., 907/376-5155, with artifacts, photos, and videos that tell you about the Last Great Race, along with sled-dog rides in the winter from Iditarod veteran Raymie Redington; there's a small fee for the rides. Summer hours are 8 a.m. to 7 p.m. daily; 10 a.m. to 5 p.m. Monday though Friday the rest of the year.

The **Museum of Alaska Transportation and Industry**, Mile 47 of Parks Highway, 907/376-1211, is a collection of industrial and transportation artifacts, all with fascinating pioneer histories. It's open May through September daily from 9 a.m. to 6 p.m. Admission is $5 for adults, $4 for seniors and students, and $12 per family.

Give the kids a chance to let off steam at **Wasilla Wonderland**, a massive, community-built playground (off the Parks Highway; turn right on Lucille and left on Nelson). It's got fabulous climbing equipment, ramps, swings, monkeybars, and a make-believe plane, car, and dogsled (get that camera out again) made of wood. Allow a little more time than you think you'll need because this place is too much fun to leave quickly.

Note: If you have more than one day to spend out of town, drive farther up the Parks Highway to **Talkeetna** (watch for the Talkeetna Spur Road at Mile 98.7 of the Parks Highway).Talkeetna is the staging area for climbs of Mount McKinley, and the town's pilots will take you flightseeing; you can also fish, snowshoe, or take a guided snowmachine trek. The town also has a handful of fun celebrations each year, including the Moose Dropping Festival in July and the Talkeetna Bachelors Auction and Wilderness Woman Competition in early December.

Or head all the way to **Denali National Park** (240 miles from Anchorage), where you can either remain on the park bus the whole time or hop off to go backpacking. Either way, you'll be treated to beautiful scenery, including the awe-inspiring Mount McKinley (unless, of course, it's cloudy that day), and wildlife that includes bears, caribou, moose, wolves, and Arctic foxes (unless they're feeling shy that day). It's important to make reservations in advance both for the bus tours and for accommodations; check the **National Parks Service** home page (www.nps.gov/dena/) or *The Milepost* for more information.

Getting there from Anchorage: *Take Glenn Highway directly into Palmer; for Wasilla, turn onto the Parks Highway at Mile 35.3 of the Glenn.*

IMPORTANT PHONE NUMBERS

Police, Fire, Emergency
911

Alaska State Troopers
907/269-5511

HOSPITALS AND MEDICAL CENTERS

Alaska Native Medical Center
907/563-2662

First Care Medical Centers
907/248-1122 or 907/345-1199

Alaska Regional Hospital
907/276-1131

HealthSouth Medical Clinics
907/562-0033 (East Anchorage)
907/345-4343 (South Anchorage)
907/694-6941 (Eagle River)

Providence Alaska Medical Center
907/562-2211

EMERGENCY CENTERS

Abused Women's Aid in Crisis
907/272-0100

Alcohol and Drug Intervention
Helpline
907/272-1174

Clare House (emergency shelter for
women and children)
907/563-4545

Covenant House (emergency shelter
for youth)
907/272-1255

Poison Control
907/261-3193

Rape Crisis Line
907/276-7273
907/278-9988, TTY/TDD machine

Suicide Prevention/Intervention
907/563-3200

VISITOR AND NEW RESIDENT INFORMATION

Alaskan Hospitality & Relocation
Services
907/563-8555

Anchorage Chamber of Commerce
907/272-2401

Anchorage Convention and Visitors
Bureau
907/276-4118

Log Cabin Information Center
907/274-3531

MULTICULTURAL RESOURCES

Alaska Women's Resource Center
907/276-0528

Bureau of Indian Affairs
907/271-4084

Cook Inlet Tribal Council
907/265-5900

Gay & Lesbian Help Line
907/258-4777

DISABILITY RESOURCES

Access Alaska
907/248-4777
907/248-8799, TTY/TDD machine

Alaska Center for the Blind
907/248-7770

Alaska Welcomes You
(accessible travel)
907/349-6301, phone/TTY
800/349-6301

Alaskan AIDS
Assistance Association
907/276-4880

The Arc of Anchorage
(mental retardation)
907/277-6677
907/272-9966, TTY/TDD machine

Alaska Center for Deaf Adults
907/276-3456
907/258-2232, TTY/TDD machine

Challenge Alaska
907/344-7399
907/783-2925, adaptive ski school

Deaf Interpreter Referral
907/277-3323
907/277-0735, TTY/TDD machine

Disability Law Center of Alaska
907/344-1002

Down's Syndrome Congress
Alaska Chapter
907/694-2545

National Federation for the Blind
907/566-2620

BABYSITTING & CHILD CARE

Carousel Child Care Centers
907/333-1231

Faith Daycare and Learning Center
907/248-6355

Gingerbread House
907/562-2568

Kee's Kiddie Kare
907/277-8943

Mt. McKinley Child Care Center
907/248-3993

Rent-A-Mom of Alaska
907/276-6667

Spenard Kiddy Drop
907/561-5513

Sunshine Schools
907/344-9435

INTERNET SITES

Alaska Women's Network
www.juneau.com/akwomen/.

Anchorage Convention & Visitors
Bureau
www.anchorage.net

Anchorage Daily News
www.adn.com

Anchorage Department of Parks and
Recreation
www.ci.anchorage.ak.us/Services/
Departments/Culture/Parks

Anchorage Telephone Utility
(city information)
www.atu.com/

City of Anchorage
www.ci.anchorage.ak.us

Department of Fish and Game
www.state.ak.us/local/akpages/
FISH.GAME/

Division of Parks and Outdoor
Recreation
www.dnr.state.ak.us/parks

Department of Labor Relocation Site
(employment and travel information)
www.labor.state.ak.us

The Milepost
(travel information and FAQs)
www.alaskainfo.com

University of Alaska–Anchorage
www.uaa.alaska.edu

TIME AND WEATHER

Air Quality Recording
907/343-4899

Current Time/Temperature
844

Road Conditions/Avalanche
Information
907/273-6037

Round-the-Clock Weather Updates
907/936-2525

CAR RENTAL

Ace Rent-A-Car
907/562-2292 or 888/685-1155

Affordable New Car Rental
907/243-3370 or 800/248-3765

Airport Car Rental
907/277-7662

Alamo Rent-A-Car
907/248-0017 or 800/327-9633

Arctic Rent-A-Car
907/561-2990 or 888/714-4690

Avis Rent-A-Car
907/243-2377 or 800/831-2847

Budget Car & Truck Rental
907/243-0150 or 800/527-0700

Denali Car Rental
907/276-1230

Dollar Rent A Car
907/248-5338 or 800/800-4000

Frontier Rent-A-Car
907/274-9959

Hertz Rent-A-Car
907/243-4118 or 800/654-3131

National Car Rental
907/243-3406 or 800/227-7368

Payless Car Rental
907/243-3616 or 800/729-5377

Thrifty Car Rental
907/276-2855 or 800/367-2277

RECREATIONAL VEHICLE RENTAL

ABC Motorhome Rentals
907/279-2000

Alaska Economy RVs
907/561-7723 or 800/764-4625

Alaska Experience RV Rentals
907/561-9800 or 888/242-4359

Alaska Panorama RV Rentals, Inc.
907/562-1401

Alaskan Adventures RV Rentals
907/344-2072 or 800/676-8911

Alutiiq RV Adventures
907/561-8747 or 800/426-9865

Clippership Motorhome Rentals
907/562-7051 or 800/421-3456

Compact RV Rentals
907/333-7368 or 800/841-0687

Cruise America Motorhome
Rental & Sales
907/349-0499 or 800/327-7799

Great Alaskan Holidays
Motorhome Rentals
907/248-7777 or 888/225-2752

Murphy's RV, Inc.
907/562-0601 or 800/582-5123

Sweet Retreat, Inc.
907/344-9155 or 800/759-4861

NEWSPAPERS

Alaska Journal of Commerce
907/561-4772

Anchorage Daily News
907/257-4200

Anchorage Press
907/561-7737

Alaska Star
(Eagle River-Chugiak area)
907/694-2727

MAGAZINES

Alaska Business Monthly
907/276-4373

Alaska Magazine
907/272-6070

SPECIALIZED PUBLICATIONS

Alaska Women Speak
907/696-0924

La Voz Latina (The Latin Voice)
907/345-8638

Senior Voice
907/277-0787

RADIO STATIONS

KRUA 88.1 FM/alternative (campus
    radio)
KATB 89.3 FM/religious
KNBA 90.3 FM/adult alternative and
    Native American
KSKA 91.1 FM/public radio
KQEZ 92.1 FM/easy listening
KFAT 92.9 FM/rhythmic format
KEAG 97.3 FM/oldies
KLEF 98.1 FM/classical
KYMG 98.9 FM/contemporary
KMBQ 99.7 FM/contemporary
KBFX 100.5 FM/classic rock
KGOT 101.3 FM/contemporary
KKRO 102.1 FM/classic rock
KMXS 103.1 FM/contemporary
KBRJ 104.1 FM/country
KNIK 105.3 FM/smooth jazz
KWHL 106.5 FM/rock
KASH 107.5 FM/country

KENI 550 AM/news and talk
KHAR 590 AM/standards
KBYR 700 AM/talk, news, sports

KFQD 750 AM/news radio
KAXX 1020 AM/sports
KASH-AM 1080 AM/business news,
   BBC

TV CHANNELS

NBC: KTUU, Channel 2
FOX: KTBY, Channel 4
UPN/WB: KYES, Channel 5
PBS: KAKM, Channel 7
CBS: KTVA, Channel 11
ABC: KIMO, Channel 13

BOOKSTORES

Barnes & Noble Bookstore
200 E. Northern Lights Blvd.
Anchorage
907/279-7323

Borders Books & Music
1100 E. Dimond Blvd.
Anchorage
907/344-4099

Cook Inlet Book Co.
415 W. Fifth Ave.
Anchorage
907/258-4544

Cyrano's Bookstore & Cafe
413 D Street
Anchorage
907/274-2599

Metro Music & Books
530 E. Benson, Ste. 9
Anchorage
907/279-8622

Waldenbooks
University Center
3901 Old Seward Hwy.
Anchorage
907/561-7644

Waldenbooks
Northway Mall
3101 Penland Pkwy.
Anchorage
907/276-2876

Waldenbooks
320 W. Fifth Ave., Space 340
Anchorage
907/276-2522

Waterstone's Booksellers
Anchorage International Airport
Anchorage
907/243-6016

INDEX

ABOUT THE AUTHOR

Donna Freedman, a staff writer with the *Anchorage Daily News*, has lived in Alaska since 1984. Her work has appeared in *Country Living*, *McCalls*, the *New York Times Review of Books*, *Parade*, *Premier*, *The Writer*, and a number of children's publications, including *American Girl* and *Girl's Life*. Freedman also reviews books for *Alaska* magazine. She is a member of American Mensa and has received a number of awards from the Alaska Press Club and the Society of Professional Journalists.

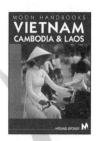

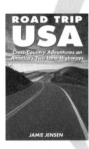

AVALON TRAVEL PUBLISHING and its City•Smart authors are dedicated to building community awareness within City•Smart cities. We are proud to work with the Alaska Center for the Book as we publish this guide to Anchorage.

AVALON
TRAVEL

The **Alaska Center for the Book** stimulates public interest in literacy through the spoken and written word. The center acts as a catalyst to bring together Alaskan readers, writers, booksellers, librarians, publishers, printers, educators, leaders, and others to promote and build an informed and literate citizenry vital to a strong democracy. The center also supports programs, events, and projects that celebrate the richness and diversity of language.

The Alaska Center for the Book is an all-volunteer organization and one of more than 30 affiliates established by the Library of Congress Center for the Book. Major projects include the annual Writing Rendezvous, a weekend of writing workshops for Alaskan authors, and the Contributions to Literacy in Alaska award, which recognizes outstanding work in promoting literacy and the literary arts.

For more information, please contact:
Alaska Center for the Book
3600 Denali St.
Anchorage, AK 99503
907/343-2805